Unearthing
the
Moment

Mindful Applications of Existential-Humanistic
and Transpersonal Psychotherapy

Edited by
Myrtle Heery, Ph.D.

Director, International Institute for Humanistic Studies

Tonglen Press

Compiled and edited by Myrtle Heery, Ph.D.
Cover photograph "Seal at Galapagos Beach" by Myrtle Heery, Ph.D.

For information about the content or permission to use, contact
Myrtle Heery at mheery@sonic.net.

Publication Information

First published in 2014 by Tonglen Press.
Unearthing the Moment: Mindful Applications of Existential-Humanistic and Transpersonal Psychotherapy

ISBN: 0989452506
ISBN 13: 978-0989452502

Tonglen Press

4940 Bodega Avenue
Petaluma, CA 94952
www.tonglenpress.com

In Memory of

Mentors
Jim and Elizabeth Bugental
Hobart "Red" Thomas

Unearthing Students
Jim Pinnell
Roberta George-Curran

Contents

Preface

WHILE THIS BOOK SEEKS TO REVEAL a broad spectrum (25 chapters) of mindful applications of existential-humanistic and transpersonal psychotherapy, it cannot "*unearth*" all applications. It is not a definitive work, but rather a search for what is possible using mindfully the subjective world of the psychotherapist and the client. *Unearthing the Moment* not only focuses on the expansion of the psychotherapy hour in the actual moment, but includes applications outside psychotherapy such as: disaster relief work, the homeless, research in Israel and Palestine, hospice and prison group settings, and shamanic work. Each chapter consistently points to the subjective world of the author and how that world influences and changes his or her objective world. This book is *subjective-based* for psychologists, psychotherapists, psychology professors, social workers, marriage and family therapists, interns, students of psychology, clients, potential clients—and hopefully other helping professionals, including but not limited to hospice workers, coaches, nurses, clergy, yoga and meditation teachers, peace and justice advocates, and business consultants.

In the paragraphs that follow, I would like to define words used consistently throughout this book.

Unearthing the Moment is the title of training program I developed along with my mentor, James F. T. Bugental, Ph.D., in 2000. Unearthing the Moment Training points to the important use of the here and now in psychotherapy, unearthing the deeper meaning of the actual moment that can bring significant change in the client's inner and outer world. All of the authors have attended four basic trainings and the majority have continued in advanced trainings.

Psychotherapy is used throughout this book to signify the 50-minute or one-hour session with a client and psychotherapist. It is not limited to one-on-one sessions, and includes couples, family, and group psychotherapy.

Client is primarily used, rather than "patient," to acknowledge the intrinsic healing of the individual seeking help. The word "patient" is traditionally used in the psychoanalytic model with more emphasis on diagnosis and interpretation.

Mindful is reserved in this book for the helping professional's state of presence in the moment, with emphasis on self-awareness, restraint in reaction, and curiosity to all aspects of the moment. Listening mindfully is encouraged and practiced in Unearthing the Moment Trainings.

Existential-humanistic psychotherapy in this book points to the possibility of human experience, which can be similar to others and unique to the individual. This therapy is process-oriented, not directed by categories and interpretations of clients, but rather pointing toward potentials and limitations of being human.

Transpersonal psychotherapy is used throughout this book to refer to the potential beyond the body and ego self. In this book, the transpersonal model explores other potentials of consciousness in relation to their applications in daily living.

In addition, I would like to clarify the mention of clients throughout this book. The clients described are often composites of multiple individuals, and all identifying information regarding a single client has been altered to completely disguise the client. Because of the human condition of being unique and similar, the cases mentioned might seem like you or someone you know, but this is not the case.

Acknowledgments

The authors who contributed to this book wrote their chapter as part of the training they attended. At the end of the fourth and final basic training session, a paper on how the participants are applying what they have learned is required for completion and certification as "A Steward of In-Depth Communication." Some participants have continued with advanced trainings, and all continue as a steward of the heart and mind in helping others.

This collection of papers was completed during trainings held from 2002–2013. Some authors attended the same training class, but most were in different training groups. To compile chapters for this book, I had the challenging job of editing essays from 18 different trainings, with six to 15 papers submitted for each training. I believe those selected show the widest lens of applications for the practice models. I want to acknowledge *all* of the participants in the trainings; *all* wrote incredible papers. Each paper is important to the subjective world of psychotherapy—thank you. And to the authors selected, thank you one and all for your hard work in editing and bringing your paper into form for an excellent chapter in this book.

Compiling a book with 25 authors who are unique and similar takes a village. For me personally, it takes the support and love of my family, friends, and colleagues. Especially important in this regard are my husband William and my son and daughter-in-law, Jamie and Patty. My dear wisdom friends, Vivian Clark and Connie Mahoney, are an inspiration for continuing to live fully after age 85! I would like to thank my mentor, Jim Bugental, who taught and continues to teach me and all the "unearthers" from beyond the physical form, the importance of being present to this moment. My spiritual guides, Irina Tweedie and Margaret Sampson, continue providing guidance from the other side.

I greatly appreciate the marvelous editors who worked with care and vigilance to bring forth clarity to each chapter: Sandy Beddow, Steven Fehl, Michelle Mullane, Amy Sharp, Elly ven der Pas, and Dana Vitorelo—thank you so much. Each of you played an important role in getting this book to the readers. I would also like to acknowledge Steve Graydon for his wonderful cover design and Susan Gumucio for invaluable production assistance.

Unearthing the Moment is the first book published by Tonglen Press, a new publisher dedicated to building bridges between academic psychology and our daily lives. Similar to the Buddhist meditation practice of Tonglen, we hope to inspire themes of giving and receiving to aid in the transformation of individuals, thus creating a ripple effect of global transformation.

Yes, we are thinking big because the practice of giving and receiving the suffering of others is just that—big. Through mindful applications of existential-humanistic and transpersonal psychotherapy models, this book expands on the experience of the helper and the helped, the giving and receiving process of transforming suffering.

Finally, I would like to express my gratitude to the International Institute for Humanistic Studies (IIHS), which sponsors the Unearthing the Moment Trainings. IIHS is a nonprofit educational organization dedicated to helping build a world community through maximizing the contribution of each person. Its mission is inspired by the compassion, courage, hope, resilience, and tolerance found in all human beings. The IIHS vision embraces the potential of humanity and approaches this vision by touching the mind and heart of each individual.

For information about IIHS training programs, please visit our website at www.human-studies.com.

—Myrtle Heery, Editor
Winter 2014

Introduction

INHERENT IN UNEARTHING THE MOMENT is the mindful application of existential-humanistic and transpersonal psychotherapy. *Unearthing the Moment* is a subjective-based book. The authors share their applications of these psychotherapy models to diverse populations, and supported by their personal experiences, give the reader insight into who the psychotherapist actually is. The emphasis is on the actual moment and searching for deeper meaning of the moment in an individual's life. All of the authors participated in a training program titled Unearthing the Moment and wrote papers as part of the final basic course. The papers I selected to include in this book were written by participants who primarily attended in different training groups from 2002–2013.

In these trainings, the authors were encouraged to increase their mindful awareness of the actual moment. Preparing participants for mindful awareness includes both outer and inner learning. In the *outer* objective world, preparation includes reading books, watching DVDs and videos, reviewing cases, and practicing in-the-moment communication in a structured setting. The goal of these objective activities is to open participants to *experience* the vast human potential in their *inner* subjective worlds. The teaching provides content that supports the individual process of inner learning.

Building bridges between the subjective and objective worlds in each participant is the goal of Unearthing the Moment Trainings. In attending to the actual moment with each participant, the searching process is enhanced— full of potential and experiencing how each participant is choosing to actually live. These trainings are based on compassion, courage, hope, resilience, and tolerance. Classes are focused on authenticity of the actual moment by honoring what is *actual* for participants, fostering choices in their objective world that actualize the participants' full potential.

In Jim Bugental's (1978) landmark book, *Psychotherapy and Process*, existential and humanistic come together in a powerful form of psychotherapy. In this model of therapy, existential-humanistic, people are not reduced into types. Instead there is continual pointing to possibility of human experience, which often overlaps and is simultaneously unique to the individual. This therapy is process-oriented, not directed by categories and interpretations of clients, but rather pointing toward potentials and limitations of being human. Humanistic values such as unconditional positive regard and empathic listening are used when the constructs and process of existential-humanistic psychotherapy are present: the existential givens, intentionality, presence, pou sto, and resistance. All of these constructs and processes are demonstrated throughout this book, but it is important to elaborate on the existential givens that are used in Unearthing the Moment Trainings.

The four existential givens of living are fundamental to this model of therapy (Heery & Bugental, 2005): embodiment, choice and responsibility, the continual draw between being a part of and apart from (or relatedness and separateness), and death (or finitude). This fourth given, death, is unique to this model of psychotherapy. Rarely is a psychotherapist trained to hold death or finitude as essential to the client sitting in front of him or her. It is in actually facing one's own death or finitude that the present moment becomes enlivened with possibilities. Enlivened because the client and psychotherapist are going to die one day, as is everyone in their lives. This brings us to a fifth given that is vital to human existence, making meaning out of our living. This gift of being alive and making the most of life right now is the experience elaborated upon by each author in this book.

The "actual in psychotherapy" needs the clinician's mindful awareness in order to bring the moment into the client's awareness and thus explore it for further in-depth therapeutic work. Too often psychotherapists and their clients unknowingly slide into conducting their "work" on a hypothetical level in which they are dealing with supposition, fictional example, story telling, and tentative speculation. Psychotherapy that sets as its goal aiding the client to make genuine and lasting life changes must concern itself with that which is actual—at least potentially rather than being content with speculative, hypothetical, or fictional steps and products. The work of the actual has been a part of the existential-humanistic model for years, but is central in Jim Bugental's (1999) book, *Psychotherapy Isn't What You Think*, which is used in the trainings.

The process of individual psychotherapy releases newfound freedoms and responsibilities in the individual. Existential-humanistic psychotherapy is concerned with communicating responsibility by integrating the gains made in psychotherapy into the world in which each client lives.

This book is mindful in bridging the existential-humanistic and transpersonal models of psychotherapy. In 2005, I wrote with Dr. Bugental the following:

> We ask ourselves and our clients to look at how we are each meeting this basic act and mystery of our existence. Mystery is infinite, not finite. Mystery is the latent meaning always awaiting our discovery, and it is always more than our knowing in the objective world. Mystery points to the subjective world where implicit meanings are waiting to be *transformed* into explicit meanings in living experience.
>
> Our *value system* is humanistic, meaning that we regard all humans as valuable and as having the potential for experiencing greater meaning in their lives. Through the processes of inner searching, we can access the human potential inherent in our being. The open spectrum of possibilities is a powerful encouragement for us—client, therapist, and supervisor—to reconceive the familiar, to attempt the new, and to explore with innocence of perception. Existential-humanistic psychotherapy is a lengthy, in-depth searching process, not a few visits to the doctor's office for a quick answer to a client's objective concerns. (p. 255)

One of the great gifts of being human is the capacity to search and particularly to search for meaning. It is not an "out there" search for an objective answer to a problem, a dream, or a symbol, but rather an "in here" search for one's full life potential with all its paradoxes and complexities. This inner search for meaning weaves individual experiences into a tapestry of meaning from inside. The individual is transformed from inside. Searching is a process of transformation from inside, facilitating transition and psychological shifts inwardly by which the individual moves the process of living from one stage of life to the next, forming patterns of beginnings and endings. These patterns become conscious and choiceful to the individual through the searching process lived in psychotherapy.

This transformation from the inside is rich with mystery. For transpersonal psychotherapy, this mystery can include but is not limited to dreams (Taylor, 2009), hearing voices (Hastings, 1991; Heery, 1987), out of body experiences (Tart, 1998) and many other experiences of anyone's subjective world. The vast possibilities of the subjective world are the bridges between existential-humanistic and transpersonal psychotherapy. Searching the subjective has possibilities beyond the body and ego self, which is exactly what the research of transpersonal psychology is about (Vaughn, 1985). Bugental (1965) actually titled the final stage of psychotherapy the ontological stage, where the client faces ontological freedom composed of actualization and transcendence. In crossing this bridge, we are finally faced with responsibility of being here in the unearthed moment. It is not a question of being in or out, as we so often hear in these polarized times, but rather a responsibility to build bridges between the subjective and objective worlds in which we live, not why we live, but *how we actually choose to live.*

In *Unearthing the Moment,* the authors share their choices as clinicians building bridges from their subjective worlds to their objective worlds, in both their personal and professional lives. The book starts with an essential ingredient to psychotherapy, the self-care of the psychotherapist (Comeau). This topic is usually an aside in training, but for me it is the essential piece of creating ongoing mindful awareness in and out of the psychotherapy room. The authors present a wide range of mindful applications serving diverse populations. *Presence* and how it influences the relationship between psychotherapist and client is elaborated upon by all the authors. There are a variety of processes including art, dreams, labyrinth, poetry, parts of the subjective self, soul searching and surfing, to assist in understanding who the psychotherapist is and how the unearthing process is manifested and utilized.

And the book moves deeply into the personal with a clinician's search for meaning in caring for her dying mother (Pinnell). This book is rich with who the psychotherapists actually are and how they care for others personally and professionally. There are a wide range of applications helping the reader to think outside the box, where many diverse opportunities to serve others with the base of existential-humanistic and transpersonal psychology exist.

I chose these papers to represent not only mindful applications of existential-humanistic and transpersonal psychotherapy but diverse processes, constructs, and populations. The diverse populations include addicts (Harrison), adolescents and young adults (Strouzas), bereaved (Haarstad), children (Sauln), clergy (Grimes), disaster relief workers (Yang), families and couples (Touch Mercer), homeless (Berry Newton), Israelis and Palestinians (Burge), prisoners (Swartout), and sports injured (Vogan).

The constructs and processes explored overlap in all the chapters. In order to assist your specific interest, the following chapters address: existential givens (Berry, Grimes, Harrison), intentionality (Heery, Strouzas), presence (Burge, Calhoon, Cronin, Harner, Hoffman, Partington, Swartout, Wasserman), pou sto (Sharp, Sauln), resistance (Cronin, Fehl, Hooper, Partington), and creativity including art (Barbee), dreams (Sauln), labyrinth (Hooper), poetry (Hoffman), shamanic journey (Harner), and surfing (Schulkin).

This book makes a clear statement that psychotherapy with a *subjective basis* for the client and psychotherapist can and does bring about objective change in the client's world. The book demonstrates over and over again how change is actualized from the inside out.

It is with great honor that I offer this book to you, to read, to savor, to be moved by the journeys of these authors. In reading this book you will visit many places and you will visit your own inner worlds. My invitation to you is to hold curiosity as you read, to be surprised.

My gratitude to the authors for their authenticity and honesty in being true to themselves and to those whom they are serving.

—Myrtle Heery, Editor
Winter 2014

References

Bugental, J. F. T. (1965). *The search for authenticity: An existential-analytic approach to psychotherapy.* New York, NY: Holt, Rinehart and Winston.

Bugental, J. F. T. (1978). *Psychotherapy and process: The fundamentals of an existential-humanistic approach.* Essex, England: Longman Higher Education.

Bugental, J. F. T. (1999). *Psychotherapy isn't what you think.* Phoenix, AZ: Zieg, Tucker, & Co., Inc.

Hastings, A. (1991). *With the tongues of men and angels: A study of channeling.* San Francisco, CA: Holt, Rinehart and Winston.

Heery, M. (1987) Inner voice experiences: An exploratory study of thirty cases. *Journal of Transpersonal Psychology, 21*(1), 73-82.

Heery, M., & Bugental, J. F. T. (2005). Meaning and transformation. In E. van Deurzen & C. Arnold-Baker (Eds.), *Existential perspectives on human issues* (pp. 253-264). New York, NY: Palgrave Macmillan.

Tart, C. T. (1998). Six studies of out-of-body experiences. *Journal of Near Death Studies, 17*(2), 73-99.

Taylor, J. (2009). *The wisdom of your dreams: Using dreams to tap into your unconscious and transform your life.* New York, NY: Penguin.

Vaughan, F. (1985). Discovering transpersonal identity. *Journal of Humanistic Psychology, 25*(3), 13-38.

1

Self-Care in Existential-Humanistic and Transpersonal Psychologies

Thea Comeau

IT SEEMS AS THOUGH EVERY BOOK on therapeutic technique ends with a chapter communicating the importance of self-care, wellness, and the therapist's ability to live a balanced life. Some of these chapters even provide handy tools, which one can implement to begin working towards active, effective self-care. I have had the privilege of training therapists about self-care across Canada and the United States, and each time I do, I am faced with the same critiques. Comments and questions like "I don't have enough time," "I don't have enough money," "I don't know how," and "Will it work?" greet me in every presentation I give. The goal of this chapter is to answer those questions with one of the most powerful techniques to enter psychology in recent history: mindfulness. Ryan and colleagues (2012) define mindfulness as "the ability to bring one's attention to experiences occurring in the present moment, with complete acceptance and without judgment" (p. 289). Mindful techniques can be used at any time, even during sessions, to help therapists be present with their clients, their loved ones, and themselves both during and after engaging in psychotherapy.

This chapter may also differ from other chapters on self-care, because it will consider mindful self-care specifically from the lens of existential-humanistic and transpersonal psychology. Both existential-humanistic and transpersonal psychologies posit that it is through connections to others, particularly through the therapeutic relationship, that individuals are impacted in such a way that change can occur (Bugental, 1999; Lajoie & Shapiro, 1992). These connections are made possible through the therapist's ability to maintain a state of presence throughout the session.

Many factors can damage therapists' ability to stay in the present moment, decreasing the effectiveness of their clinical work. Ironically, the act of connecting with our clients can impact us in such a way that present-centered connection becomes very challenging. As therapists, we encounter material every day that has the potential to be highly noxious, and affect both our work and our personal lives. Few professions require that one be exposed to another individual's worst experiences numerous times a day, most days a week. Yet this is the work of a psychotherapist.

Therapy Can Cause Depletion

Hearing these stories can have numerous negative effects, which may result in conditions as serious as secondary trauma, burnout, vicarious trauma, and compassion fatigue. Figley (1999) says that secondary trauma is the effect, such as changes in behaviour or emotions, which can arise after being exposed to another person's traumatic experience. Burnout is a more chronic condition, defined as ". . . a state of physical, emotional, and mental exhaustion caused by long-term involvement in emotionally demanding situations" (Pines & Aronson, 1988, p. 9). Vicarious trauma involves a shift in the internal experience of a therapist, which impacts him/her negatively, after being exposed to a client's trauma (Pearlman & Saakvitne, 1995). Some therapists may even begin to vicariously develop symptoms of post-traumatic stress, such as hypervigilance or avoidance, following exposure to clients' traumatic narratives. Finally, in the same way a muscle can become fatigued after use and be less effective, counselors can experience compassion fatigue and become less effective in their work. Compassion fatigue is a decrease in a therapist's ability to care for and show compassion for his/her clients due to the exhaustion that can arise from witnessing the suffering of other people (Figley, 2002). All of these conditions preclude the therapist's ability to be present while conducting psychotherapy. While this is likely concerning for all therapists, from an existential-humanistic and transpersonal psychology perspective, the ability to achieve presence is the foundation for all therapeutic work. All therapists are compelled to avoid these outcomes, yet the impacts are exceptionally salient for those therapists employing these models in which the person of the therapist is their most powerful tool.

As I write this, I hear the echoes of many students I have taught, who see this information as an ominous prediction of their experiences as therapists. Though many therapists struggle with the above afflictions, many avoid their impacts completely. Those who do successfully avoid these fates engage in regular effective, *mindful* self-care. Many training programs espouse the value of participating in regular self-care, yet they do not prepare therapists for how to select self-care, how to engage in it effectively, and how to know when it is needed. It is here that mindfulness can be used to facilitate building effective self-care skills that can allow therapists to remain present in their personal and professional lives. In fact, engaging with mindfulness skills alone has been shown to decrease stress and anxiety and increase self-compassion in therapists (Shapiro, Brown, & Biegel, 2007).

Three Component Self-Care Model

Baker (2003) identified three elements of effective self-care: self-awareness, self-regulation, and balance. Self-awareness refers to individuals' ability to look within themselves and identify when and what type of self-care will meet their needs at any given point. Self-regulation refers to the ability to act on this identified need for self-care in a way that is effective and helpful. Balance refers to a therapist's ability to maintain space within his or her life for both professional and pleasurable pursuits. Mindfulness practice will allow therapists to engage meaningfully with each of these three components of self-care, to ensure the time and resources they dedicate to self-care will adequately meet their needs and work to prevent secondary trauma, burnout, compassion fatigue, and vicarious trauma.

Self-Awareness

The development of mindful skills is essential for the attainment of self-awareness, the first ingredient in effective self-care. It is important to note within the context of self-awareness, therapists are encouraged to observe their individual experience in an accepting, nonjudgmental stance. The goal is merely to identify areas within themselves in which they are feeling depleted. Such areas may be physical, emotional, psychological, or spiritual. One technique that can help decrease stress in the present and provide us with insight regarding needed self-care is the body-scan intervention, often associated with Mindfulness-Based Stress Reduction (Kabat-Zinn, 1990). During the body scan, one slowly, mindfully connects with each part of the body, observing sensations, emotions, and thoughts that are triggered with each lingering attention. This simple act of observation can provide important information about the ways we store stress and possible means of rectifying these stressors before they devolve into compassion fatigue, burnout, or vicarious trauma. I often use body scanning at the end of particularly draining days, to identify in which ways I am feeling most drained.

Specific to working from an existential humanistic perspective, self-awareness can often also include a reflection on one's stance with respect to the givens. Just as our clients struggle between freedom and responsibility, meaning and meaninglessness, connection and isolation, and life and death, so too do we. In understanding the ways we are impacted by the therapeutic work we do, it is important to examine how our balance amongst the givens may be toppled by this work. For example, often when working with trauma victims, I am viscerally confronted with a sense of anger at the lack of responsibility often taken by the offenders of violent crime. This leads me to feel powerless, as though I am responsible to facilitate healing in the face of their poor decisions, and without the freedom to prevent their continued violent behavior. This type of self-awareness may require more cerebral types of self-awareness activities. I often use free journaling, which helps me get my thoughts and ideas down on paper, again helping to identify the givens with which I am struggling.

Mindfulness also plays an important role in the use of self-care in transpersonal psychology. This school of thought focuses on attaining levels of experience that transcend the typical ego, exploring the ultimate potential of the spiritual realm. Seated, mindful meditation can simultaneously allow a therapist to connect to his/her deeper spiritual self while gently exploring and observing the impacts of therapeutic practice on the spiritual self, noting any sense of depletion.

Self-Reflection

Once you have identified areas in which you are feeling depleted, it is important to engage in self-reflective practices to identify and conduct effective self-care for those areas that are most depleted. This often requires much practice and experimentation to identify which self-care activities will be most effective. For example, when engaged in body scanning, I often notice my stomach is upset at the end of particularly disempowering days, like when I have clients with serious suicidal ideation. With this information in mind, I transition from self-awareness into self-reflection, or deciding upon and enacting self-care to rectify the depletion that is making my stomach hurt. For me, the act of cooking a good meal at the end of the day encompasses many types of self-care. It provides physical nourishment, psychological calm through the routine of following a recipe, and reinstates a sense of emotional control, nourishing the heart as well as the body.

Again, transitioning into a consideration of the givens, we can also choose to enact self-care to rectify the balance between our existential struggles using self-reflection. For example, if I am feeling like I have little control, or am weighed down by responsibilities and have little choice, I try to find some form of self-care that makes me feel free and as if my time is my own. Often in my work, difficulties arise when working with authority figures, such as police or child protective services. They are often less efficacious than I might hope, and I struggle to understand why my clients are not protected or supported in the way that I had hoped they would be. I often feel like I have little choice or power in how these things are handled, and it leaves me terribly frustrated. In times like this, I might go for a long walk and leave my cell phone, watch, or any other device to tell time at home. This experience allows me to feel free to connect to my surroundings on a deeper level, and often leaves me feeling rejuvenated and capable of facing the responsibilities of life and work. By choosing to disconnect from things I cannot control, even time, for a little while, I find I am better able to identify the things for which I am responsible and can control, and those I am not and cannot.

If I am struggling with connections with friends or family, I seek out self-care that is fun and interactive, and makes me feel part of something. Working in the treatment of trauma, I often feel apart from the general public, as they have limited contact with such horrific human experience, and I struggle to find something to feel a part of. I often experience being alienated from people who do not do the type of therapeutic work that I do. Very few individuals can comprehend the degree of difficulty that can arise from sitting for hours a day with clients describing some of the worst parts of society. So I seek self-care with my work colleagues, who understand the demands of the work and the need for self-care. I have started facilitating compassion fatigue workshops in the office for all the staff to participate in self-care together. This provides an added source of connection, decreasing the isolation that can arise from therapeutic work and adding more balance to the struggle with this given.

A major part of my work involves facing the finite nature of life, whether that be physical or spiritual. Many of my clients experience a great degree of loss as a result of their victimization. They may grieve virginity, a relationship they previously had with their offender, or a general sense of safety in the world around them. A sad reality of working with adolescent trauma survivors is the possibility of one of my clients dying by suicide. Almost every week, I sit with individuals who self-harm or are suicidal. As loss and finitude are central in my work, I find my struggle with the finite nature of existence, both that of myself and others, can be extremely difficult. When I have found myself faced with the absolute knowledge that I will die some day, and struggle to understand my place in a temporary world, I often seek self-care that makes me feel connected to my body in the present moment. I have spent many an hour running, doing yoga, and working out in an effort to connect to being alive in the present moment, knowing that is all I have, and coming to some degree of peace with that.

Closely tied to the struggle to comprehend and accept the finite nature of existence is the need to find meaning in the life we do have in the present moment. Many therapists report that the work they do injects a great deal of meaning into their lives. I see purpose for my existence in helping people cope with trauma using the knowledge I have gained over my years of training. Yet there continue to be times when I feel disconnected from the meaning in my life, and ask questions such as, "Who am I?" "Why am I here?" "What do I contribute?" At these moments, it is key to seek self-care that addresses these needs. I volunteer with a not-for-profit in Canada and around the world building houses for individuals who are struggling with residential challenges. This work helps to provide such meaning in my life, as it makes me feel as though I have made a tangible, quantifiable change.

Self-reflective self-care can also be used with transpersonal psychology to facilitate healing and connection on a spiritual level. Once self-awareness practices have indicated that you are feeling depleted at the spiritual level, self-care can be enacted to rectify this damage. Many creative modalities provide opportunities for expression that can serve to refill spiritual depletion arising from the practice of psychotherapy. I have found drawing or painting with my nondominant hand to be an effective and soothing tool to allow an outlet for the spiritual angst that can arise when practicing therapy. Many therapists identify a range of spiritual practices in which they engage to nurture and heal the spiritual bruises that may arise through this work.

Balance

Finally, Baker (2003) reminds us that not only is it important to be self-aware and engage in self-care in the moment, it is essential that we build lives of balance, which can accommodate the necessary steps to engage in regular effective self-care. Research has shown that psychologists who maintain a strict work-life balance reported greater job and career satisfaction, fewer psychosomatic complaints, higher satisfaction with their family, and a significantly more positive sense of emotional well-being (Burke, Oberklaid, & Burgess, 2003). Again, mindfulness can facilitate this essential component of self-care. As therapists live in progressively more mindful ways, they can become aware of the ways in which they are not using time effectively, are engaging in unnecessary or unhealthy practices, and they can detect the need for self-care more quickly. For example, in my early days of clinical practice I would check my e-mail between every session, perhaps in an attempt to balance the given of connection/isolation. However, as I began to develop a regular mindful practice, I began to notice that not only was this habit not helping to fill my need for connection, it was leaving me feeling rushed before the next session and more alone, especially if I did not receive any e-mails. Mindfully attending to my needs in this way has helped me establish a new routine of leaving my office and greeting at least one other person in our clinic prior to commencing my next session. This activity is effective in helping to balance my struggle with this particular given, but it has also helped me to create a bit of balance in my daily schedule, so I begin each session feeling refreshed and grounded.

Conclusion

The purpose of self-care for therapists is to ensure they are able to continue their psychotherapeutic practice in ways that are safe for both client and therapist alike. From an existential-humanistic and transpersonal perspective, effective practice requires a deep presence, which cannot be attained by therapists who are struggling with burnout, compassion fatigue, or vicarious traumatization. Mindfulness is a key ingredient to successful self-care practice—facilitating self-awareness; engagement in self-reflective self-care; and the construction of a balanced practice and life. This chapter provides many ideas for self-care strategies that I have found effective. Perhaps the most important contribution mindfulness can make to therapist self-care is the identification of the methods that work best for each individual therapist. Self-care must be customized to accommodate each therapist as he/she balances the personal and professional.

Mindfulness provides the map that can lead to a well therapist, balanced practice, and hopefully a balanced life.

References

Baker, E. (2003). *Caring for ourselves: A therapist's guide to personal and professional well-being.* Washington, DC: American Psychological Association.

Bugental, J. F. T. (1999). *Psychotherapy isn't what you think.* Phoenix, AZ: Zeig, Tucker & Co., Inc.

Burke, R. J., Oberklaid, F., & Burgess, Z. (2003). Organizational values, work experiences, and satisfactions among Australian psychologists. *International Journal of Organizational Analysis, 11*(2), 123-135.

Figley, C. R. (1999). Compassion fatigue: Toward a new understanding of the costs of caring. In B. H. Stamm (Ed.), *Secondary traumatic stress: Self-care issues for clinicians, researchers, and educators.* (pp. 29-36). Lutherville, MD: Sidran Press.

Figley, C. R. (2002). Compassion fatigue: Psychotherapists' chronic lack of self-care. *Journal of Clinical Psychology, 58*(11), 1,433-1,441.

Kabat-Zinn, J. (1990). *Full catastrophe living: Using the wisdom of your body and mind to face stress, pain and illness.* New York, NY: Delacourt.

Lajoie, D., & Shapiro, S. (1992). Definitions of transpersonal psychology: The first 23 years. *Journal of Transpersonal Psychology, 24*(1), 79-98.

Pearlman, L. A. & Saakvitne, K. W. (1995). *Trauma and the therapist.* New York, NY: W. W. Norton and Company.

Pines, A. & Aronson, E. (1988). *Career burnout: Causes and cures.* New York, NY: The Free Press.

Ryan, A., Safran, J. D., Doran, J. M., & Muran, J. C. (2012). Therapist mindfulness, alliance and treatment outcome. *Psychotherapy Research, 22*(3), 289-297. doi: 10.1080/10503307.2011.650653.

Shapiro, S. L., Brown, K. W. & Biegel, G. M. (2007). Teaching self-care to caregivers: Effects of mindfulness-based stress reduction on the mental health of therapists in training. *Training and Education in Professional Psychology, 1*(2), 105-115.

2

The Essence of Presence

Ilyssa Swartout

"But I don't want to go among mad people," Alice remarked.
"Oh, you can't help that," said the Cat: "we're all mad here.
I'm mad. You're mad."
"How do you know I'm mad?" said Alice.
"You must be," said the Cat, "or you wouldn't have come here."

—Lewis Carroll, *Alice's Adventures in Wonderland,* 1865

I HAD COME HERE. *Here* was many miles from nowhere. *Here* was hot; it was rigid; it was uncomfortable, helpless, sad, dirty, stark, and very orange. I opened my car door and stepped out onto the burning hot, soft, rubbery blacktop. I opened my trunk, took off my open-toed shoes, one at a time, and tossed them into the trunk of the car, donning my other shoes. I thought with a strange sort of resentment, "This is mad, wearing closed-toed shoes in 115-degree weather." I reached down and lifted out my box of materials, checking it carefully to make sure I had everything. I mused at the awareness of my privilege, "I am here checking to see if I have it all, and they have . . . have what? Nothing! I am about to walk into *madness*," I whispered under my breath. This was the madness of the system, the mad-looking faces, the mad thoughts, the mad temperaments, and the madness of not having an identity aside from a number.

Walking into the plain brown building, I showed my identification badge as I walked through the metal detector greeting the on-duty officer, "Good afternoon, Officer Hernandez," receiving a mere grunt in return. I could feel my hands tighten around my box of materials, which somehow felt soft and warm in contrast to the greeting I had just received. This was the first human encounter I had experienced upon walking into the dark, hollow, institutional building. I continued onward as the large door closed behind me with the startling sound of cold, hard, lifeless metal. I stepped into a narrow hallway, which included one window that looked into an office. Met with a second officer, I again presented both sides of my identification badge, which lay hanging around my neck on a soft ribbon. When my identity was confirmed, a second large metal door opened. I exited the hallway and officially entered the State Prison.

Looking around, I saw high fences topped with shiny barbed wire, dirt fields shrouded with hovering clouds of brown dust, old brown picnic tables, officers with deadpan expressions, and . . . my clients. Catching their eyes and seeing their faces, I was sure to smile at each soul I encountered. I understood that human beings are continually in relationship with one another—that life is lived in relationship. This situation, however, resembled nothing more than *madness*. I began to feel as if I truly *was* Alice, whirling down, down, down the rabbit hole, though I felt that I might be entering the depths of hell or perhaps the depths of my soul; this was clearly not Wonderland!

Intentionality and Embodiment

I felt the gentle tug and bounce of my identification badge as I marched on to encounter these women, contemplating the question, "What makes a therapeutic relationship effective?" I had previously found that,

> At a fundamental level throughout our lives, human beings are in relationship. We engage in friend relationships, love relationships, casual relationships, and at times harmful relationships. An inquisitive

psychotherapist may ask, "What makes the psychotherapeutic relationship effective? Is it particular therapist characteristics such as: gender, age, ethnicity, religious beliefs, theoretical orientation, or therapeutic skill and technique? Are there certain client characteristics that are either congruent or incongruent with therapist characteristics? Is it a portion of these characteristics, or none of them?" (Swartout, 2001, p. 37)

In my dissertation research, I had explored the depth of this question from the vantage point of the relationship of the therapist's soul and existential being. I had desired to make these words come to life, to infuse my heart's blood into the veins of this project so that it would mean something more than just a right of passage to a degree. I wanted the fruits of my research to be used to make a real difference in the lives of human beings.

My thoughts continued to turn inward to my profession as a psychotherapist, and to why I chose to practice at the State Prison. I questioned my intentions: *Was this something that would add meaning to my life? Was this a way of resolving an existential crisis?* I did not fully know the answers yet. I did know I was entering this place because of real people with real concerns. I would work with real women with real names, real faces, and real identities. These were women who happen to be human beings, yet who have been robbed of their essential humanness by being referred to as inmates with numbers. These were women who were being defined solely by their crimes, rather than as women with names and accomplishments.

In this place, it was difficult for a woman to experience feelings, to become emotionally vulnerable, and to contemplate new ideas generated from participation in therapy groups. I pondered: *Could I ask them to be vulnerable for a time, in a closed community, and to then have them by necessity put their feelings away upon exiting this room? Could I ask them to entertain accessibility by embracing whatever happened in therapy? Could I make this experience matter and have an effect on them?*

Bugental (1987) has written that, "Opening oneself to another's influence is significantly investing in that relationship" (p. 27). *Would they invest themselves in this therapeutic relationship? Finally, would they be able to express themselves and let themselves be truly known by one another?* Bugental elucidates this process, stating, "This involves disclosing without disguise some of one's subjective experiencing, and it requires a willingness to put forth some effort" (p. 27). *Would these women come to feel safe enough to lay aside some defenses?*

Finding Presence in Prison

And so my relationship with these women began. Week after week I trekked out to the State Prison. One clanging metal door closing behind another, I entered the group room. After several minutes of preliminaries, the 15 group members were gathered together in a circle. Life and the course I had chosen had put me in this place, a place that was as foreign to me as China, yet as familiar as sitting at my kitchen table.

In the beginning, resentment spewed forth from the group members. For many weeks and several months, I would hear variations of closed or challenging statements: "I'm fine, I have nothing to say." "I'll be upfront with you, Swartout, I ain't talkin' tonight." "What do you know about us, Miss Goody Two-Shoes? I bet you never did a wrong thing in your life." "So, Swartout, tell me, how long does it take you to put on your makeup?" "Don't ask me anything tonight, 'cause I'm good; I'm angry; I'm hot and tired. There, now you have my three feelings. I pass." It was resoundingly clear. Many women did not want to be there, to feel, to expose their souls and hearts. Their anger, hurt, and regrets were ever-present. I persevered week after week and month after month as I learned to embrace the heart of a dove through the hide of a rhinoceros.

One day after the usual routine upon arrival, I looked up and saw Mona. Upon first meeting Mona, she'd had me at, "Hi, doc, whaz up?" Mona's sparkling earnest eyes transfixed me. This day, Mona met me before the group began, stating, "Iz real tired tonight doc, but I came anyways. Is it OK if I go back a little early? I need ta eat, shower, and call home." Feeling fully rooted in the present moment, I answered, "Sure, it's OK, Mona. You can leave at the break." I felt that in a system that denied these women so much in the way of gratification, I must open a way for them to attend to their emotional and physical needs; I proceeded to treat them as human beings.

Sorting-It-Out

After one year of meeting six hours per week, most of the women grew to know each other well, to trust each other, and to trust me. The three-hour block twice a week became a time of soothing balm for these women. The women who could no longer stand their pain learned to allow what happened in the group to matter and to have an effect on them; they began to put effort into disclosing their subjective experiences. This accessibility and expressiveness did not come easily. The trust came out of days, weeks, and months of experiencing my presence and commitment. The women learned to trust me as a human being, to trust my consistent presence, to trust themselves and each other, to trust in the belief that inner change is possible, and most importantly, to trust and commit to the therapeutic process. The day I knew that they felt this as well, was the day they no longer called me Dr. Swartout, but nicknamed me Dr. "Sort-It-Out." In my heart, I knew they were *my* women, *my* group; this was a place of personal transformation, as their lives and stories unfolded slowly, poignantly, and sadly.

There were so many. Holly was confused and filled with rage. She had a long history of sexual, physical, emotional, and institutional abuse. It was very difficult for her to tell her story. No one tried to be more invisible than Bev, yet without much success, as she fidgeted in the hard, institution-issued chair. Like Bev, Laura would try to make herself invisible. Her camouflaging would manifest whenever the discussion would focus on physical abuse. Emotionally, she would disappear just like when she was a child, when she learned early on to stay out of the way and to not make a sound.

Sharon was abandoned by her mother when she was 8 years old and had tried to fill that void with drugs, alcohol, and men ever since. Nancy came from a good family, yet became involved with abusive men and soon became an alcoholic. Joan talked about her emotional abuse as a child, and about never being allowed to be a child. Susan's ex-husband kidnapped her two daughters. She soon resorted to alcohol in order to cope with the loss, resulting in three arrests and her incarceration.

These women were filled with painful memories; they were filled with guilt-ridden hearts as they remembered the infants, children, family, and pets they had to leave behind when they were incarcerated. Themes of hopelessness, helplessness, anger, deep sadness, and regret pervaded the group sessions. These were the women of this group. These women were now in an environment designed to take away their power and their identities. I could feel my internal struggle in this truly maddening situation as I would agonize and question myself: *How in the world can I lead them to find their power and souls again, from this place?*

What I did know is that therapists are continually faced with individuals coming through the doors to therapy seeking their own souls. Individuals relate stories of looking for this deepest aspect of self in a myriad of places: in relationships, in lovers, in substances, in play. Yet, as therapists, we cannot give others anything that does not already exist within them; we cannot create what is not present in the soul of the other. What we can do is to bring into existence the favorable conditions, the motivation, and help to make the internal visible. Nothing more.

As I gained bits of hope during this experience, my thoughts progressed toward the existential views of the human being. In my dissertation research, I had reported that,

> The existential human being is a singular individual who is unique and irreplaceable, who creates meaning in his or her subjective world through relationship with others. The existentialist views an individual with his or her uniqueness, freedom, responsibility, and will to find meaning in life, through understanding normal guilt, hostility, and anxiety. While some scholars criticize and find existentialism lacking on psychological grounds, other scholars believe existentialism may have much to offer, and psychology much to gain. Since the individual is unique, existentialists insist it is difficult to describe individuals under the laws of predictability. Frankl (1965) stated, "A real human person is not subject to rigid prediction. Existence can neither be reduced to a system nor deduced from it" (p. 169). (Swartout, 2001, p. 64)

The lives of these women *were* being reduced to a system, the prison system. I was on a mission to help them discover their uniqueness.

Sensation of Presence

A therapist can be considered a lover of music, eager to hear the themes and variations of a client's story-music over and over and over again. A therapist is also a nostalgia buff, never tiring of hearing about the good old days, and the bad old days (Storr, 1990). The business of therapy is not a scientific enterprise. It is an art demanding that the therapist be congruent and never adopt the concept of the client as an object to be manipulated, diagnosed, and dissected. Therapy is more like a greenhouse where the growth of the client and therapist alike occurs as a result of trust, empathy, understanding, and unconditional positive regard. (Swartout, 2001, p. 64)

The women were always very grateful to me around the holidays, for it was during those sessions that I nurtured their unique creativity, bringing all sorts of materials for them to make cards to send to their loved ones. I would play music, and watch them enter their own worlds and develop their creative flows, some singing or humming to the music. At times I would walk around and ask them to show me what they were making. I hoped I was the *good-enough mother* (Winnicott, 1982/1960) for whoever needed one at that moment. Some would relate stories of childhood while coloring with the crayons, while sprinkling the glitter, or while using watercolor paints. Some stories shared brought warm feelings, while others brought regrets. These were *their* stories and I was willing to listen to each one, and sometimes more than once or twice. I hoped that for these women it was not too late to have happy childhoods (Robbins, 1980).

One day, I discovered that the perfume I wore aroused the women's sense of smell. "I know that you're here 'cause I can smell ya, Doc." "I like your perfume, Doctor Sort-It-Out. All we get to use for perfume are those scratch and sniffs in the magazines." Knowing that the sense of smell was the only sense that transmitted impulses directly to the emotional center of the brain, I decided that perfume was going to be a way into the present moment for these women.

Following the essence of my perfume, I helped them recognize memories connected to smells in their lives, enabling them to bring these experiences into the present moment. I helped them experience the present moment and the healing that happens within the moment. They were so accustomed to being in another place and time, to being pulled into the past or out into the future. I knew that being in the moment in the environment of the State Prison was something they wanted to escape from, even if fleeing was only through their imaginations. Yet, I also knew that bringing attention to their sense of smell would be bringing their awareness to their internal states, to other possibilities of being that could expand into the lived moment. I believed that this momentary relief would give them the strength that self-awareness brings, and hoped it would give them back some of their power. The fragrance of the perfume could lead them to share their positive subjective experience with me, with each other, and with themselves.

The Essence of Presence: Increased Freedom

It is the world of your own soul that you seek. Only within yourself exists that other reality for which you long. I can give you nothing that has not already its being within yourself. I can throw open to you no picture gallery but your own soul. All I can give you is the opportunity, the impulse, the key. I can help you make your own world visible. That is all.

—Herman Hesse, *Steppenwolf*, 1927, p. 175

In closing, I am once again reminded of what I know about being a therapist. I recall the words I have expressed in earlier work, now infused with new life and heart through my experience with these women.

The therapeutic relationship is the necessary starting point of every therapeutic encounter. The therapist and client, two existential human beings, can establish a bonded alliance, creating a collaboration and intersubjective communication. This intersubjective communication is the intuitive therapist sensing the client going beyond words. It is through the client/therapist intersubjectivity an entity called the "third essence" emerges.

The third essence is the unknown piece of each therapeutic dyad. It is the part of the therapeutic relationship uniquely developed between the therapist and the client, and is different from all other therapeutic dyads because it is based on the subjective world of the client and the therapist at particular moments in time. It is more than the therapeutic techniques of interpretation, clarification, support, and guidance. It is on the other side of technique, as the therapist orients therapy almost entirely around the center of the therapeutic relationship, believing only in the present therapeutic relationship precipitating long-lasting life changes. The third essence is a corrective relationship the client can assume as an added component of the client's relationship with self, obtained through relationship with the therapist. This allows the client to self-create ongoing life changes, regardless of the therapeutic techniques employed by the therapist. This is the objective of therapeutic encounters and is the orchestration of psychotherapy. (Swartout, 2001, p. 65)

I had done my time at the State Prison with no regrets. I left the steel chambers of the prison with inspiration to continue to assist others who, while perhaps physically free, remained imprisoned within their own invisible walls. I knew I had orchestrated a therapeutic symphony composed of the subjective experience of the women in my therapy group. Each individual played a different song with a different instrument. An underlying rhythm resounded, playing "Trust in the Process and Look Inside Yourself." To my ears it was harmonious, and I named the song "Increased Freedom." I knew the women were not physically free yet, but they had learned the essence of how to free their hearts and souls. They had experienced the essence of presence.

References

Bugental, J. F. T. (1987). *The art of the psychotherapist: How to develop the skills that take psychotherapy beyond science*. New York, NY: W. W. Norton.

Carroll, L. (1865). *Alice in Wonderland*. United Kingdom: Macmillan.

Frankl, V. (1965). *The doctor and the soul: From psychotherapy to logotherapy* (2nd ed.), (R. Winston, & C. Winston, Trans.). New York, NY: Vintage. (Original work published 1946)

Hesse, H. (1927). *Steppenwolf.* New York, NY: Bantam Books.

Robbins, T. (1980). *Still life with woodpecker*. New York, NY: Bantam Books.

Storr, A. (1990). *The art of psychotherapy* (2nd ed.). New York, NY: Routledge, Chapman and Hall.

Swartout, I. (2001). The interplay between client and therapist subjectivity promoting therapeutic change highlighted in the existential-humanistic model, including a proposal for future research. (Unpublished doctoral dissertation). Arizona School of Professional Psychology at Argosy University, Phoenix.

Winnicott, D. W. (1982). Ego distortion in terms of true and false self. In *The maturational processes and the facilitating environment: Studies in the theory* of emotional development (pp. 140-157). New York, NY: International Universities Press, Inc. (Original work published 1960)

3

Excerpts From Nomadic Reflections of an
Existential-Humanistic Psychotherapist

Deborah Partington

ON A VERY BASIC LEVEL, PSYCHOTHERAPY is about the interaction of two psychological forces coming together, that of the therapist and that of the individual seeking recognition of the therapist, to achieve a certain end. Dr. James Bugental (1999) suggested that as therapists we must be constantly aware of what the client is doing to us. Preceding the business of what the client is doing to the therapist is the concern of what the health care system is doing to the therapist and to psychotherapy in general. I have been working in community mental health for the past several years. My current position is as an in-home therapist to adults who find it challenging to leave their homes to seek mental health treatment at a clinic. Without the health care system, these individuals would likely not receive needed treatment; yet, the system sets expectations of treatment. To be a therapist within the system, I realize I need to make peace with my own quarrels with the system.

Given here are excerpts from a longer essay, *Nomadic Reflections of an Existential-Humanistic Psychotherapist* (2005), which I wrote as I explored my arguments with the system. James Bugental's (1987) statement, "Being a therapist is being a nomad," (p. 271) inspired the title.

Define Your Terms, Please Excerpts

Language reflects the tenor of the times. It is through our language that we gain insight into our thought processes, hence our own evolution; language guides our own paths of being. Agreeing on a vocabulary gives us a foundation for discussion. *Behave* is to "conduct oneself in a specified way" (*American Heritage Dictionary* [*AHD*], 1992, p. 167). Behavior then is the "actions or reactions of a person in response to external or internal stimuli" (*AHD*, 1992, p. 167). The Middle English roots of behave are "be" and "have" (*AHD*, 1992, p. 167) or "to be in possession of" (*AHD*, 1992, p. 828). Behavior, logically, then is a possession, apropos for a society that espouses material gain. To focus on behavior before examining underlying causes for the behavior seems to be putting the proverbial horse before the cart.

Mental means "of or relating to the mind" (*AHD*, 1992, p. 1,128). The definition of *mind* is "The human consciousness that originates in the brain and is manifested especially in thought, perception, emotion, will, memory and imagination" (*AHD*, 1992, p. 1,148). The terminological shift from *mental* health to *behavioral* health is significant. Behavioral health points towards a fascist approach to treatment, which dismisses human vagaries such as emotions, will, and imagination.

I do not use the phrase *a fascist approach* lightly or to simply to create shock value. Fascism is a political philosophy based on a centralized authority of "oppressive dictatorial control" (*AHD*, 1992, p. 663). Interesting, the term fascist comes from the Italian via Latin meaning of a bundle of sticks that has been bound together and is typically used in the construction of fortresses, sea walls, and dams. Thus, the implication is that individuality is dispossessed for a common utilitarian purpose. Indeed, mental health's systemic preoccupation with behavior-based treatment plans, short-term behavioral goals, and medication compliance aim toward submissiveness with system regulations. This utilitarian approach has little to do with psychotherapy. It has a lot to do with treating individuals as their diagnosis. The language of the behavioral health system is utilitarian and evokes linear efficiency. Clients have plans and goals congruent with what the system thinks is in their best interest.

The language of the system points to an antilogy, that is, a self-contradiction. The terms SMI (seriously mentally ill) and CMI (chronically mentally ill) are still widely used. Yet, *behavioral* health systems have replaced *mental* health systems. I have yet to hear either the terms "seriously behaviorally ill" or "chronically behaviorally ill." Thus, it appears that at some level we still view behavior as being under the influence of mental processes, perhaps even driven by mental processes. Yet, current consideration of the problem points toward alleviating behavioral rather than mental processes.

I am a practicing psychologist. *Practice*—a word rich with meanings. On one hand it refers to the profession in which I am engaged. The *American Heritage Dictionary* (1992) defines practice in several ways: "to do or perform habitually or customarily; to do or perform repeatedly in order to acquire or polish a skill; and to work at, especially as a profession" (pp. 1,421-1,422). The first meaning is problematic when the practice of the system, that is, what it does habitually or customarily, and the practice, that is, the profession, of the psychologist are incongruent.

The system wants to fix the person who is perceived as having behavioral defects. Counseling programs train therapists to assemble a toolkit of therapeutic techniques to repair the behavioral defects. Psychotherapy focuses on processes of listening and relating to clients in their own moments, their own presence. It involves allowing clients freedom to trust in their own decisions and to honor their own paths. As a practitioner in the system, I ask myself if it is possible to work in this situation. More importantly, is it possible to do authentic work in this system?

I Want Tools Excerpts

I recently met with a woman, a consumer in the behavioral health system, in her home. "I want you to tell me what to do," she stated. "I want tools." Not a unique request. I suggested I did not know what she should do, but I was willing to help her figure out what she wanted to do. She was insistent on wanting tools, to the point where I felt I would be more helpful if I were a hardware store. After I left, she contacted her case manager and demanded another therapist. I recommended that she work with a very brief solution-focused therapist. Still, two thoughts crossed my mind: First, I am curious to know what kind of individual would so readily turn her life over to a stranger to be fixed—much as we, in the event of a roadside emergency, turn our vehicle over to an AAA mechanic for repairing. She stated she did not want to be listened to. That was a waste of her time. Nevertheless, the emergency roadside mechanic seems an apt metaphor for what treatment has become. Second, psychotherapy appears to be a matter of fixing problems. People want tools to make their lives run more smoothly, but seem reluctant to understand mechanisms that interfere with the smooth purring of their lives. It is one thing to talk about the tools of the mechanic, quite another to engage in the learning process of being a mechanic.

Tools. Toolkits. Objective measurements. Charts. Plans. The language we have adopted to describe therapy is one of problem-solving, much the way one would go to a hardware store and consult with the staff about the correct size and threading of a screw or length and width of a nail to secure a fixture. As therapists, we are expected to carry a toolkit. Our clients want tools. They want services. The logical direction of this discourse is that the therapist is a service center.

"Cart Before the Horse" Model Excerpts

My limited experience has taught me that telling people how to fix their lives usually has one of two outcomes: They will follow your directions to the word, and then blame you because the resulting assemblage does not work, or they will not do as you suggested because that would require they change, and the requirement would be imposed on them from without. Perhaps both of these responses germinate from a desire in each of us to see ourselves as unique individuals. Kierkegaard (1959) comes to mind, speaking far more eloquently than I with my reliance on clichés: "One must know oneself before knowing anything else . . . it is only after a man has thus understood himself inwardly, and has thus seen his way, that life acquires peace and significance" (p. 46).

Instead of focusing on gathering a weighty toolkit of the trade, to achieve a utilitarian end, I prefer to think that as psychotherapists we should be building our vocabularies—our communication skills, our skills at therapy to help integrate the fragmented conversations (maladaptive or problematic behaviors) of our clients. Tools in the hands of a master roofer will help to construct a watertight covering, which is useless without the walls of the house.

Authenticity and the System Excerpts

In 1967 R. D. Laing admitted a woman, Mary Barns, to London's Kingsley Hall, the home of Laing's anti-psychiatric movement. Joseph Berke, a psychiatrist, treated her, not with medications, but with an authentic relationship. He had the presence of mind, and training, to recognize in her smeared feces an attempt to communicate.

> Mary smeared shit with the skill of a Zen calligrapher. She liberated more energies in one of her many natural, spontaneous, and unselfconscious strokes than most artists express in a lifetime of work. . . . I remember the words of John Thompson [a psychiatrist], "Be aware of the ways by which men will reveal themselves!" (Barnes & Berke, 1971, p. 236)

Berke gave Mary paper and crayons. Through psychotherapy, she found a way back to a meaningful life. At the publication of her account of her journey through illness, she was living independently.

> Joe reminded me, Ronnie [R. D. Laing] says, "Life is therapy and therapy is life". . . . In a particular way, Joe recreated me, reformed me. I was able to let him, because I trusted him. This trust has been rewarded. Since the spring of '67 I have grown up. To an increasing extent I have become much more involved with people both at Kingsley Hall and in the outside world. Also I have had two successful exhibitions of my paintings. Sometimes I have felt like going down again, but never so strongly as before." (Barnes & Berke, 1971, p. 212)

I position myself as a practicing existential-humanistic psychologist, even in the system. To establish an authentic relationship with the clients means that I must first accept them at the point where they are, not where they are going with treatment goals, just as Dr. Berke accepted Ms. Barnes's smearing feces on the living room wall. That was where she started her journey back. By not imposing goals from without, but by allowing her to blossom from within, she met her treatment or recovery goals of living independently, engaging in socially accepted behaviors, and more.

Being present also means I must figure out who I am with this client. Can I be empathic? What kind of commitment can I make to this relationship? Am I able to make a commitment to this relationship? Although these may sound like academic questions, they are very real ones for me and perhaps for anyone who has spent any amount of time engaged in the psychotherapeutic process. No matter how long or short the therapeutic encounter may be, presence can still be a quality of the moment. Bugental (1986) defined presence as "the quality of being in a situation in which one intends to be as aware and as participative as one is able to be at that time and in those circumstances" (p. 222). Starting with the present moment is the beginning of being authentic with another person. It is in this moment that we have come together. I posit that it is possible to be an existential-humanistic psychotherapist within the mental health system. The system is not responsible for the personal qualities of authenticity and presence that we bring to the therapeutic hour. If we are authentic—and being authentic means owning our own moments, our feelings, our decisions, in short, our practice—then it is important to be on guard against falling into the pit of blaming the system. It is too easy to dismiss the hassles and shortcomings of mental health treatment on the expectations of the system.

Don't Blame the System Excerpts

To blame the system seems to be creating resistance, which may then interfere with practice of psychotherapy. The existential-humanistic approach is to create my own space within the system. Define my own terms. Define my own meaning. It goes back to the issue of mental versus behavioral health. The system cannot control my mind — how I perceive the clients and how I hold them in my presence. It can set limits on the time I have with the clients. It cannot set limits on authenticity I bring to the therapeutic encounter. That is my responsibility.

Through our work we create the reality in which we perceive and behold our clients. Psychotherapists also comprise the qualities of emotion, perception, will, and imagination. The imagination, Kierkegaard (1959) stated,

> Is what providence uses in order to get men into reality, into existence, to get them far enough out, or in, or down in existence. And when imagination has helped them as far out as they are meant to go—that is where reality, properly speaking, begins. (p. 243)

Imagination refers to the holding of a mental image that is "not perceived as real nor present to the senses" (*AHD*, 1992, p. 901). Through imagination, we hold the mental image of hope for our clients. They may come to us thinking that they are flawed and that the flaws are inevitable and indelible. We see in their struggles for meaning fertile ground for a richer life. Imagination also refers to the "ability to deal with reality through the creative power of the mind" (*AHD*, 1992, p. 901). Psychotherapists, it seems, should be intimately in tune with imagination, that process and that quality in us that allows each of us to perceive each individual as a unique apotheosis of mental and behavioral processes.

I find the core of my practice remains the same, and embraces presence, holding and caring for the client, challenging the client, and confirming the client's increased sense of self. How that looks alters, and should alter, from client to client if I am being truly authentic. It is when I find myself voicing platitudes and becoming more worried about meeting system requirements and identifying clients as service plans that I realize I forfeit my own authenticity and presence. Bugental (1986) stated, "Presence is carried into effect through mobilization of one's inner (toward subjective experiencing) and outer (toward the situation and any other person/s in it) sensitivities" (p. 222).

Through presence, through our imaginative faculties, we watch the boats, our boats, fashioned by our practice, our words, and our presence, participate with the current. We watch them skip along the water, be shuffled by rocks and twigs and floating beer bottles, and trust in the meaning of our work. Practice is what allows us as psychotherapists to take in the whole river. I like to think that the more authentic the therapeutic alliance is, the longer the boats will float.

Addendum

Dark brown is the river.
    Golden is the sand.
It flows along forever,
    With trees on either hand.

Green leaves a-floating,
    Castles of the foam,
Boats of mine a-boating—
    Where will all come home?

—Robert Louis Stevenson, *Where Go the Boats,* 1885

A lion's share of a decade has passed since I completed the Unearthing the Moment series of workshops and wrote *Nomadic Reflections of an Existential-Humanistic Psychotherapist.* My career has shown me paths I had not anticipated. For example, I had not planned on staying in community mental health. Nor had I planned on being the training director for one of Arizona's largest psychology internship programs. Making the commitment to remain in community mental health has increased my ability to be a transpersonal psychologist, to consider larger potentials. I reflect back to a question I posed in the essay: Is it possible to be an authentic therapist when the managed-care concern is with sculpting behavior and having both therapist and client conform to demands of the mental health system? How is transpersonal work possible in an environment of excessive paperwork, psychotropic medications, limited sessions, and on the acquisition of tools rather than on dealing with existential concerns, which in my experience is what motivates people to seek therapy?

The structure of the system has allowed me to focus on who I am and what I bring to my work. I bring a deeper sense of practice, because my identity as a therapist has ripened as I transition from early career to mid-career psychologist. If I am a psychotherapist then that is part of my identity and I cannot so easily separate one facet of my identity from another. *Practice* and *identity* fuse together, and with this fusing, I am pulled more and more into transpersonal work.

Joining practice and identity pulls me more and more into presence. Being present to existential questions is to wear a seamless garment, where past and future are knitted into the present. To spend too much time in the past is to wear only half the garment. To focus only on the future is also to be only half dressed. The present is where we are fully dressed—fully in the moment where we fully endorse the experiences of the other person.

As I go deeper into my work as a psychotherapist, I am more acutely aware of the need to create a seamless language between my professional self and my personal self. Is it possible to aim to engage in I-Thou (Biemann, 2002) relationships in the therapy office and not have them outside of the office? Can I strive to develop I-Thou (Biemann, 2002) relationships with private-practice clients and ignore that in my community mental health clients? I don't think so. The personal authenticity that is necessary for the art of psychotherapy permeates all areas of living. The issues I struggle to find meaning with in my personal life equal the issues my clients struggle with. Where do I find meaning? What values do I hold? How do my daily actions and thoughts shape my life? Is this the life I am meant to live?

To honor the work the client is doing in therapy also means honoring the work that brought us both to this point. My presence is my identity. As long as I railed against a system, the frustration became part of my identity. If I allow the system to be what it is, then I free myself to be what and who I am. In other words, I am freed to get on with my own work as a psychologist and supervisor. Community mental health has offered a wealth of internship opportunities and is an excellent training ground for psychotherapists of any philosophical and theoretical orientation.

My own understanding of the language of psychotherapy is shifting and evolving. I no longer cringe when I hear the word, tools, though I prefer the word, skills, because that implies learning and growth. I am still of the opinion that existential challenges are not fixed, but worked through by developing necessary skills. Over the years I have learned skills, that is, developed a presence, that have allowed me to live in relationship with the health care system, even if I disagree with it at times. Through my practice, I am able to watch the system, and like all living organisms, evolve.

Community mental health has intensified the journey toward greater relationship between practice, identity, and presence. It frees me from having to search for clients. I am never at a loss for them. I am thrust into their experiences daily, which means the connection between us must be forged within a relatively short period of time.

I opened my original essay with the words from Robert Louis Stevenson's (1885) poem *Where Go the Boats?* I recalled the childhood poem as I was walking along the canal that stretches across Phoenix, channeling water through the desert-bound city. The boats are metaphors for life and for the work we do as psychotherapists. I see in the boats an image of the purposeful coming together in therapy. While they retain the original material, be it paper, wood, or fabric, these crudely crafted boats have undergone a metamorphosis, just as Mary Barnes underwent a metamorphosis from psychiatric patient to productive artist. That to me is the transpersonal work of therapy. The client has become more than the elements that brought him or her to therapy. Whatever the client chooses to call it—skills or tools, insight or presence—that quality is now integral to his or her identity. The same goes for the therapist whose practice keeps presence, who keeps the art of psychotherapy, alive.

References

American Heritage Dictionary of the English language (3rd ed.). (1992). Boston, MA: Houghton Mifflin Co.

Barnes, M., & Berke, J. (1971). *Mary Barnes: Two accounts through madness*. New York, NY: Harcourt Brace Jovanovich.

Biemann, A. D. (Ed.) (2002). *The Martin Buber reader: Essential writings.* New York: Palgrave Macmillan.

Bugental, J. F. T. (1986). Existential-humanistic psychotherapy. In I. L. Kutash, & A. Wolf (Eds.), *Psychotherapist's casebook: Theory and technique in the practice of modern therapies* (pp. 222-236). Northvale, NJ: Jason Aronson.

Bugental, J. F. T. (1987). *The art of the psychotherapist.* New York, NY: W. W. Norton.

Bugental, J. F. T. (1999). *Psychotherapy isn't what you think.* Phoenix, AZ: Zeig, Tucker & Co., Inc.

Kierkegaard, S. (1959). *The journals of Kierkegaard* (A. Dru, Trans.). New York, NY: Harper & Brothers.

Laing, R. D. (1967). *The politics of experience.* London, England: Penguin Books.

Partington, D. (2005). *Nomadic reflections of an existential-humanistic psychotherapist.* Unpublished manuscript.

Stevenson, R. L. (1885). *A child's garden of verses.* London: Longmans, Green and Co.

4

A Yearning for Home, A Yearning for Self:
The Existential-Humanistic Therapeutic
Approach to Working With Families in the
Crises of Poverty and Homelessness

Makenna Berry Newton

SINCE THE RECESSION OF 2008 thousands of families in the San Francisco Bay Area have found themselves with no place to call home. The economic crash, followed by constriction in the job market and no relief for expensive housing in the Bay Area, reduced some families that were just getting by (or that previously had lived well enough) to the ranks of the homeless.

Some of these families were fortunate enough to gain entry into one of the few transitional housing shelters in the Bay Area. These shelters usually provide services for basic needs such as shelter, food, and safety. Individuals and families may also have access to referrals for off-site and on-site mental and physical health treatment. Mental health services are provided to help shelter residents recover from the effects of the stressors often associated with homelessness and poverty—i.e., stress, anxiety, and depression—as well as struggles with trauma, abuse, violence, and substance abuse.

A few years ago, I had the good fortune to provide mental health care to families living at a transitional family shelter. It was an excellent opportunity for me to begin my practice by serving people who shared similar stories of the poverty, struggle, and resilience I had also experienced in my youth. I know the general narrative of losing it all. My work as an intern therapist at the shelter integrated my personal history with the skills I had learned in my Ph.D. program and in the Unearthing training.

It is my intention to present the application of existential-humanistic (EH) psychotherapy with those experiencing homelessness as a narrative rather than as a research paper since my work at the shelter contained very little controls, measures, or scientific inquiry. This will be a story that weaves together the many threads of the lives of the families that I was privileged to sit with during my tenure.

There are six areas within the existential-humanistic psychotherapy framework that I will focus on in this chapter. These are intentionality, choice/relinquishment, a part of/apart from, anger, self, and presence within the framework. This piece would not be complete if I did not reflect upon what was most challenging and joyous about the experience. Hopefully, in the end, the story of one therapist's practice of using existential-humanistic psychotherapy with those experiencing homelessness will be able to provide the reader with a sense of how this approach can be helpful—and at times not so helpful—with this community.

Foundations

The model of existential-humanistic psychotherapy provided me with a foundation of therapeutic practice that required me to see the mothers, fathers, daughters, children, brothers, and sisters as who they were, not what they do. I was able to see that they were not solely ruled by their behaviors. They were human beings experiencing life. "We are processes, not things. We are humans, *be-ing*. We are the *ing* of our doing. We are not what we do, but the do-*ing*. We are not what we think, but the think-*ing*." (Bugental & Bugental, 1984). Breaking past the one-dimensional viewpoint of seeing my clients as homeless, or poor, or as an addict, was the first critical step in my practice. I realized that if I were to work in the EH framework, I had to move past the therapy of simply questioning and correcting behaviors. This is why, over the past few years I shifted my language around this topic. I no longer use the term "the homeless," rather I speak about those who are "experiencing homelessness." This change in language reflected a shift in my perspective of how I saw my clients. In the humanistic spirit of Bugental, I saw my clients as human beings who were experiencing life, and that being homeless was an experience, not an identity. The community I worked in was more than just "the homeless." They were families who were human beings in the experience of being without a home.

In practice, I found that the experience included physical, social, and personal needs. My clients shared a common foundation of yearning that they carried with them into the psychotherapy room. This was a yearning for a home: a physical home and a psychological home. I found a connection between the yearning and the concept path of intentionality in EH psychotherapy.

Intentionality

"Intentionality is the meaning we express by our living" (Bugental & Bugental, 1984).

Intentionality is expressed through a flow of experiences: wishing, wanting, willing, action, actualizing, and interaction. In my psychotherapy office, intention was presented as vague yearnings, restlessness, and hungering for a home, or perhaps a home that they may have had or wanted since their childhood. It's easy to assume that if we simply give the homeless a house, their lives will brighten and slip into place. I found in my work that underlying this immediate need of shelter there was a yearning that went beyond the solid structure of four walls.

Sitting in session with a young mother, I listened as she flowed through moments of tearful concern and worry over an uncertain and unknown future. She had never been in a place in her life where the concept of her own home was even a possibility, and this very possibility of having her own home brought her to a place of concern. "Yet it is the impetus of concern that brings most clients to therapy, motivates their continued participation, and strengthens their resolve to put into actuality in their lives the gains that truly life-changing therapy makes possible" (Bugental, 1999, p. 63). It was in this place of concern this mother searched along the path of intentionality, flowing through wishing, wanting, willing, action, actualizing, and interaction all in one session. Like many mothers, she wished for a home for her family, wanted a place for her family, was willing to take action, but struggled with actualizing and interaction. Her struggle with actualizing was rooted in her personal history of uncertainty, trauma, abandonment, and violence.

The temptation was to walk her through her past in order to discover the historical source of her struggle, but that wasn't necessary. Her history was there in that present moment and she did not need to dive into the past, because the demons, fears, and pains were right there with her, holding her back from taking the steps to a new life. We could explore the presence of those demons in the moment as it related to her making important choices about her future.

I recall hearing her saying over and over how she wanted a good home, since providing a home is what mothers do for their children. What was her intention? Was it to have a good home? Was it to be a good mother? Or was it both? In this session, we danced around the logistics of a new house, what it would look like, whether it would have a yard or a lot of sunlight. We went back and forth like this for a good portion of the session. I did my best to be with the ebb and flow of her feelings in that moment. But then she began to speak about how she wanted to be a good mother and how good it would feel to be one, and I said, "So, you want to be a good mother." For her, being a good mother was both joyous and frightening. The joy was in the possibility of finally being able to provide a home for her children on her own as a good mother. The fear was also in that same possibility. She had never done this before. Prior to this she had long relied on others, who in the end were not reliable. She did not trust her own ability to make this dream come to fruition or to maintain it. Imagine how difficult it would be to try to actualize through the human experience of moving between the excitement and fear of building a new life. I had a deep faith in her since by this time she was beginning to gain awareness of her own needs. She did eventually find a home, but of course, there were a few times when her fear pulled her back to old, harmful patterns. If it were not for the supportive container of shelter staff and our psychotherapy relationship, I do not believe she would have even gotten to that point. Hopefully she has continued to follow her dream. In my time at the shelter, I sat in the place of intention with many other clients. One young man wanted to see his mother be happy and to fulfill his personal dream of being an artist. There was a group of sisters who all differed in their perception of the family in the shelter, but I found that their wanting was similar in that they wanted a home and for their sisters to succeed in life.

The aspect of existential-humanistic therapy discussed here, intentionality, can be an effective tool in the work with this community. It allowed me to explore the unique experience of each client in this particular challenging and painful period in his or her life. Being able to place the experience of my clients into the framework of intentionality allowed me to see how they were moving toward their goals in life. Intentionality frames the pursuit of dreams as a series of steps beginning at wishing and ending at interaction. The young mother moved from wishing for a new home to finally interacting with her achievement—the new home.

The beauty of the existential-humanistic therapeutic approach is that age, race, gender, spiritual background, or personal history does not seem to be an obstacle. To me, there is a universal yearning that can be discovered through the path of intentionality. It was not as if the diversity of the clients did not matter: on the contrary, it did, but it was not an obstacle. How one is in the world is informed by his or her age, race, gender, spiritual background, and personal history. All of these aspects will inevitably impact what and how one wishes, wants, wills, acts upon, actualizes, and interacts with his or her intentions in life. We all wish, want, will, take action, actualize, and interact, but in all of this I still needed to be willing to see the entirety of the person who chose to sit with me by acknowledging the presence of race/ethnicity, class, and gender in the therapy room as well.

A Part of/Apart From

This given emphasizes the uniqueness of how we relate to ourselves and to each other. The thrown condition of *a part of/apart from* speaks to my clients' experience of homelessness. For my clients, their former life no longer existed. They could not go "home" and sit at their dining table or sleep in their own beds. From the perspective of existential-humanistic psychotherapy, there may be a felt sense of being apart from their former lives. The sense of separateness extended beyond the loss of the former life. It crept into the experience of suddenly entering a new community and not being able to adjust or relate to this new place in life.

A mother came to a session full of a kind of strength and angry fire that could light a thousand lives. She reflected that she felt she was not like the *others* at the shelter. "I'm not like these people; I was never on food stamps; I was always able to make it, and now I'm here." She was saying that she was apart from, but in reality she was now a part of, since she lived there at the same shelter as "these people." The internal conflict that she suffered from boiled over in a number of occasions and took the form of anger and rage at the system that she was now a part of.

Anger was a regular encounter in the therapy room. The source of anger ranged across the three key areas discussed in the basic existential-humanistic hypothesis of the three conditions when anger occurs. These are: expectations were not being realized; disappointment at the injustice or unfairness of the situation; and a feeling of lack of control (external locus of control) or the power to change their circumstances (IIHS, 2009). Anger was not the only reaction to the existential given of a part of and apart from. At times the anger showed up as stress, depression, or self-destructive behaviors that would result in Ask To Leaves (ATLs), which is the final action taken by shelter staff to have a resident dismissed from the program.

The experience of homelessness put some of my clients face to face with the condition of being a part of and apart from (Heery & Bugental, 2005). Their stories of loss reflected their experiences of losing what was once considered to be their own. They were no longer a part of the life that they had worked to have for themselves or their family and, as a result, were now apart from this former life. As a therapist, it was helpful to be able to see this life in the shelter in terms of dealing with separation, loss, and isolation. Although my clients did not use these terms to describe their current experience, it was one that I could be acutely aware of because of the existential-humanistic perspective in therapy. I could be open to understanding and having empathy for their thrown conditions (Bugental, 1965).

Choices/Relinquishment

In existential-humanistic psychotherapy we speak of choice and relinquishment. There is always choice, even when one feels none is present. But in choice there is relinquishment. This was one area that I drew strength from and focused on more often than not in the psychotherapy room. Relinquishment, losing in some form, is always part of life and is not, in itself, a sign that something has gone wrong. At times, my clients had to let go of things to which they were attached. The letting go of things had nothing to do with whether or not the things were good or bad. This was hard work. One mother made a choice for her family that led to the relinquishment of an abusive relationship. There was comfort in her relating with the father of her children, but there was an enormous amount of pain from the abandonment and verbal abuse that she suffered while in this relationship. In order for her to move past this pain, she had to make a choice that involved not only the relinquishment of the relationship, but of her ideal of family, which meant that she had to let go of her vision of herself as the mother with this man as father. It was a hard and painful journey that led her to becoming a resident at the shelter. She took a chance that many mothers in abusive relationships try to take. In her case, she was fortunate in that her abusive partner did not attempt to track her down to harm her or her children. She often reveled in her good fortune, but still remained pained at the choice that caused her to lose the life that she had accepted. While at the shelter she also struggled with letting go of other ways of being that she had created during her life, especially letting go of friendships that would have reconnected her with her abusive partner.

The children I saw in psychotherapy had to make choices on their own even if they did not really have too many choices about where they were at the time. Some of the children tried hard to exercise their ability to make choices. They fought with their parents while struggling to satisfy their wants and needs. At times, working within the area of choice and relinquishment was incredibly difficult, because I was faced with trying to help my clients navigate through the choosing and letting go. Initially, I would step in fully to help them along the way, but I found out that this was not entirely helpful, because I did not know the complete story of what was happening in my clients' lives. Other times, I would step away entirely and quickly discovered that my clients were making choices that were not at all helpful. The caseworkers and other staff let me know when this happened, and I was left helping to pick up the pieces from the ill-fated decision. I am choosing at this moment not to disclose detailed accounts of specific situations, primarily because retelling these poignant moments in practice would simply reveal too much information about my clients.

Choice and relinquishment are always present in our lives. In the lives of my clients who were working to recover from the loss of their previous lives, what they chose to do and what they let go of was very critical to their overall success at the shelter and ultimately in their lives. It is also important to note that as the psychotherapist, I was always in the place of choice and relinquishment. I had to make choices about when and how to work through psychotherapy with a client. I had to let go of some of my intentions since it became clear over time that what I thought would be good, was not necessarily beneficial. I also had to choose when to fully take hold of a client in order to prevent disaster. Finally, I had to (and still do) sit with some of the choices I made that in hindsight were not the best. For now, I continue to choose to let go of the pain and embrace the deep lessons I learned from my clients and supervisors during that time.

The Present Moment and Presence

My clients came into psychotherapy with immediate concerns about their living situations, interpersonal relationships, searches for a job, and receipt of government assistance. There was always a sense of urgency present in the room.

Usually they wanted mainly to deal with whatever crises they were trying to manage at that time, and this urgency would eclipse any possibility of working with past trauma, suffering, and loss that may have been the underlying issues in their lives. These underlying issues were often foundational to their current struggles. It might have been helpful and healing to work with my clients on these issues, but as my supervisor reminded me on numerous occasions, I did not have the luxury of time. It was rare if I could see a client for more than four sessions, and given the timeframe, it would have been difficult to even begin to dive into the depths of my clients' lives. Having to deal with the confines of limited time, this provided no better place or moment to work within the existential-humanistic framework of presence and present moment.

Presence refers to a state of being aware and engaged as much as one can be at that moment. There is a need to be sensitive to one's own emotional state as well as that of a client. The three components of presence in existential-humanistic therapy are: accessibility, expressiveness, and immersion (IIHS, 2009). Accessibility was vital in this work; it is allowing oneself to be open to whatever happens in a session and for every aspect of the session to matter or to have impact on oneself. Letting my clients know that what they were saying and doing mattered to me lent a level of comfort to both clients and myself. I believe that my clients understood that I cared about what they were feeling and were going through at those moments.

Expressiveness speaks to allowing one to share with clients their experience of the present moment and even bits of one's [the therapist's] personal life. I trod the water of disclosure very carefully. I did not want the sessions to become about me, but rather to be more about me sharing in my clients' experiences by reflecting back to them what I felt or thought in the moment. Self-disclosure helped on a few occasions, especially when clients were curious about my motivation for working at the shelter. Retelling my own personal story of living without a home, and how that led me to choose to work at this community, was often met with appreciation and a deep sense that I had been very close to their lived experience.

Immersion occurs when the therapist is deep within the work and is open to the full experience of the therapeutic relationship. This is characterized by letting down personal guards and being open to expressing ourself with a client. Immersion is not about losing oneself in a psychotherapy session; rather it is about allowing one to be completely in the session and focused with intention—on being there with the client. Diving deep into the moment with a client can be difficult, especially when the moment may contain some stress and/or trauma that could be hard for the therapist to be with. At times, the practice of immersion was difficult for me to manage with many of my clients. This could have been due to my lack of experience or that it was not appropriate at the time. Immersion was difficult to achieve at times, mostly due to my own need to be protective of my emotional self. But immersion can open doorways that would normally be closed in therapeutic approaches that champion a more distant onlooker interaction between client and therapist.

I believe that presence was a powerful part of the therapeutic process in sessions, and before and afterwards as well. Being there for myself when I had a long day with hard sessions helped me to rebuild my psyche for the next day's work. This usually involved listening to some favorite music on my long drive home or just taking a moment before I went to bed to sit in complete silence. I suppose it was my way of immersing myself in myself.

I found that being there—being present for all of those that I met at the shelter—was a powerful and potent aspect of healing. I was accessible as much as I could be, in whatever happened in the lives of the parents and children I saw. Everything mattered. I would catch the quiet dismissals of stress or sadness whenever I sensed a shift in their body or expressions. Something was there and it mattered. I expressed my concern to them with the intention to flow into the therapeutic conversation. At times, it seemed that my clients were just as curious and perhaps even concerned for me. I was often asked for my own reports of how I was doing that day. I did not lie, but I usually would take the road of discerning disclosure, i.e., would the self-disclosure serve the client, serve our relationship, or serve me? Questions I have learned to ask myself through the Unearthing trainings.

Immersion was an aspect of my practice outside of the psychotherapy room as well. I would arrive early and float around the site saying hello to staff, checking in with case managers, and greeting old and new residents. This was part of my practice of being *a part of,* even though as the therapist I was *apart from.* I worked hard to maintain a balance between these two concepts and it was important for me to engage and be present with the community in order to feel content with life there and to be effective as a therapist. I was not only physically present but emotionally present as well.

This act of presence usually garnered more referrals and moments of quick informal sessions in the hallways or the yard. It seemed that more residents were able to see the potential benefit of having another ally who was interested in their mental and physical well being, beyond the basics of shelter, food, and safety.

The Potential of the Approach

The EH approach is unique in that it recognizes that people have experiences that are unique unto themselves. "In this model of therapy, people are not reduced into types. Instead there is a continual pointing to possibility of human experience, which often overlaps and simultaneously is unique to the individual" (IIHS, 2009).

I believe that what is unique about using existential-humanistic therapy with this community is that this approach has a great advantage when working with those who are going through the process of entering a social care system. This system demands that individuals reveal their personal assets and histories in order to receive services. Because of that, in order to receive services from that system, in some way they have to become an object within the system. It is almost as if the self must be dissolved in order to receive assistance, and to some extent that is true. For example, most of the shelters in the Bay Area do not afford their clients the luxury of private rooms. Some agencies are able to offer this to a very limited number of families, such as the agency I worked for, but most others put families into shared spaces. This prevents anyone from having any real privacy. Parents are often confronted with situations of other parents disciplining their children. Food spaces and meals are shared. Dietary needs are difficult to support. Rooms can be searched. Curfews are often enforced on adults. These curfews were considered unreasonable by some of the parents at the shelter. The pain of losing one's own individual freedom and space was difficult for many of my clients. Private space and personal freedom were luxuries.

In EH psychotherapy, the client is honored as a human being. In the shelter system I worked in, the humanistic energy of honoring the humanity of the families was foremost on the minds of the shelter staff. It was a unique place in that there was always an effort to honor everyone there. Still, it was hard for many family members to deal with the loss of self and freedom in the shelter. In the psychotherapy room, we could openly explore the topics of self and freedom as they related to the immediate situation and as they related to people's internal feelings.

Challenges to the Work

Remaining in the moment was a challenge. One day a mother walked in furious and anxious about yet another time when staff had, as she put it, stifled her, or put up roadblocks to her progress. I was unsure about the validity of her facts, but that didn't matter. At that moment, her anger flowed into my own. Her anger was based upon the fact that she was black, and that is why she felt she was hassled. I was drawn into the issue because I shared her past, based on my own history as a black woman who has felt stymied by others. In our session her pain and anger became mine, and I flowed down her river not stopping along the way. James Bugental speaks of *pou sto*, "A *pou sto* is a place from which to exert power, a place to ground one's work, a base of operations. It needs to be solid, well founded. The psychotherapist needs a firm *pou sto*."(Bugental, 1999). My *pou sto* was to remain outside of the client's internal experience and to find a base within my own experience in the moment of the session. I chose this since I am aware of my own tendencies to merge with others, and remaining within myself helped me along the way in my internship. In this case, I had lost my *pou sto* in personal desire or an impulse of empathy. There was a therapeutic alliance, but it was more than what was needed. It took me a while, but I managed somehow to pull back into myself so that I could sit still in the moment while she was able to express her annoyance. Then a shift happened for both of us. I was there and no longer wrapped up in her experience and she became aware of what she saying. Perhaps that was because I was not immersing myself in her emotional pain rather I chose to take my *pou sto* and be present as witness. She finally stopped, then dropped inward and started to cry. I asked her as gently as I could where she was at that moment, and then she began her work.

I found myself drawn on more than one occasion down the path of distraction with the mothers, daughters, and sons who shared the therapy room with me. As the internship came to a close I discovered the power of pulling into the present moment. I put on my here and now rabbit ears (Yalom, 2002) and paid attention to the stories that they told about their day at the shelter. I never gained a good sense as to whether or not clients liked me or approved of my sessions. I was happy to have numerous women show up for the optional support group I held and to hear from the caseworkers that the women who attended appreciated the space. That space was intended to give them the opportunity to be with each other as women and as mothers.

I struggled with my *pou sto* on many occasions. In my attempts to create ease in therapy, I would begin sessions with a generic and ineffective inquiry such as, how are you? My supervisor would tease me a bit and tell me that I wasn't peeking over the fence and chatting with a neighbor. I believe that I was truly unsure of my *pou sto* as a therapist in the beginning of the internship. I had to begin to see my clients fully. I had to watch them as they came into session, notice how they moved, check out their energy, and see if they made eye contact. Doing this seeded many of my good sessions. Doing this allowed for my clients to know that I did actually see them, fully. If they arrived limping into my office, well we were certainly going to check in on a physical level first. Then after we determined that they could actually be there, we could explore the potential mind-body connection.

In the end I discovered that the EH approach is only as good as the psychotherapist. This approach requires that the psychotherapist be willing to be more than just a blank wall for the client to write upon. The psychotherapist must be willing to engage in an internal and external process of being with the client and with whatever is happening in the therapy room. The psychotherapist must be willing to be aware of what the client is bringing into the session as well as what the psychotherapist is (or is not) bringing in as well. Here is where the deeper challenge with EH therapy with this community lies, in the place of giving the psychotherapist the training necessary to be able to sit with the deeper social, cultural, and psychological struggles of poverty and the issues that are often related to these problems. This includes what I had mentioned earlier in this chapter: race/ethnicity, class, gender, spiritual background, and other aspects of diversity in our communities.

In working with those who were experiencing homelessness, I found that I was able to hold an awareness of their life situation by being respectful. Not blind, not overly optimistic, just respectful of the fact that my clients were now struggling with financial and emotional hardship. I had to hold in awareness that I did not know all of the answers, or that I was the benevolent therapist helping those in need. I had to respect the resulting social inequity that was present in the room. I was going home to sleep in my own bed, and my clients were not.

When the EH psychotherapist brings full awareness to psychotherapy, this intention creates a relationship based on commitment, mutual respect, freedom, choice, and responsibility. It is also an approach that is nuanced in such a way that it makes it challenging, at least for early-career psychotherapists, to use this in all situations. It is not as if the psychotherapist would sit down and immediately begin discussing or using the term intentionality in a session. Rather, the psychotherapist would step into psychotherapy with the framework and understanding of intentionality while working with clients.

It is also critical to be aware that it may be easy for the psychotherapist to focus on the self and I in EH therapy. Much of what has been written in EH therapy (Bugental, 1965) uses those terms in its teaching. It is important as a therapist to be open to the understanding that there are differences in how people see themselves. The vision of "self" may be more oriented towards we and community rather than self and I. The concepts that are espoused in EH therapy are relevant to the human experience, but it must be understood that that relevancy may only go so far. The EH psychotherapist must be willing to relinquish the possibility that this approach is for all, but can delight in the potential that it can be helpful to many.

Self

Where I stand in my own experience of living is part of the therapeutic process. The therapeutic orientation that I chose reflects my own perception of my being. I can easily relate to the dichotomy of human existence, referred to as the givens of existential-humanistic psychotherapy. What keeps me going in life and allows me to make it through all of the challenges and successes is my intention. Within the existentialist-humanistic model of psychotherapy there is movement from impulse to action as intentionality. I wish, want, will, act, actualize, and interact, as much as those I worked with in session wished, wanted, willed, acted, actualized, and interacted in their daily lives. I deeply appreciated the accessibility of the existential-humanistic process, in that it inherently assumes the empowerment of individuals to transform their lives.

References

Bugental, J. F. T. (1965). *The search for authenticity: An existential-analytic approach to psychotherapy.* New York, NY: Holt, Rinehart and Winston, Inc.

Bugental, E. & Bugental J. F. T. (1984). Dispiritedness: A new perspective on a familiar state. *Journal of Humanistic Psychology, 24,* 49-67. doi: 10.1177/022167884241004.

Bugental, J. F. T. (1999). *Psychotherapy isn't what you think.* Phoenix, AZ: Zeig, Tucker & Co., Inc.

Heery, M. & Bugental, J. F. T. (2005). Listening to the listener: An existential-humanistic approach to psychotherapy with psychotherapists. In J. D. Geller, J. C. Norcross, & D. E. Orlinsky (Eds.). *The psychotherapist's own psychotherapy: Patient and clinician perspectives* (pp. 282-296). New York, NY: Oxford University Press.

International Institute for Humanistic Studies (2009). *Ways that may help an angry person.* Petaluma, CA: International Institute for Humanistic Studies.

International Institute for Humanistic Studies (2009). *Givens and intentionality.* Petaluma, CA: International Institute for Humanistic Studies.

International Institute for Humanistic Studies (2009). *Marking our place in time: Historical roots and the present emphases of existential-humanistic psychotherapy.* Petaluma, CA: International Institute for Humanistic Studies.

Yalom, I. D. (2002). *The gift of therapy.* New York, NY: HarperCollins Publishers.

5

⌒

The Existential-Humanistic Givens: A Personal Exploration

Christopher T. Harrison

THE EXISTENTIAL-HUMANISTIC APPROACH to psychotherapy is guided by four simple yet profound givens: (a) finitude, (b) being a part of and apart from, (c) embodiment, and (d) choice and responsibility (Heery and Bugental, 2005). These principles provide a road map to follow on the journey through "each client['s] . . . singular topography" (Heery & Bugental, 1999, p. 27). Beneath the four givens lies the potential for authenticity, "a way of being in the world in which one's being is in harmony with the being of the world itself" (Bugental, 1981, p. 33). The being of the world is, at least, partially defined by these givens of existence. Authenticity, therefore, entails an ability to accept the givens as they manifest throughout life, in all its myriad forms. Thus, the core task of psychotherapy is the search for authenticity, a phrase coined by James Bugental in his book so titled. Existential-humanism recognizes the uniqueness of each human being's experience in the world; the givens may be conceptually universal, but are experientially unique.

The purpose of this chapter is to explore the four givens from my perspective as an individual and clinician. Personal reflection provides an opportunity to integrate the material that was presented over the course of the two-year Unearthing the Moment Training and allows for a review of how the work has affected me. I will dedicate a section to each given and conclude with thoughts on the importance of focusing on communication in psychotherapeutic healing.

Finitude

We begin dying from the moment we are born, a paradoxical fact easily forgotten in the fast-paced culture of modern life. Death is the first given under review because, arguably, it is the most powerful; so powerful, in fact, that we have created a culture that does its best to deny its existence. We demean death's power through film and television, where actors' characters kill and are killed with brutal regularity, while the actors live on to conduct press tours in celebration of their achievements. The denial of death may be a cause of intense suffering; it is definitely a primary cause of inauthentic living.

The existential-humanistic orientation is defined by its careful consideration of the impact of finitude on the lived experience. One of the few certainties in life is death, and the manner in which one deals with this universal truth is of paramount importance. A lack of awareness around one's mortality is akin to believing one can function optimally without sleep or food; the latter statement is so ridiculous it is laughable, yet finitude, the key ingredient for the sustained nourishment of authenticity, is skipped so frequently it has become forgotten. I chose to study and practice existential-humanistic psychotherapy because I believe life cannot be truly lived without an acute awareness of death.

Death is the most significant limitation we face as humans beings. Regardless of the power we acquire or the wealth we obtain, there is no escaping the ticking clock of our own demise. How can we live fully without realizing our mortality? How can we live honestly without admitting the ultimate limitation we face? The search for authenticity begins when we allow ourselves to contemplate our deaths. Death has figurative and symbolic meaning, along with the literal, and fortunately we have many opportunities to practice dying throughout our lives. The humanistic side of this paradigm focuses on the birth created from death. Developmental psychology is rife with examples of this process; to move from childhood to adolescence, the child dies, to move from adolescence to adulthood, the adolescent dies, and to move from adulthood to old age, the adult dies. The natural world provides countless lessons of peaceful death like the rising and setting of the sun and the gentle whisper of fallen leaves as they journey gracefully to their final resting place.

Death, in its literal and figurative manifestations, provides cause to consider life's meaning. This given is critical because it unearths the ultimate question of life's purpose. When we are able to fully embrace our mortality, something changes. The ego is transformed because it recognizes itself as but a transient life form attempting, with all its might, to generate permanence. My clinical work is, in part, guided by my clients' holding of their own mortality. In my training, I worked with at-risk adolescents who had no awareness of the certainty of their own deaths. Many of them had experienced the death of loved ones, but that had done little to awaken thoughts of their own mortality; death remained something that happened to other people, not them. Developmentally it makes sense that these teenagers were not in touch with their mortality; they were just beginning life and an overt focus on death could have been an indication of pathology. Death, then, was worked into the therapy through alternative means. The symbolic aspect of death became primary, as many of my clients had experienced tremendous upheaval in their home lives. We discussed the premature loss of childhood and the grief of losing parents to addiction, divorce, or prison. The trauma experienced by these young people had a direct impact on their formation of meaning. Many of them were very depressed and saw life as a burden to be shouldered. The future was too distant to consider, and getting through each day was their first concern. Holding onto this first given in therapy provided me with an anchor with which to maintain consistency from session to session. Death and meaning go hand in hand, without some consideration of death, authentic meaning can become unimportant.

I had one client who experienced significant loss and trauma very early in life. His mother was a drug addict; his father left the house before my client was born. My client was left to raise his two younger brothers until his grandmother finally stepped in to care for the children. He is a shining example of death's ability to fuel rebirth. He was headed down the same path as his mother. He began using and selling drugs at around 10 years old, he was struggling to make it to school, and generally did not care if he lived or died. Eventually he moved to a new town with his grandmother and brothers and was given the opportunity to be a child. Our work focused on the figurative loss of his parents and his innocence. He consistently commented on how grateful he was to have experienced such traumatic loss at an early age because it provided him with meaning. He had come to believe that his life's purpose was to make something of himself, to give back to those who have experienced similar circumstances, and to overcome the challenges of his childhood by becoming a strong and successful man. He had found profound meaning in his suffering and, like the forest fire that clears out old growth to provide space for the emergence of new life, he had been reborn.

Like the young man described above, my personal growth and search for meaning has been significantly impacted by my consideration of death. I experienced an extremely traumatic loss at the age of 14 when my uncle died instantly in a freak ski accident while skiing with my brothers, my cousins, and me. My life was forever changed that day. I realized that my life too could end in an instant, just like my uncle's did. At first, this realization led me to feel quite depressed. Meaning was stolen from me. I asked myself what purpose life had if it could be taken away so suddenly and capriciously. Slowly, my depression gave way to appreciation for each moment lived. I have experienced several losses since my uncle's death, and I consider my mortality each and every day. By embracing mortality, I am liberated from its nihilistic grip because I now realize that death has transformative potential, as evidenced in all of life's natural cycles.

The existential-humanistic paradigm is defined by its focus on finitude. The existential part of the equation awakens us to the power of death and the potential loss of meaning that frequently accompanies it; the humanistic perspective provides the realization that death is but an opportunity for rebirth. Taken together, existential-humanism acknowledges the power of suffering and allows for its transformation into something that evokes meaning. Ultimately, finitude provides each of us the opportunity to live authentically, for death and rebirth are the most basic elements of nature's harmony.

A Part of and Apart From

The second given is the notion that we are at once a part of and apart from different things in our lives. I had not been introduced to this concept before the Unearthing the Moment Training and, of all the givens, it has had the most profound effect on me personally and professionally. I had spent the vast majority of my life attempting to be a part of everything. I am the last born of seven children and often felt excluded growing up, due to the sheer size of my family. My life was dramatically impacted by my experience of feeling apart from my family as a child. I, of course, did not have the ability to identify that experience as a child, but reflecting on it as an adult has provided tremendous meaning. Had my life been dictated by a need to be a part of? Was it really OK to be apart from, or did that mean something was wrong with me? How was I to decide when to be a part of or apart from? These were some of the questions I wrestled with over the two-year Unearthing the Moment Training. The questions opened a variety of deep insights into my experience of self in the world.

It became clear as I worked with the givens that they were providing the building blocks of meaning and identity. Consideration of this very simple premise, a part of and apart from, had opened a deep probe into the nature of my identity as a human being. I discovered that I had been far too willing to sacrifice and/or ignore parts of myself to fit in with the "popular" crowd. Somehow it became ingrained in my psyche that being a part of was all that mattered; perhaps my early childhood experience of being apart from my family engendered such a strong conviction. I struggled with alcoholism for years, an addiction fueled by my need to fit in; I lost my virginity long before I felt ready because I felt I needed to in order to remain a part of the group of friends I had formed in high school. At one point in my life, I prided myself on the fact that I was a social chameleon, easily able to adapt to any situation and fit in without a problem. I have since learned that in doing so I forgot about myself; others formed my identity, and meaning was generated externally. This period of my life coincided with the death of my uncle, and I battled between an internal sense of meaninglessness and external need to be a part of something to try and make up for that loss of meaning. This illustrates the interrelation of the givens; they are themselves a part of and apart from one another.

My profound experience with this particular given has impacted my clinical work most dramatically. My interest in working with adolescents was likely generated from my experiences as an adolescent, when I was most wounded. Perhaps that wounding was born out of my ignorance that it is, in fact, OK to be apart from certain things. The removal of this ignorance illuminated the sheer necessity of being apart from and provided the realization that I had willfully chosen to be apart from a great many things in life. Adolescence is the most crucial period of identity development. The propensity for teens to focus externally in forming their identities creates the need for a particularly strong focus on this given for this age group. If I had possessed explicit knowledge of this given as a teen, I may have made different choices. Existential-humanistic psychotherapy provides a unique opportunity for teens to explore their attitude and emotions around being a part of and apart from certain groups, gangs, classes, etc.

The population I worked with while completing the training was especially at-risk with regard to gangs. Many of them felt they had to be a part of a gang for safety, security, and income; or, they felt terrified at being apart from gangs for fear of being assaulted or killed. The consideration of being apart from gang life was scary and unimaginable for some, while the experience of being a part of gangs was equally daunting. A focus on this given provided room for my clients to explore the feelings they had on both sides of the equation. They, like me, were able to probe more deeply into the nature and sources of their identity. Clearly, this given had a profound impact on my personal growth and clinical work.

Embodiment

Ultimately, we are all a part of the human race. The bodies we inhabit make that so; correspondingly, we become apart from the human race when the body dies. Though presented in a linear manner for the purposes of clarity, the givens constantly interact with one another. The energy generated through that interaction becomes the "stuff" of life. For example, we can only be a part of the human race if we are first born into a human body, which also dies, leaving those still living apart from the person they once knew. Thus, the primary experience of being a part of and apart from begins and ends with the body.

Early psychological theories did not place much emphasis on the body as a reservoir for emotional holding. The body, following the medical model, was an object that performed certain functions to support life. The mind was a separate entity that acted on the body through the application of reason and logic. This separation of mind and body was, perhaps, most dramatically exemplified through Descartes' work, and his philosophy deeply informed the early developments of psychotherapy. Recent theoretical and empirical developments however, have discovered that the body and mind cannot be separated; the two are one and any separation of them creates a false dichotomy. I will leave aside transpersonal thought on the existence of the soul and its presence before and after the body is born and dies as those issues, though important, are not directly relevant to the current topic. Somatic psychology has become a respected discipline in the field and serves as a testament to how the existential-humanistic approach was, in this regard at least, ahead of its time.

As with the previous two givens, the clinical focus on the body involves how conscious one is about one's body. Does one recognize the different types of movement one makes when discussing particular issues? What is the quality of one's breath in and out of the lungs? How tense or relaxed does one's musculature tend to be? These are some initial considerations taken into account when working with clients on this given. The idea is to work from the inside out. If not aware of the manner in which they hold their body in different situations, it is unlikely they are in touch with their more subtle energy systems. Emotion is energy in motion, and that energy is generated from and passes through the body. The more we can assist our clients in getting in touch with their gross anatomy, the more successful we will be in helping them discover the deep emotional rivers that flow through them. Recent trauma research has uncovered fascinating details on the importance of cellular memory. It is becoming increasingly more accepted that the brain is not the only organ with memory.

My personal psychotherapy, meditation practice, and course work in somatic psychology have taught me a great deal about my body. I have become more aware of how and where I store anxiety, I have experienced the deep emotional reservoir that sits beneath my skin, and I have trembled in fear as I revealed parts of myself to my therapist and to my own conscious mind. The body is a great educator, and making it a focus of therapeutic work opens doors that talk therapy alone could never approach.

Working with teenagers on body awareness was an interesting endeavor. Objectification of the body may be strongest in the adolescent population. I called certain patterns of movement to the attention of many clients and received awkward and surprised reactions. The sheer ignorance that many of us carry with regard to our bodies is astounding, me included until recent years. Awareness of patterns and recognition of comforting, supportive postures enables one to wake up to the fullness of one's humanity and ultimately serves as another opportunity to live authentically, for if we can learn to live in harmony with our bodies, we can learn to live in harmony with the larger body of the manifest world.

Choice and Responsibility

The final given is choice and responsibility. Discovering one's experience of these two ideas provides invaluable information about the way the world is experienced. The most quintessential aspects of existentialism, in my opinion, are death and the role of choice and responsibility. An acute awareness of death provides one with intimate knowledge that they are, in fact, limited. How do we choose to proceed with our lives with knowledge of this ultimate limitation? What level of responsibility do we accept for the choices we make knowing that we may not be around to see their end result? This area is ripe with ethical and moral implications that are far too complex to address in this chapter, but the fact remains that choice and responsibility are at the very core of consciousness and meaning making.

This given is important for psychotherapy because therapy begins with the client's choice to enter the therapist's office for the first time. The client assumes responsibility for paying for the session and treatment begins.

Again, the goal of therapy in this model is to assist the client in living an authentic life. A core feature of authentic living is gaining consciousness around choices, or recognizing that choice is or is not present in one's life. The three givens are once again profoundly interrelated to this one. Does one choose to face one's mortality? Does one take responsibility for being a part of or apart from decisions made by family, friends, and colleagues? Does one choose to recognize the treasure trove that exists within one's body?

Although I have chosen to write about this given last, it is, for me, the place where therapy begins. I am acutely aware of my clients' relationships to choice and responsibility in all of my sessions. I feel it is the most tangible and informative of the givens. Most teenagers are just beginning to wrestle with making their own choices after living a life dictated largely by the choices of their parents. Others are traumatized by the level of responsibility they have been forced to assume because of the poor choices or difficult circumstances of their caregivers. In very simplistic terms, everything boils down to choice and responsibility. One can choose to work toward living an authentic life or choose to ignore the fact that they have any choice at all.

I constantly monitor my own relationship to this given. While completing the Unearthing the Moment Training, I frequently felt anxious and overwhelmed by the responsibilities of my graduate program but became relieved when I reminded myself that I made a choice to enter the program and had the freedom to get out if I wanted to. I struggled with responsibility in my clinical work and realized the struggle was born out of my choice to occasionally take on the problems of my clients as if they were my own. I had areas in life where I felt my choices were very limited and worked to realize that I was choosing to see it that way. Choice, responsibility, and freedom (another existential ideal not included in the givens) are intertwined in a web that begins with birth and ends at death.

Conclusion

The four givens provide the framework for the existential-humanistic approach to psychotherapy, but are only given life through the art of authentic communication. The key to this method of work is how the givens are communicated to the client in the most appropriate and well-timed manner. Discretion is an ingredient not often discussed in the context of psychotherapy, yet it is among the most important considerations to contemplate in clinical work. Above all, psychotherapy is about communication, in that it helps to shape how one communicates to others and, more importantly, how one navigates the landscape of internal communication. The givens provide sign posts along the journey of inner transformation. They are visited time and again in a spiral cone that oscillates from the surface of our consciousness to its depths and back again. They serve as a map to help lead the way to wholeness and harmony, and deep communication is the tool that blazes the trail.

The Unearthing the Moment Training provided me with tremendous personal insight and professional development. It served as a GPS of sorts for the journey down my path of inner growth. The paradoxical simplicity and profundity of the existential-humanistic model is astonishing and, I believe, my journey down its path of knowledge and wisdom will continue for years to come.

References

Bugental, J. F. T. (1981). *The search for authenticity*. New York, NY: Irvington.

Bugental, J., & Heery, M. (1999). Unearthing the moment. *Self and Society, 27*(3), 26-27.

Heery, M. & Bugental, J. F .T. (2005). Listening to the listener: An existential-humanistic approach to psychotherapy with psychotherapists. In J. D. Geller, J. C. Norcross, & D. E. Orlinsky (Eds.), *The psychotherapist's own psychotherapy: Patient and clinician perspectives* (pp. 282-296). New York, NY: Oxford University Press.

6

Integrating Existential-Humanistic Theory
Into a Weight Management Program:
The Given That We All Live in a Body

Christopher S. M. Grimes

THIS CHAPTER IS A REFLECTION on the application of the existential-humanistic therapy orientation as a means of conceptualizing the work I do as a psychologist leading a multi-disciplinary team of clinicians providing weight management services. Through the process of reflecting and writing this chapter, I hope to clarify how the interventions and techniques employed as part of the weight management program fit within the existential-humanistic theoretical orientation.

There are four givens of human existence (Heery and Bugental, 2005). An additional fifth given was also discussed during the Unearthing Training (IIHS, 2008): These five givens are (a) we all live in a body; (b) we will each die; (c) freedom to make choices and responsibility that comes with making choices; (d) we each experience being a part of and apart from; and (e) we each seek to make meaning. In this chapter I will reflect on the given we all live in a body and its application to weight management.

Before beginning the reflection, it may be helpful to provide background information to set the context. For the last five years, I have been serving as Clinical Director of the Program for Psychology & Religion at St. Louis Behavioral Medicine Institute. A couple of years ahead of my joining the staff at St. Louis Behavioral Medicine Institute, a weight management program had been developed for the treatment of obesity among clergy and religious women and religious brothers of the Catholic Church. The program was begun after a survey of church leadership revealed obesity, and the associated physical diseases and impairments, to be a substantial concern that was impairing the ability of priests, religious sisters and religious brothers, to minister and carry out the duties of their assignments. Upon assuming the responsibility of Clinical Director, I inherited the weight management program, which has been successful at helping obese clergy and religious reduce their weight and increase their participation in exercise and other health-supportive behaviors. The Program for Psychology & Religion has long taken an integrative and multi-disciplinary approach to treatment. The reflection provided in this chapter was written as I approached my first anniversary in the role of Clinical Director, and was written as a means of reflecting on how existential-humanistic theory relates to the work being done through the weight management program.

The Program for Psychology & Religion has history and reputation for approaching treatment from a multi-disciplinary perspective, and the current treatment protocol for the weight management program reflects this preference. Each client who presents for the weight management program is evaluated by a physician, a psychologist, a physical therapist, a nutritionist, and a spiritual director. This comprehensive assessment results in an individualized treatment plan. The general components of the outpatient intensive program include the client participating in twice-weekly individual therapy, once weekly spiritual direction, once weekly nutritional counseling, monthly consultations with a physician and psychiatrist (if needed), and monthly assessment by a physical therapist. In addition, the client participates in several group therapies during the week including: interpersonal group, cognitive-behavioral therapy group, mindfulness group, art therapy group, spirituality group, nutrition group, and fitness and active lifestyle group. The goal of the treatment program is to help the clients achieve healthy eating and exercise behaviors, weight loss, and later weight maintenance, while at the same time increasing their self-awareness, their ability for self-monitoring, and their overall well-being (psychologically, physically, socially, and spiritually).

Within this context, I want to reflect upon how the program is addressing the given of living within a body. This seems like an appropriate starting point for exploring the application of the existential-humanistic theoretical orientation to a multi-disciplinary weight management program for religious professionals. (Any client discussed in this chapter represents an amalgamation of individuals in order to protect anonymity and confidentiality.)

The Given: We All Live in a Body

I have chosen to focus on the given of embodiment because it seems to me that clients presenting for help with weight loss are most aware of this given of existence. As Schneider and Fitzgerald-Pool (2005) observe, clients who present symptoms of disordered eating, including compulsive over-eating, are expressing through their symptoms problems with being-in-the-world. Schneider and Fitzgerald-Pool note that clients who experience problems with eating are likely to be living predominantly within the physical dimensions while neglecting other dimensions of existing.

Many of the clients who enter the weight management program have been struggling with obesity for many years. It is not uncommon for middle-aged clients to report they have been overweight since adolescence or childhood. Many have previously tried weight loss strategies, but most often with only small success or temporary changes. Over the years they have made accommodations to their body. Sometimes coming to feel that achieving long term weight loss is hopeless, they have adapted their behavior to fit what their obese body will and will not allow them. They have, for example, reduced or eliminated routine physical exercise and may have adopted a sedentary lifestyle.

I once worked with a minister from the western United States who, as a young adult, enjoyed taking advantage of the beautiful splendor of mountains and lakes through fishing, hiking, and biking. However, as the client's level of obesity gradually increased, to the point of being 200 pounds overweight at the time of entering treatment, the individual had stopped all outdoor activities. We found through the course therapy, however, that the love of the outdoors had never left, but instead it had been overshadowed by difficulty experienced when attempting to participate in those previous hobbies. It took so much physical effort for the individual to carry the extra weight that the once pleasurable activities had grown to be experienced as work, and the fun was lost.

The weight management program begins with a concern for the body. Individuals entering the program are assessed by a board-certified internist who evaluates their current state of physical functioning. Besides their struggle with obesity, many clients also have other associated health concerns such as diabetes, hypertension, and hyperlipidemia. This is one reason a multi-disciplinary approach, which takes seriously the given of living in a body, is important in weight management treatment. Once cleared by the physician for physical exercise, one of the first parts of the treatment plan to be constructed is an exercise routine. Another critical part of the initial assessment and early treatment for obesity is a nutritional assessment and development of a healthy meal plan that will meet the client's daily nutritional needs, while also promoting weight loss. Both exercise and meal planning are an ongoing and vital component of the overall treatment plan. Because of the physical effects of obesity, beginning with a focus on the body is necessary, and appropriate, but it is not, in my opinion, sufficient by itself.

One of the ways in which the weight management treatment program attempts to help clients move beyond a focus entirely on their body is through the practice of mindfulness meditation. One of my current responsibilities is leading a mindfulness group. In my reading of literature on mindfulness, I have come to see the principles of mindfulness as very consistent with the emphasis on the inner-subjective found in existential-humanistic therapy. In the literature, the practice of mindfulness is often described as cultivating non-judgmental awareness of the client's experience in the present moment (Segal, Williams, and Teasdale, 2002). I conceptualize mindfulness as a form of self-empathy: It is a process by which clients are encouraged to identify the thoughts and feelings that are present for them in the moment and to put off judgment or criticism. The goal of mindfulness practice is to help clients develop greater awareness of their thoughts and feelings in order to allow greater ability to make choices, as compared to reacting to a thought or feeling impulsively or automatically. In other words, mindfulness is the practice of unconditional positive regard and empathy toward the self in the present moment, with the goal of moving toward greater congruence between thought, feeling, and behavior. Through incorporating practices such as the mindful body scan and sitting meditations, clients are encouraged to consider the ways in which their thoughts and feelings relate to their physical sensations, and how their physical sensations relate to their thoughts and feelings.

In the existential-humanistic model, naming what is in the room is part of our psychotherapy work. I have been especially careful to attune to this during my work with individuals in the weight management program. I am a slender Caucasian male, approximately 5 feet 8 inches tall, and weighing 125 pounds. This fact can be paradoxical for clients working on weight issues with me, intimidating and motivating. When the alliance between my client and myself or in a group is sealed with safety and trust embedded in confidentiality, I might ask, "How are you feeling working with a psychologist who is physically small and relatively fit?" I know by asking this question I may be inviting deeper issues such as jealousy, envy, and shame about their weight. But it is also leaning into the positive potential of each person in the room with weight issues. First, in a group they are not alone creating the experience of universality and second, by having a physically small group leader, they can hold hope that they too can move toward caring physically, emotionally, and spiritually for themselves. These two cornerstones, universality and hope, are essential to successful existential-humanistic group work (Yalom, 2005). My self-disclosure calls attention to and uses what is actual between the client and myself, leading to the release of new choices for the client, thus implementing more of the existential givers—a part of and apart from, choices and responsibility, and meaning-making.

Sometimes, answers to this question about a client's feelings regarding working with a slender and fit therapist, open up the individual or group to a very important existential given with eating disorders—we will each die.

Beginning to touch on issues of death such as death anxiety is intertwined with care of the body, eating, and exercise. Taking care of myself physically is a priority, as I am a father of three young children and feel strongly that I want to be alive and participating in their lives and my professional life giving guidance to others as long as I can. I talk openly with my clients and group members about using death anxiety as a motivator to be fully alive now in a healthy body.

At first, many clients have a hard time understanding the importance of developing a broader context from which to understand their struggle with obesity. Over time they come to develop greater sensitivity to the physical and emotional states associated with hunger, stress, sadness, joy, etc. They also begin to understand the relationship between emotional states and eating behavior. As the value of this mindful awareness begins to take hold for clients, they often express it by stating something like, "I used to think if I just dieted and exercised, that alone would be enough for me to lose weight, but now I understand it is more important that I achieve a healthy and balanced lifestyle."

When clients are able to verbalize awareness that the behaviors that have lead to their obesity are more complicated than what they eat or how much they exercise, they are able to open to a deeper kind of work in therapy. They are now ready for deeper exploration of other existential concerns beyond embodiment, which Schneider and Fitzgerald-Pool (2005) suggest are important to the therapeutic process in the treatment of eating problems. It is this deeper existential-humanistic psychotherapy that, I believe, helps move clients toward lasting, transformational changes in their approach to life.

Conclusion

This is just the starting point. In this chapter I have reflected upon ways in which the awareness of the limitation of life in a body is applicable to the treatment of weight management. But there are four remaining givens, which because they are common to all humans, must have application to weight management treatment. It is my intention in the future to explore how, using these givens as a foundation for understanding weight management, clients can facilitate the development of a depth-oriented approach to psychotherapy to complement the multi-disciplinary integrative approach already in use. Through this reflection I have come to realize how important it is for clients to confront the limitations of living in a body, and how working through these limitations while getting more in touch with the relationship of the mind, body, and spirit is the starting point for deeper therapeutic work.

References

Heery, M. & Bugental, J. F .T. (2005). Listening to the listener: An existential-humanistic approach to psychotherapy with psychotherapists. In J. D. Geller, J. C. Norcross, & D. E. Orlinsky (Eds.). *The psychotherapist's own psychotherapy: Patient and clinician perspectives* (pp. 282-296). New York, NY: Oxford University Press.

International Institute for Humanistic Studies (2008). *Givens of the human condition*. Petaluma, CA: International Institute for Humanistic Studies.

Schneider, K. J., & Fitzgerald-Pool, Z. (2005). Eating Problems. In E. van Deurzen and C. Arnold-Baker (Eds.), *Existential perspectives on human issues: A handbook for therapeutic practice*, (pp. 58-66). New York, NY: Palgrave Macmillan.

Segal, Z. V., Williams, J. M. G., & Teasdale, J. D. (2002) *Mindfulness-based cognitive therapy for depression.* New York, NY: Guilford.

Yalom, I. D. (2005). *The theory and practice of group psychotherapy* (5th ed.). Cambridge, MA: Basic Books.

7

Season-Ending Sport Injury and Existential Impacts

Rex R. Vogan II

SPORT, LIKE LIFE, IS COMPLETELY UNPREDICTABLE from one moment to the next. A focused and determined athlete may do everything in his or her power to prevent an injury by attempting to train hard, eat right, and mentally prepare for each practice and competition. In fact, many athletes tend to believe they can, through skill and effort, control their own destiny. But, within a split second, the immortality many athletes feel can come crashing down with a sharp and awakening pain of reality. Injury is blind to race, age, gender, and skill level. According to Williams and Andersen (2007), approximately 23 million athletes are injured each year. Ironically, these numbers continue to rise despite advances in athletic equipment and rule changes promoting safety and protection for participants. Even with enhanced technology and a greater understanding of the human body and how it works, injuries continue to occur.

Serious injury is one of the most emotionally and psychologically traumatic experiences faced by an athlete (Heil, 1993). When sudden injury occurs, athletes may experience every emotion in the psychological lexicon: depression, anger, fear, tension, disgust, anxiety, and panic, to name a few

(Lynch, 1988). Danish (1986) stated that injury can be highly stressful because it not only threatens physical well-being, but acts as a threat to the athlete's self-concept, belief system, social and occupational functioning, values, commitments, and emotional equilibrium. For the injured athlete, it is not uncommon to experience a loss of independence and social mobility (i.e., loss of status), a decreased capacity to perform, greater exposure to pain, and thoughts about disfigurement, permanent disability, and death (Hobfoll & Stephens, 1990; McDonald & Hardy, 1990).

Season-ending injuries, like career-ending injuries, are usually quite severe and often require surgery followed by several months of rehabilitation. When a severe injury occurs, it is common that the injured athlete copes with an excess of medically based information, the loss of physical capability, the emotions of withdrawing from a desired activity, and a dependency on others to fulfill daily needs (Flint, 1999). When an athlete no longer participates as a result of a season-ending injury, there is a separation and alienation from the people and activity with whom the athlete is essentially unified (Thomas & Rintala, 1989). In some cases, unfortunately, coaches pay little attention to injured athletes because they are no longer useful to the team or perhaps because coaches feel awkward around injured athletes and do not know what to say or do (Weinberg & Gould, 1999; Wiese-Bjornstal & Smith, 1999). For those athletes who sustain a season-ending injury, isolation may be felt more frequently and with a higher intensity because coaches and teammates may "write them off" for the entire season. This perceived lack of support from teammates and coaches, while already feeling disconnected from their sport due to physical restrictions, will likely make the physical and mental recovery that much more difficult to cope with.

From the existential-humanistic perspective, the four givens of existence include embodiedness, finitude, choicefulness, and being a part of and apart from (Heery & Bugental, 2005). It appears that these themes are especially relevant when discussing the injury experience of athletes. For example, injured athletes routinely find themselves separated and isolated from their coaches and teammates, and are left to find meaning in a life without athletics. Although a physical death has not occurred, a symbolic death of their identity and invulnerability often takes place. As a result of these existential dilemmas, many athletes may be unprepared to deal with the magnitude of their recovery.

When an individual is confronted with the givens of existence (i.e., certain intrinsic properties that are an inescapable part of every individual's existence in the world), internal conflict may arise due to this awareness. For an athlete who is faced with an injury, embodiedness may have profound implications. These individuals dedicate their life to training and being in superior physical condition, and when the body fails them, the betrayal felt can be overwhelming. The examples that follow have been disguised for purposes of confidentiality.

In working with a 26-year-old female, semi-professional triathlete who sustained a compound fracture of her tibia and fibula, her experience of the loss of fitness, independence, and place on the team increased her fear and the emotional difficulty for her. Her injury challenged her perceptions of invulnerability and identity as an athlete, and in describing what it was like to acknowledge the difficult aspects of this process, she stated,

> So, I couldn't use my hands, for example, because with the crutches um . . . I couldn't carry anything, so that was probably one of the first things that I was learning, and I had to learn to ask for help, so that was one of the harder transitions that I made. Because again, asking for help was admitting that I needed help, and that was a sign of weakness.

In describing how she took her health for granted, she explained that if someone had granted her three wishes before the injury, she would have only needed two, but now that she was going through a season-ending injury, she would need all three. She stated,

> Before I only needed two [wishes] because happiness to me is love and money, so I have the love and the people I need and then the money to have fun and to enjoy it with, but now I have added health, so I do need that third wish whereas before, I just had it, it was just taken for granted [her physical health].

Similarly, a 22-year-old male, collegiate soccer player who tore his anterior cruciate ligament, stated,

I mean it is upsetting me that I can't play. It's hard to just sit there and watch and hear people complain about, oh practice was tough today, and then I'm sitting on the sidelines going, man, I wish I could play. So, it's, it's tough to sit on the sidelines.

In describing the most difficult part of his initial injury experience, he stated,

Just not being able to do what I want to do. I can't work and money is tight. I had two jobs before this, and I can't work. I just can't do the things that I want to do, and that's the hardest part. Like when my buddies go out and play football and I can't do that. That's probably the hardest part, just the restrictions that I have.

In discussing the totality of his injury experience, he stated,

It's not, it's not just a sport injury, it's an everything injury. It's a . . . it just affects your entire life. It affects the way you sleep. It affects the way you get around. It affects your relationship with people. It affects your work. It affects your school. It affects a lot of things and I don't think I really realized or imagined that it was going to have this big of an impact on my life as it has.

When young adults who are in elite condition are suddenly restricted physically, put in a position of dependence, and uncertain of the impact an injury will have on their ability to play, their life is opened to the reality that all things change. Although this change was not chosen, asked for, or even welcomed, it is the truth of their life that can either be embraced and used to find deeper meaning and purpose, or used as an opportunity to deny a given of existence and strengthen one's denial and avoidance of what it truly means to experience life as a human being.

From the existential point of view, a core inner conflict is between awareness of inevitable death (i.e., finitude) and the simultaneous wish to continue to live; yet the fear of death can be experienced on many different levels. For example, one may fear pain, worry about the act of dying, regret unfinished projects, or mourn the end of personal experience (Yalom, 1980).

Additionally, the person may have a symbolic death associated with a certain role, relationship, or aspect of their identity.

The committed athlete usually lacks the opportunity to develop a well-rounded identity outside of sport. With a self-identity constructed solely from athletic participation, injury may be especially difficult because the athlete has little to maintain his or her self-worth. In addition, compounding a potential identity crisis, any physical impairment that prohibits active involvement in an athlete's sport, whether temporary or permanent, is cognitively, emotionally, and behaviorally challenging (Pederson, 1986).

For the semi-professional triathlete, her realization of how much worse her injuries could have been resulted in the athlete reflecting on life and death, as she explained,

> A lot of people said about my injury, "It could have been worse, you could have lost your life, or been paralyzed." I could have gone head first into that telephone pole; so yeah, it could have been worse. I mean, that could have been a spinal injury, I could have been paralyzed, and I try not to think about that.

When asked how she dealt with the reality that her accident could have resulted in her death, she answered,

> I deal with that with avoidance and denial, as much as I can . . . living with the idea of being young and healthy [is what she attempts to do] this [her injury] is definitely a reminder [of her mortality] . . . it's not supposed to happen until your seventies or eighties [that you become aware of death].

In another attempt to minimize the severity of her injury and take her mind off her mortality, she preferred to outwardly show strength and confidence, even if that did not coincide with how she felt. She stated,

> I use denial and avoidance so much . . . I really just try to keep a face of positivity, optimism, and confidence. How much behind that was congruent to what I was feeling . . . let's just say they did not match up all the time.

When asked if this incongruity was self-driven, she said,

Yes, because it did not match my schema of being independent and being strong and not showing weakness . . . the pounding of that message I can really link to coming from my mom . . . I created "I'm strong, be strong, don't show weakness" message, because to be vulnerable or to show vulnerability, I would be weak, and to be weak I could be hurt, and that would be bad.

Although the athlete did not want to fixate on how close to dying she came (i.e., her head missed the telephone pole by inches), this severe accident had an overwhelming effect on her experience with life. Her injury was perceived as a threat to her physical life, the meaning she derived from competing, and shattered her illusion of invulnerability. She was unable to see that being strong and injured can co-exist, and therefore, felt ashamed and vulnerable to the outside world. Even though she utilized avoidance, denial, and repression to deal with the flood of death anxiety, she could not escape from the reality that one day she will die.

For this athlete, it appears that as long as she projects the image that she is getting ahead, progressing with her rehabilitation, or accomplishing goals, the awareness of death anxiety will be countered, and her fears of not returning to competition will be hidden. Consequently, she chose not to deal with her true internal emotions in the hope that they would magically disappear.

Choicefulness refers to the fact that the human being is responsible for and the author of his or her own world, own life design, and own actions. According to numerous authors, accepting and taking responsibility for the injury has been noted as an important part of coping more effectively with the injury and rehabilitation process (Bianco, Malo, & Orlick, 1999; Brewer, Van Raalte, & Petitpas, 1999; Gould, Udry, Bridges, & Beck, 1997a, 1997b; Shelley, 1999; Udry, Gould, Bridges, & Beck, 1997; Vogan II, 2003). Not surprisingly, injured athletes who feel a sense of control and personal responsibility for their recovery are more invested in the rehabilitation process.

Injured athletes are confronted with daily choices, from choosing to be compliant with their rehabilitation and maintaining a positive attitude, to making choices that support their healing or sabotage their progress. For the semi-professional triathlete, during her experience in the hospital after her surgery, she was able to quickly realize within two days after surgery, that how she dealt with this injury affected her environment. She explained,

> The lesson that I learned the second day in the hospital, when my anger was my most showing emotion . . . was how I perceived this injury and how I live with it, how I deal with it was being reflected with the nurses. So, at that point, when I was showing anger and really feeling sorry for myself was mostly what it was, they were mirroring that emotion, so I was getting that back. That was a real quick and dirty lesson that if this is what I show, this is what I am going to get back, and this is definitely not the response that I wanted.

She also realized that taking responsibility for mental and physical recovery needed to be a priority. She stated,

> I had to be a grownup real quick. It was kind of like part of me wanted to be a kid and be taken care of and doted on, but I just saw in a few instances that this isn't going to work. So, I made a conscious decision at this point forward, that how I perceive this injury and how I present with it better be positive.

When discussing his choices on how to cope with his injury initially, the injured lacrosse player stated,

> Um . . . yeah, it's probably not the best thing, but I've gone out socially a lot more. I've gone to the bar a little more, probably drank a little more than I would if I was in season. I try not to drink when I'm in season but now it's not as hard for me to go to the bar and have a few drinks . . . so yeah, I guess I have done that to kind of cope with it.

Responsibility for all human beings accounts for existence and authorship of one's own life. According to Yalom (1980), "to be aware of responsibility is to be aware of creating one's own self, destiny, life predicament, feelings and, if such be the case, one's own suffering" (p. 218). The injured lacrosse player utilized a form of escape through alcohol as a way to deny the reality of his injury. However, the semi-professional athlete was able to realize the importance of taking responsibility for her actions, words, and perceptions of her injury. By understanding the influence she had on her own recovery, she was able to shift her relationship to her injury.

The last given of existence is being a part of some situations and apart from others. For injured athletes, being isolated and apart from their team, coaches, and sport participation is a given. Consequently, it has the potential for the athletes to truly realize that regardless of their current injury status, participation in their sport will always be limited due to the natural aging process of the human body. However, the intensity of the isolation felt can be positively or negatively influenced by the injured athlete's choices, as well as by his or her teammates and coaches.

The injured lacrosse player stated,

You don't feel as much a part of the team when you're not out there. You learn a lot about the kids when you are playing with them. You learn how different people play and everything. Like our freshman this year, I'm not getting a chance to feel them out. I can't really feel how they play or anything like that, so I'm sure it's going to be more of a learning experience when I have to actually go out there and play with them. I mean, I can talk to them and get to know them off the field but it is different when you're on the field.

However, for this athlete, his coach made a choice to keep him involved. The athlete stated,

He was real upfront with me. He said he wants me to help out on the sidelines, he knows that kids kind of, at least some of the kids, look up to me so he knows that I can be an encouragement at times or just be an extra pair of eyes. So, maybe I can see something that he doesn't see, or as far as defense goes maybe I can tell a younger guy that he could do something that the coach doesn't really see or something like that.

In contrast, a 21-year-old male, collegiate basketball player who suffered an anterior cruciate ligament tear, discussed his coaches not contacting him. He stated,

No, not as far as phone calls, but if I see them in the halls or whatever they will ask but, it's kind a . . . I expected more, to be honest with you. I expected maybe a phone call here or there saying, "How are you doing?" "What does it look like when you are getting surgery?" That type of thing, but I mean, it just seems like I am really way on the back backburner.

In summarizing how the lack of contact from his coaches affected him in dealing with his injury during the midpoint of his rehabilitation, the same athlete explained,

Um, it's more of a business, so I think the knee is kind of like, you're kind of like damaged goods. You're on the back burner, you're not a priority. So that's just, I mean that's another part of the frustration that comes along with the injury.

When his rehabilitation was complete, the athlete expressed what he wanted (i.e., expected) from his coaches. He stated,

Lunch would be cool, or any type of get together to say, "How are you doing? What can I do to get you ready for the season? Could I set up something with the trainers?" Or, "Come up to the gym, and we can run sprints and I'll help you with your shot," or something like that, you know, just . . . someone there that you know they're going to help you. That is what I have wanted all along.

The semi-professional athlete described her experience with accepting help and allowing her support system to contribute to her healing, when she stated,

Coming from this kind of thing where it is "just me" outlook, and then realizing how important my social system, my social supports are, just came down on me like a brick . . . the most pleasant brick. Bricks, I should say, because I had people who were just acquaintances that came out and really reached out. My swim coach had the whole community there arrange meals to drive by my house. Where my tendency would be to withdrawal if I'm feeling anything that is not positive, people were pulling me out. My boyfriend was mostly responsible for that. So, I didn't really have a lot of time to feel sorry for myself because I was surrounded by supporters. It was humbling. That was probably one of the most humbling experiences of my life, just to see the support I got, and just showed how, again, grateful and lucky I am to have friendships and connections like this.

It is clear that the effect, positive and negative, of feeling a part of versus apart from one's social support and team has profound impacts on the experience for the injured athlete. Since the athletes cannot control how others will respond to their injury, it is vital that the individuals work through their anger, disappointment, and betrayal if support is not provided. Otherwise, resentment and bitterness have a high probability of sabotaging the recovery process. Unfortunately, the collegiate basketball player was not able to make a return to his sport for his senior season, in large part due to lack of support and the negative impact it had on his motivation, dedication to rehabilitation, and hope of being a part of the team once again.

Since most human beings deny the existential truths we all live with, when an injury or illness unexpectedly occurs, most individuals will be ill prepared to properly deal with the emotional and physical consequences. Athletic injury does not occur subtly; it is often a traumatic and overwhelming experience where the injured athlete feels disoriented and uncomfortable in his or her own skin. The injured athlete cannot escape the magnitude and new reality of life, even when there are attempts to deny it as long as possible. Therefore, it is crucial that the existential givens (i.e., embodiedness, finitude, choicefulness, and being a part of and apart from) that an injured athlete faces are appropriately dealt with, to enhance recovery and personal development.

References

Bianco, T., Malo, S., & Orlick, T. (1999). Sport injury and illness: Elite skiers describe their experiences. *Research Quarterly for Exercise and Sport, 70*(2), 157-169.

Brewer, B. W., Van Raalte, J. L., & Petitpas, A. J. (1999). Patient-practitioner interactions in sport injury rehabilitation. In D. Pargman (Ed.), *Psychological basis of sport injuries* (2nd ed.), (pp.157-174). Morgantown, WV: Fitness Information Technology.

Danish, S. J. (1986). Psychological aspects in the care and treatment of athletic injuries. In P. E. Vinger, & E. F. Hoener (Eds.), *Sports injuries: The unthwarted epidemic* (2nd ed.), (pp. 345-353). Boston, MA: John Wright PSG.

Flint, F. A. (1999). Seeing helps believing: Modeling in injury rehabilitation. In D. Pargman (Ed.), *Psychological basis of sport injuries* (2nd ed.), (pp. 221-234). Morgantown, WV: Fitness Information Technology.

Gould, D., Udry, E., Bridges, D., & Beck, L. (1997 a). Coping with season-ending injuries. *The Sport Psychologist, 11*(4), 379-399.

Gould, D., Udry, E., Bridges, D., & Beck, L. (1997 b). Stress sources encountered when rehabilitating from season-ending ski injuries. *The Sport Psychologist, 11*(4), 361-378.

Heery, M. & Bugental, J. F. T. (2005). Listening to the Listener: An Existential-Humanistic Approach to Psychotherapy with Psychotherapists. In J. D. Geller, J. C. Norcross, & D. E. Orlinsky (Eds.), *The Psychotherapist's Own Psychotherapy* (pp. 282-296). New York, NY: Oxford University Press.

Heil, J. (1993). *Psychology of sport injury.* Champaign, IL: Human Kinetics.

Hobfoll, S. E., & Stephens, M. A. P. (1990). Social support during extreme stress: Consequences and intervention. In B. R. Sarason, I. G. Sarason, & G. R. Pierce (Eds.), *Social support: An interactional view* (pp. 454-481). New York, NY: John Wiley & Sons.

Lynch, G. (1988). Athletic injuries and the practicing sport psychologist: Practical guidelines for assisting athletes. *The Sport Psychologist, 2*, 161-167.

McDonald, S. A., & Hardy, C. J. (1990). Active response pattern of the injured athlete: An exploratory analysis. *The Sport Psychologist, 4*, 261-274.

Pederson, P. (1986). The grief response and injury: A special challenge for athletes and athletic trainers. *Athletic Training, 21*, 312-314.

Shelley, G. A. (1999). Using qualitative analysis in the study of athletic injury. In D. Pargman (Ed.), *Psychological basis of sport injuries* (2nd ed.), (pp. 305-319). Morgantown, WV: Fitness Information Technology.

Thomas, C. E., & Rintala, J. A. (1989). Injury as alienation in sport. *Journal of Philosophy of Sport, 16*, 44-58.

Udry, E., Gould, D., Bridges, D., & Beck, L. (1997). Down but not out: Athletic response to season-ending injuries. *Journal of Sport and Exercise Psychology*, 19, 229-248.

Vogan II, R. (2003). Living through a season-ending injury: An exploratory study. Unpublished master's thesis, Ithaca College, Ithaca, NY.

Weinberg, R. S., & Gould, D. (1999). *Foundations of sport and exercise psychology* (2nd ed.). Champaign, IL: Human Kinetics.

Wiese-Bjornstal, D. M., & Smith, A. M. (1999). Counseling strategies for enhanced recovery of injured athletes within a team approach. In D. Pargman (Ed.), *Psychological basis of sport injuries*_(2nd ed.), (pp. 125-155). Morgantown, WV: Fitness Information Technology.

Williams, J. M., & Andersen, M. B. (2007). Psychosocial antecedents of sport injury and interventions for risk reduction. In G. Tenebaum & R. C. Eklunds (Eds.), *Handbook of sport psychology* (3rd ed., pp. 404-424). New York: Wiley.

Yalom, I. D. (1980). *Existential psychotherapy*. New York, NY: Basic Books.

8

‿⟶

Finding Your Balance

Gina Touch Mercer

In order to keep our balance, we need to hold the interior and
exterior, visible and invisible, known and unknown, temporal and
eternal, ancient and new, together. No one else can undertake this
task for you. You are the one and only threshold of an inner world.
This wholesomeness is holiness. To be holy is to be natural, to
befriend the worlds that come to balance in you.

—John O'Donohue, *Anam Cara: A Book of Celtic Wisdom*, 1996, p. xvi

AS A YOUNG THERAPIST, I desperately wanted an instruction manual
called "How To Help People." When clients, often older and worldlier than
me, would come into the psychotherapy room, I wanted to instill hope and
confidence. Even though I was completing my doctoral training, I truly didn't
know what to do when the door closed.

Using History To Find My Way

I'd accumulated 12 years of education beyond those of my Italian-
American parents. In that time, I learned how to diagnose the psychological

problems I could see around me. Steeped in my family-of-origin enmeshment, I paid attention to the patterns and people that were stuck. I could provide abundant advice on how everyone should behave, because that's how the people of my world tried to be "helpful." But beyond that, I needed to learn more in order to truly help. My teachers said I should have a theory that could help me explain what I was doing to help people change, though the formality and elucidation of that process eluded me for years.

I turned to my naturalistic observations: I could see that family obviously had much to do with how well, or how ill, individuals might become. And I drew from sources of history. Through years of reading about the holocaust and slavery, I understood the deep and pervasive impact of culture on a person's formation, as I flinched from the oppression and aggression of power. But I was most drawn to the depth of pain and suffering and the curative peace of transformation.

I understood that many factors could influence personality and psychological functioning, but I couldn't identify a single theory or describe how to help people change.

Informal Education

Being a novice, I didn't realize I could depend on informal training and life experience to figure out how to help. I had been taught to play the piano by nuns who then trusted me to play the organ at church, and I had parents who were deeply religious. These experiences shaped in me a spiritual rootedness, showed me the bond between respect and trust, and helped me appreciate the enduring gift of relationship.

As a very small child, I had a turned-in foot that made it hard to walk, and my parents took the pediatrician's advice to enroll me in ballet class. I immediately loved both the elegance and discipline of dancing, and spent years literally finding—and holding—my balance.

If only I had realized I had received a foundation in kindness, responsibility, humanity, spirituality, and creativity, it may have been easier to articulate my theory.

Becoming a Professional

Since I was becoming a "professional," I valued formal education and knowledge. During graduate school, I luckily met three supervisors who showed me how to help. I gratefully swallowed every teaspoon of guidance I received. One mentor told me, "The client will say this . . . or this . . . and you can say this . . . or that. . . ." The first time my client said "this," I knew what to say! And when I said "that" and she in turn said "this," again I knew what to say! This was my earliest experience of "self-efficacy" on my way to actualization as a fully functioning therapist.

Another supervisor directed me to Bowen (1993), the multigenerational family systems therapists, and to genograms. Using those, I could finally show persisting patterns in black and white! I also learned about the concept of "individuation," which illuminated the broader context of "this and that," and became the platform for my one-size-fits-all "treatment plan" . . . to help people achieve independence (my early, naive understanding of "individuation"). I became enthralled with "I" statements and "assertiveness training" and realized I had so much to teach my clients! I could help them communicate their personal desires and once-suppressed feelings and needs with crystal precision, and they would in turn get those needs met. Not only was I helping, I was becoming an expert!

Becoming a Real Professional

It took the next 10 years of clinical experience, 10 more years of teaching clinical psychology and family and couples theory and psychotherapy, nearly 20 years of marriage and parenting experience, and the last three years of existential-humanistic training to "birth" the kind of help I might offer now.

In teaching graduate students and in living through my own midlife stages, I have become able to distinguish "individuation" from independence, freedom, separating or even autonomy. I now maintain that those definitions and interpersonal stances alone are narrow and insufficient to help people change. That kind of individuation doesn't teach a person how to give or accept love and intimacy, although it may help him or her to differentiate from a dysfunctional family and form a sense of self. In focusing on the intentional choices and ongoing processes of *balancing* separateness and intimacy, simultaneously being a part of and apart from (Heery & Bugental, 2005), I think I better understand, appreciate, and practice the concept of individuation, now that I have matured into being a part of and apart from as a basic existential given in living a healthy life within a family system.

A Balancing Act

Despite my growth, I see how hard it is to shift and regain the balance of individuation and intimacy in our most significant relationships, especially as we leave and enter new lifecycle stages. Harder still is it to maintain this balance in the multiple systems and roles that define us. But deep within ourselves, within each couple, between each parent and child, underlying every family, and woven through all systems, is a matrix of separateness and belonging. How we change—or stay stuck—seems connected to how we navigate this matrix.

The Dance

In the past year, my husband and I learned to dance the tango, and now we finally move as a unit, even as we dance separate steps. I'm no longer trying to lead to resist his power; he's no longer stepping on my feet because he has no idea where I'm going; and we don't have to stay in one place, locked in delirious embrace, in order to feel a part of.

The tango metaphor somehow helped me to define myself as an evolving humanistic family therapist and characterizes my emerging way of helping. I have needed the dance floor, the years of watching Italian relatives fight in my kitchen, and all the years of reading on my own and in graduate school, to learn about individual and family dynamics, and to understand how to help. I also needed the past 15 years of practicing psychotherapy, the teaching experience and the students who needed my precision and clarity, the nurturance of supervisors who were "good parents," and colleagues who, like sisters and brothers, could help me recognize what I myself, and other people, need most.

Compassion

My connection to an existential-humanistic consultation group provided the next steps. Intrigued by the name, "Unearthing," I dipped my foot in the new psychotherapy training ground. From the first meeting, I found another home. The group is gilded with caring and support, with honesty and wisdom, and with women who, like the aunts of my childhood family, provide guidance, security, and cherishing.

It is in all of these climates that I have grown.

How To Help

If I could describe my orientation as a psychotherapist now, it would encompass the philosophies and concepts that have always mattered to me and the values I have always held. My intention is to embody my values in family psychotherapy providing a role model for family members to experience their individual and collective strength by using their own voice within the family system.

Seeing families in distress means I, the psychotherapist, need to be clear on where I stand, sometimes referred to in existential-humanistic psychotherapy as *pou sto* (Bugental, 1999). My pou sto for the families I see is listening with an open mind and heart to relieve isolation; genuine compassion to accompany the family suffering; deep respect for heritage and culture (while recognizing their maladaptive forces); preparation and support for the realities of human and family life; recognition of the complexity and impermanence of living; perspective and hope in changing dysfunction; and reconnection to the ancestry and stories we inherit and inhabit, often without our knowledge or choice.

A Case Example

To illustrate this and to "actualize" the recommendation for a "unified" theory (Appel and Ken-Appel, 2010; Magnavita, 2012), I would like to present some case material I recently used in an advanced family and couples psychotherapy course to describe how I've come to integrate my Bowenian family systems training with the concepts and processes of existential-humanistic theory. The clients I present are an amalgamation of many couples' and families' stories, and are not meant to disclose the confidential history of any couple I have met.

The couple I met was young, both in their late 20s, and married for three years, with a 2-year-old daughter. They were both white, from upper middle class backgrounds, and had moved 3,000 miles away from their families for "good jobs" and "a fresh start." Both were employed in major companies, which provided on-site child care. They came in for psychotherapy after the wife's second affair, the first having occurred when they were engaged.

After I shared this presenting information with my class, we conducted a 10-minute role-play of the intake. I then asked the students watching and those role-playing the spouses to share their reactions.

Common reactions included vilifying the wife and identifying with the husband, despite his wanting to take their daughter and return to his family, 3,000 miles away from her mother. We talked about how to "join" this couple, and see the family unit as the client, offering neutrality and managing countertransference towards the "villain" (W), the "victim" (H), and the daughter (the other "victim").

We talked about biases, assumptions, countertransference, collusion, and the impact of gender roles, religion, and culture on learned morality. Then I talked about valuing *both* clients as people of worth, explaining the emptier concept of neutrality through the foundational existential-humanistic concept of "unconditional positive regard" for each.

Then we role-played the next several exchanges:

T1: "As you tell me about all that you've been through in the past three or four years, I wonder how you have stayed together to this point?"

W1 (immediately): "He's been the one holding us together. I'm the one who did this; I need help. He's been so forgiving. So incredible."

H1: "I really loved my wife, but I don't know if I can survive this. This is the second time! I've already told her this, but just so you know, I'm 99 percent sure I want a divorce."

W2: "I don't want that, but I can understand why he does. I really don't know why or how I could hurt him like this. I don't deserve his forgiveness, or his loyalty. I don't know if I can even be helped."

H2: "I don't know if I can stay any longer."

W3: "Do you think you can help us? Help me?"

T3: "When you both decided to come here, what did you imagine would happen?"

W4: "That you could help me, help us, figure out why I did this— again—and help me stop once and for all. Maybe then he wouldn't leave with our daughter."

H4: (Shakes his head.)

T5: (To Husband): "What you imagined might be very different. Can you describe what you envisioned? I'm also wondering about your reaction to what W just said."

H5: "I know she wants me to make a decision right now. But if I do . . . (trails off)."

W6: "I really understand why he would want to leave, but I don't want that! I don't want to lose him . . . or Ariel, because of my stupid mistakes!"

H6: "I really wish you had thought about us sooner. I really loved you, and wanted us to be a family, to stay a family, but now I just look like a fool for trusting you. I truly loved you."

W7: "I know you didn't deserve this. Any of it. I just wish we could go back in time . . . that I could have come here sooner, that I would never have hurt you."

T7: "It seems like you both wish you could love each other again. I am struck by the caring that comes through even though you are suffering so much."

After this exchange, I asked my students again to share what they were experiencing as they listened. Some asked why I thought the wife was suffering, and why I didn't answer her questions directly about whether I could help. I invited the students to move closer to their inner experience, away from content of the discussion and how they felt about the content; to what was occurring inside them as they listened more deeply to our interaction. I asked them to pay attention to the shifts of mood in themselves and in the room, and they noticed that it had become "sad," but quickly moved to ask how I was "seeing suffering" in the wife, or considered her to be "caring" when maybe she was just feeling guilty.

I talked about reframing (a main technique from my systems training) the real and palpable pain and suffering of their existential isolation, loss, and fears of future losses (Heery & Bugental, 2005). I noted that my intention was to acknowledge this pain, while trying to provide some hope in response to their question by recognizing their bond. I also shared my intention to avoid blaming and scapegoating or siding with either of the spouses against the other as I tried to maintain unconditional positive regard for both. And I shared my genuine sadness for this young couple and family with so little support.

This tapped into my countertransference, what this couple's story was touching inside of me and I shared with my students (Bugental, 1999). I had been part of a young couple with little support, since I made the choice to leave home. In my family, moving away to gain independence was punished; it wasn't the choice prescribed. Also in my culture, and in the broader patriarchal society, the wife's loyalty to husband and children was an unquestioned given. It might be acceptable for Italian (or other) men to "stray," but never for a woman.

My humanist and feminist beliefs and my existential and multigenerational training allowed me to transcend some biases my upbringing had cultivated. Also, I fully expected this couple's story to have more substance beneath the surface. I intended to ask about their family of origin histories to bring to awareness in the present, the unfinished business this couple had inherited and how they might use their connections to the past to make conscious choices for the present and future.

After disclosing my own countertransference reactions in class, I asked the students to think about the sources of their countertransference. One spoke about a family betrayal, some about religious beliefs, and many about personal choices they would never make. Before returning to the role-play, I asked the students to have compassion for this couple, for both people, and to remain attentive to their own personal reactions as the couple's story unfolded.

Returning to the role-play, I asked both spouses if there was anything in their families or their history that in any way resembled what was happening in their relationship. The wife answered immediately, saying:

W8: "My father had multiple affairs, and my mother took him back every single time! I hated him for it, and I felt like she was weak! I always wished she would put a stop to it. I almost wish H would leave me, even though I don't really want that. But I know I don't deserve him because of how much I hurt him."

H8: "Nothing like this ever happened in my family. My parents loved each other, they still do, and I never even saw them fight."

T8: "So when W was growing up, she was more like Ariel, but now she feels more like her father?"

W9: "Well, I mean, I'm not, I don't want him ... I don't want to do this to Ariel or to H. I can't believe it's so simple that I would just repeat my father's pattern. Like I said, I hated him for it, and really wanted him to leave. But my God, I hope Ariel doesn't feel that way about me!"

T9: "I don't think it's simple at all. I'm just wondering how both of your families' earlier experiences might somehow connect to what you're facing now."

H9: "There is no connection for me or my family. Like I said, my parents are still happily married. This never happened to them."

T10: "I'm wondering then if anything really significant did happen in your family, even if it didn't involve an affair."

H10: "Nothing really. Nothing that relates to this at all."

W10: "His parents are actually the ones who suggested that he and Ariel come back to live with them. They want to provide a stable home for her."

H11: "I'm not sure what I'm going to do yet."

T11: "It sounds like you see how complicated all of this is."

H12: "Not of my choosing."

W12: "I know. I'm so sorry."

T13: "H, I'm sorry if it feels like I'm pressing you. But I wonder about what it was like to grow up in your family. I've heard a little about what it was like for W growing up. What was it like for you?"

H14: "Well, pretty normal. I played sports. I got good grades. And like I said, my parents were happily married."

T14: "Did you grow up with brothers or sisters?"

H15: "I have . . . I had a younger sister. She died when I was 6."

T15: "H, I'm sorry. You were both so young."

H16: "It's fine. I'm fine. It was a long time ago."

T17: "How did you and your parents live through that?"

H17: "My mom was very religious."

T18: "So how did she survive? And how about your father, or you?"

H18: "I'm not sure why we're talking about this. How does this have anything to do with anything?"

T19: "I'm sorry if talking about this brought up more painful feelings or memories."

H19: "That's not what I'm here to talk about."

T20: "I'm sure it doesn't feel connected. But maybe talking about this could give some continuity to who you are, and some perspective to the decision you're trying to make now. It may connect this important, unfinished history from your past to what is happening in your life right now, or uncover how you cope with life's tragedies even now."

At that point, I asked for a timeout in the role-play and asked the students to describe what it felt like to role-play and to watch these spouses.

The "husband" immediately became tearful, disclosing that he genuinely felt sad for this man. I turned to the "wife" who sighed and said she'd been "holding her breath" since I said that "she" was like Ariel. She really hadn't seen any connection between the affair and her "husband's" history until realizing he may have been trying to replace his sister with Ariel, for himself and his parents. The "husband" added that he actually felt more confused about unsure about what he would do about the marriage.

I asked the role-playing "wife" how it was to hear her "husband" say this. She said she felt stunned and pulled between feeling sorry for herself as a child, and sorry for her "husband" as a child. She said she was much less focused on the affair, feeling guilty, or even worried about their future.

I then turned to the class for their reactions, and by this point, their earlier conscious countertransference reactions had dissipated. The students wanted to hear more about this couple, and what happened to them in therapy. Of course, they wanted a happily-ever-after ending . . . like the couple as newlyweds, thinking this was possible by putting the past behind them.

I shared more information about how the husband's family coped after his sister died, by choosing never to talk about her again, almost pretending that she was never born, in order to survive the grief and guilt. We talked about how this might have impacted his ability to experience any emotions, or his emotional presence and intimacy in the marriage. They were not surprised to learn that the wife's father continued to have affairs, each time being forgiven (but not forgotten) by the mother in order to keep the family together. I noted that her mother had been hospitalized four times for depression, and that her father was not allowed to meet his granddaughter, because his daughter could not forgive him for what he'd done to her mother and to her.

We talked about how these two people's histories intersected and how their choices had much to do with unfinished emotional traumas from their own childhoods. In merging family systems theory/therapy with existential-humanistic philosophy, we could see how this couple learned to distance and separate from each other even as they tried to be a family.

How Change Happened

Working with this family, and teaching my students about how to work with families like this example, required a blending and weaving of traditions and time. By unearthing the spouses' feelings and unfinished suffering from the past, we could look together at how history continued to influence their choices and could even dictate their future. We looked directly at how as therapists, our own countertransference, assumptions, interpretations, and biases could interfere with compassion and alliance, between ourselves and the couple, and between the spouses. We actually experienced how developing compassion and uncovering the existential constructs of thrownness and isolation could become a path to healing prior *and* recent tragedies and to finalizing the story with the hope of a happier ending for each member of this family.

To highlight the overlaps between my Bowen and existential-humanistic training and the philosophies and processes that most speak to me, I will point out the terms and concepts that I have tried to synthesize. I begin with a quote of Appel and Ken-Appel (2010) that guides their recommendation for a unified theory: "Human beings exist in multiple substrates" (p. 273). I believe this includes us, as psychotherapists.

Many of the most significant concepts of family systems psychotherapy can be interpreted and understood by some of the existential givens and basic constructs.

Joining: To *become a part of* the family while remaining *apart from* it.

Neutrality: Having unconditional positive regard and compassion for each client in direct and indirect treatment, as well as for their suffering.

Individuation: The ability to balance the *intrapersonal* processes of reason and emotion; and to balance the *interpersonal* processes of simultaneously being *a part of* and *apart from* significant others. Individuation allows one's self and others the ability to exercise "Freedom/Choice," which is defined as the ability to fully and consciously merge reason and emotion in making decisions while honoring the choice and freedom in others to make choices.

Horizontal and vertical stressors: Predominant factors and patterns that create "thrownness" or falling into life experiences and contingencies not of one's choosing; having contingencies and circumstances beyond one's control.

Homeostasis: The state of existence in systems comprised of rituals and patterns to establish and maintain order; often used to deal with, attempt to avoid, or forestall grief, impermanence, and finitude.

Conclusion

In their analyses, Sprenkle, Davis and Lebow (2008) and Bott (2001), identify the "common factors" in therapy that transcend the specific treatment modality or approach and that are typically responsible for change in therapy. These include: (1) conceptualizing difficulties in relational terms, (2) disrupting dysfunctional relational patterns, (3) expanding the direct treatment system, and (4) expanding the therapeutic alliance.

Consistent with the perspective of the multigenerational family therapists, I believe that grieving past unresolved losses and finishing unfinished business can permit choices that redirect the course of an individual's and a family's life. I believe that the "work" of psychotherapy and the way I can help is to identify and repair dysfunctional patterns in the here and now, bringing closure to recapitulating suffering from the past or causing additional pain and suffering that can persist and expand through generations. I believe that the presenting psychological problem often relates to the unfinished stories and patterns that can be traced back though multiple generations of a person's family and to both sides of a couples' ancestry. With the psychotherapist's adept ability to bring this history into the present with compassion and unconditional positive regard, coupled with the client's courage to explore these patterns, new choices and taking responsibility for these choices emerge into a mature, healthy family.

In combination with the essential, foundational elements of the existential-humanistic focus on the present client-therapist relationship (Bugental, 1999), acknowledgement of the multi-dimensional spheres of personality (Appel and Ken-Appel, 2010), and the contributions of multigenerational family systems theorists, I can articulate my voice in psychotherapy and how I endeavor to help people change.

To transform pain in families, I bring my heart's compassion into the room. I bear witness to choices of compassion and respect as families transform their history into a present and future that embody hope.

References

Appel, J. and Ken-Appel, D. (2010). The multipath approach to personality: Towards a unified model of self. *Psychology, 1,* 273-281. Irvine, CA: Scientific Research Publishing. url=http://www,scrip.org/journal/PaperInformation.aspx?paperID-3058.

Bott, D. (2001). Client-centered therapy and family therapy: A review and commentary. *Journal of Family Therapy, 23,* 361-377.

Bowen, M. (1993). *Family therapy in clinical practice.* Lanham, MD: The Rowman & Littlefield Publishers, Inc.

Bugental, J. F. T. (1999). *Psychotherapy isn't what you think.* Phoenix, AZ: Zeig, Tucker & Co., Inc.

Heery, M. & Bugental, J. F. T. (2005). Listening to the listener: An existential-humanistic approach to psychotherapy with psychotherapists. In J. D. Geller, J. C. Norcross, & D. E. Orlinsky (Eds). *The psychotherapist's own psychotherapy: Patient and clinician perspectives* (pp. 282-296). New York, NY: Oxford University Press.

Magnavita, J. (2012) Advancing clinical science using system theory as the framework for expanding family psychology with unified psychotherapy. *Couple and Family Psychology. Research and Practice 1*(1), 3-13.

O'Donohue, J. (1996). *Anam cara: A book of celtic wisdom.* New York: Cliff Street, HarperCollins.

Sprenkle, D., Davis, & Lebow. (2008). *Common factors in couple and family therapy, the overlooked foundation for effective practice.* New York, NY: The Guilford Press.

9

Learning Presence From the Pros—My Kids

Kate Calhoon

What we know matters, but who we are matters more. Being rather
than knowing requires showing up and letting ourselves be seen.

—Brene Brown, *Daring Greatly*, 2012, p. 16

AS PSYCHOLOGY STUDENTS WE ARE TAUGHT the nuts and bolts
of theory, diagnosis, treatment approaches, and more. There are checklists
of symptoms and how-to guides for best practice treatments for many of the
most common psychological struggles. I recall clinging to these absolutes early
in my training because they gave me some sense that I could achieve a measurable and concrete level of competence. I come from a lifetime of wanting
(a little too much) to "do it right." As a result, I sought more reading, more
supervision, and more checklists. Surely if I applied myself I could do this
thing called psychotherapy just right, like a 4th grade spelling bee or gold-star
penmanship.

Once I began to see clients, I was frequently thwarted in the execution
of my well-prepared psychotherapy plans. My rigid mental preparation often
proved to be more of a distraction than an asset. My inner critic was working

hard. However, I began to notice that my natural curiosity and acceptance of clients proved to be powerful ingredients for creating connection and promoting growth. If I had the insight to understand this dynamic at the time, I might have recognized that my ready willingness to accept clients precisely as they were mirrored my own secret desire for unconditional acceptance of myself. But, alas, I wasn't there yet. Consequently, I would revisit each session afterward and try to figure out exactly what worked and what didn't so I would be prepared again for our next session.

During my internship more than one supervisor urged me to trust in the power of the relationship, to focus on the here-and-now experience, and to prioritize presence over preparedness. Presence seemed obvious, insufficient, and dauntingly difficult to capture on a checklist. I could hear what they were saying, but could not yet implement their words of wisdom.

Over the last eight years working with clients as student, intern, post-doc, and now, licensed psychologist, I am finally convinced that presence is indeed at the foundation of meaningful psychotherapy. Presence is the vehicle by which safety, trust, authenticity, connection, and the transformative experience of being seen arrive in the psychotherapy room. An informed and intentional therapy approach is certainly important but falls short without a heavy dose of presence. To be honest, I sometimes still struggle with the inner critic in the form of self-doubt: "Am I enough?" "Am I doing it right?" My clients, too, are prone at times to seek only the same quick, concrete solutions that I once wished to provide them. I see it as my job to keep us searching toward the inner experience of the client, which is an essential guide for our work.

A Parent Learns

Perhaps the best teachers of presence in my life have been my two young sons. Their complete lack of self-consciousness and ability to give themselves fully to the moment are inspiring. When my kids play, they enjoy singular focus on the fun at hand. When they dance, they do so with reckless abandon. They waste no time secretly wondering what I think about their hair or a joke they just made. When they cry, they are unfiltered and unapologetic for the outpouring of emotion. When they say, "I love you," they mean it from the heart and "to dinosaur land and back."

In addition to their day-to-day modeling of being present in the moment, on occasion my boys have given me a profound experience and teaching about presence and relationship. One such recent experience occurred with my son, Nathan. He is newly seven years old, toothless in the front like a thug, and a sweet and sensitive old soul. He's not a big talker, unlike his verbose little brother.

While getting ready for bed one evening, Nathan told me that he had observed that his grandparents on my side of the family talk more than the grandparents on the other side. He next commented that I talk *way more* than Dad. The following conversation ensued:

ME: Do you think I talk too much?

NATHAN: Yea. Sometimes I think you do.

ME: *(Debating silence versus a response.)* Well, that's good to know.

NATHAN: You know, my teacher asks me 68 questions all day long and then I get home and then you ask me a bunch of questions. And then Dad gets home and he asks me a bunch of questions. Sometimes it's too much. I don't like to talk *that* much.

ME: You're right. I can see how that might be a bit much. I'm glad you told me.

NATHAN: *(Silent.)*

ME: *(Unable to be silent?)* Well, I am very curious about you and love to hear what you think and feel. So, I guess I need to figure out how to ask some questions, but not too many questions.

NATHAN: I can give you one idea. The question that I really don't like is when you ask me what happened that was interesting at school. You don't need to ask me. If it was interesting, I would tell you.

ME: Good point. I'll try to remember that.

NATHAN: *(Silent.)*

ME: *(Unable to be silent?)* Well, I know I ask you a lot of questions when you seem upset. I care about you and I want you to know that I notice. How do you feel about those questions?

NATHAN: (*Long pause.*) Well, those questions are good. But here's something you should know . . . (*Pause*)

ME: (*Breathless, this ought to be good!*)

NATHAN: You'll need to ask me that question 13 times . . . you know, "How are you, Bear?" "Are you OK, Bear?" "What's up, Bear?" And on the 14th time, I'll tell you exactly what's going on. So, you need to keep asking me and then I will tell you.

ME: Thank you for telling me, Bear. I hear you, and it means a lot. And no more questions about interesting school days . . . I promise!

This bedtime exchange felt like a gift to me. I was struck by its clarity and honesty. It teaches me about the importance of silence and patience. It teaches me about the importance of presence and persistence. It teaches me about honoring each other's differences in styles and needs. It teaches me about searching within to discover what we need from others and having the courage to tell them. It teaches me to wait for meaningful sharing from my children rather than trying to pry it out of them. It teaches me about the joy of honest communication and connection. It teaches me that I *am* enough. I am grateful Nathan can tell me these things and that he does. I am grateful for the laughter and tears this story brings me as I type it now.

Lessons Learned

My work is integration of personal and professional lessons that remind me of the essence of presence from my exchange with Nathan.

Lesson #1: Stay curious and enjoy the mystery of others

Not only am I incapable of forcing my son to reveal his true self via questions and prodding, but also I am reminded that I will never fully know him in his complex entirety. He is not simply an extension of me and his dad, but rather his own unique constellation of feelings, sensations, opinions, experiences, and thoughts—and these too are ever changing. Dr. Bugental (1999) reminds us that, "Mothers, despite popular sentiment, many times do not know their children fully—to their frustration, and, often to the children's relief" (p. 187).

With some of my long-term clients, I find it is easy to fall into to the trap of believing I know them well enough to predict their thoughts, feelings, and experience. This need to know everything grossly underestimates their capacity for growth and mystery of what is unknown. I will not know everything about them and what is held for them alone is sacred for them. Furthermore, I risk communicating that their patterns are predictable and fixed, thereby reinforcing a sense of hopelessness in my clients about finding a new way of being. My motto is to stay open and stay curious.

Lesson #2: Presence should not feel like a fishing expedition

One of the messages I heard loud and clear from my son was to avoid going fishing for interesting tidbits about his life. My repetitive questions about interesting school days revealed my desire to be "in tune" with his experience, but my method proved to be more of a hindrance than a help. Throwing out random and vague questions in hopes of landing on a meaningful exchange is likely to distract from, rather than elicit, real connection. I picture the vast space of the ocean before me and foolishly trying to scoop up a certain kind of rare fish with my bare hands while blind-folded. It is futile at best.

I notice that I retreat to random questioning when I am uncomfortable and uncertain about where I stand with a person. It is not that my inquiries are disingenuous, but rather they leave little room for a dialogue to unfold organically. When I remind myself to trust presence and *be with* the spontaneous moment, I can embrace or diffuse my anxiety. Awareness of this tendency has been a powerful starting place for me to experiment with new ways of being.

I shudder to think of the many times I have cast out vague questions in hopes of tapping into my clients' lives. James Bugental (1999) urges the therapist to "avoid dependence on questioning. Questions subtly move the energy locus to or toward the questioner" (p. 162). So much of the noise of everyday life can drown out the inner experience of the subjective that I do not wish to further contribute to this distraction in the psychotherapy room. It has taken me many months to migrate away from the Q&A approach with one particular client, "Kim," a mid-50s, divorced mother of two children. Kim was seeking therapy to address her depression, conflict avoidance, and difficulty choosing healthy mates and building healthy relationships. Her demeanor was gentle and soft spoken. In our initial work together she would bring little energy, content, or emotion to our sessions. Though I hated to admit it, I found myself bored and irritated. So, I went fishing and came up empty. Running out of questions, I finally settled into the room and trusted that her inner experience would be a much richer focus for our work. This was awkward at first and she frequently giggled at or ignored my observations of her sometimes-closed eyes, rubbed temples, and sighs. In summary—for much occurred between here and there—Kim now directs her own sessions and dedicates more energy to searching inwardly rather than responding politely to her kids, her boss, and her therapist. She is finding *her* voice and a sense that it is worth sharing during the psychotherapy hour. It is powerful and humbling to bear witness to her transformation and its many ripple effects in her life outside psychotherapy.

Lesson #3: Silence is golden

Not only have I found it important to limit my questioning, but also to speak less overall. I am prone to talk entirely too much. I believe my over-talk is another misguided effort to be enough. However, like author Elizabeth Gilbert (2006) of *Eat, Pray, Love,* I am working toward "no more verbal tap dancing for pennies of affirmation" (p. 190).

Silence has produced profound results with many of my clients. In particular, I think of "Mike," a mid-30s musician and intellect who has squirmed, and then flourished, with silence in our sessions. He once described his communication as "essay form"—well constructed packages of the thoughts he deemed most palatable to the outside world. His inner world was hidden to me and others, even to himself. It has been easy at times to get lost in verbal world play with Mike because it is entertaining, and he is often insightful. With the help of the Unearthing trainings and supervision, I have steered us more toward such things as his here-and-now experience, the meaning of his bouncing left leg, and the artwork he doodles while we talk. These interactions have proven to be our most powerful points of connection and change for him accepting new ways of expressing himself.

Lesson #4: Be yourself

I am convinced that dogs, kids, and clients have an uncanny sense for all things phony. My son once told me that he noticed his grandfather had two laughs—the one that meant he was really having fun and the one that meant he was pretending to have fun. My kids are quick to tell me when I am placating instead of listening, pretending instead of being present. Early in my work, I often had the sensation of watching myself play the role of psychotherapist. Like the judgmental fly on the wall, I would observe and dissect my every move and statement, making it impossible to actually be present in the moment at all. My out-of-body experience was born out of the familiar uncertainty of, "Am I enough?" Carl Rogers (1961) suspected that it was therapists' fear that holds us back from full disclosure of self:

> We are afraid that if we let ourselves freely experience these positive feelings toward another we may be trapped by them. They may lead to demands on us or we may be disappointed in our trust, and these outcomes we fear. So as a reaction we tend to build up distance between ourselves and others—aloofness, a "professional" attitude, and impersonal relationship (p. 52).

Perhaps what I have revered as professionalism is self-protection in disguise. At times, I am drawn to deeper interactions with my clients and wish to share more authentically. For example, I have a young female client with whom I have worked for over a year. I experience her as bright, likable, resilient, and dynamic. I have noticed my more playful side comes out with her, and I have questioned its appropriateness. I consulted with my supervisor, Dr. Louis Hoffman, who discouraged me from censoring too much and urged me to bring as much of myself to the room as I can. This suggestion was a relief because I find that I feel most at home and connected with my clients when I can bring my complete self to the room. It is no coincidence that my clients are looking for the same permission to be seen and accepted in their whole form.

These relationships require a certain amount of risk and vulnerability. One aspect of these relationships is the encounter, a way of relating in which both people are impacted and changed through the connection that is made . . . it seems unrealistic to help clients improve their relationships and ability to make deep connections if we are unwilling to go there with them in therapy. (Hoffman, 2009, p. 15)

Lesson #5: Persistence pays

My exchange with Nathan reminds me how important it is to be patient and persistent in being present with others. His message to me was that he wanted to be known but wanted me to stay with him until he was ready and/ or able to show me. Few clients will offer up their vulnerable selves simply because I suggest they can trust me and it will make for fantastic therapy. I earn their trust over time through the vehicle of presence. I earn their trust by being willing to be vulnerable myself, not detached and overly clinical.

Over the past few months, I have had the difficult experience of having two new clients terminate early in our work together. In both cases, these clients were traumatized by past hurts, and both were deeply yearning for and afraid of attachment and interpersonal vulnerability. I had offered my presence and the prospect of connection with their inner world and with me. They liked this idea initially, but were unnerved as we began our work. In the end, they expressed disappointment that I had not provided them quick relief or sufficient skills to "fix it." I pictured my textbooks and techniques and wondered what I might have done wrong. It has been tempting to scurry back to something more concrete, but these days I work to find strength in my *pou sto* (Bugental, 1999), my inner stand that change takes time and courage along with many other variables, more than any checklist of quickly fixing another human being's pain.

A Work in Progress

I end this written exploration with a knowing that I am still growing and developing as a person and as a psychotherapist. Instead of racing to some intangible finish line, I wish to better embrace the process of becoming and its many rich surprises and challenges. As I have been trying to capture these ideas onto paper, it seemed no accident to have stumbled upon the poem "Done," by motherhood website creator, blogger, and "Zen Mommy" Suzanne Tucker (www.mymommymanual.com). Indeed, undone may be the most enlivening place to be.

Done

What if I was done?
Complete
Leaving me incomplete
Longing to be
A work in progress
Rough around the edges
Potential yet realized
Hidden in the folds of the me yet spread
I want to live in the sticky, sloppy, slippery now
To roll in the uncertainty of freedom and choice
To remember each breath, and in each know that I am love
I am enough
I am now
It is what I have
For I am Undone.

—Suzanne Tucker, 2009

References

Brown, B. (2012). *Daring greatly.* New York, NY: Penguin Group.

Bugental, J. F. T. (1999). *Psychotherapy isn't what you think.* Phoenix, AZ: Zeig, Tucker & Co., Inc.

Gilbert, E. (2006). *Eat, pray, love* New York, NY: Penguin Group.

Hoffman, L. (2009). Introduction to existential psychology in a cross-cultural context: An east-west dialogue. In L. Hoffman, M. Yang, F. Kaklauska, & A. Chan (Eds.), *Existential psychology east-west* (pp. 1-67). Colorado Springs, CO: University of the Rockies Press.

Rogers, Carl. (1961). *On becoming a person: A therapist's view of psychotherapy.* London, England: Constable.

Tucker, S. (2009, September 17). *Done.* Message posted to http://lookingglasslane.com/wordpress/2009/09/everyone-is-crazy/

10

⸺

The Pou Sto:
Finding a Place To Stand Your Lever

Amy Sharp

EXISTENTIAL-HUMANISTIC PSYCHOTHERAPY, developed by James Bugental (1999), combines the theories of existential and humanistic psychologies to form a unique way of approaching an individual in the psychotherapeutic setting. A significant concept expounded by Bugental is that of the *pou sto*, a concept related to the psychotherapeutic presence of the therapist. This chapter presents a description of the concept of the pou sto, its value for the therapist and role in conducting therapy, and ends with my experience of pou sto, both personally and professionally.

The term pou sto comes from Archimedes, an ancient Greek scholar who once said, "Dos moi pou sto kai kino taen gaen," or "Give me a place to put my lever, and I shall move the world" (Bugental, 1999). Pou sto is the position in which one places the lever and is the "starting point which determines the general direction" (Fisher, 1909, pp. 321-322) one takes. The foundation of the pou sto is necessary as it is from this place that all else emerges; for example, structure, technique, and method (Fisher, 1909).

Within the field of existential-humanistic theory, Bugental (1999) described the pou sto as the "place from which to exert power, a place to ground one's work, a base of operations" (p. 85). The therapist illuminates the pou sto by consciously determining "intentions, limits, and availability" (Bugental, 1999, p. 85). For example, what responsibility will the therapist accept in relationship with clients, and what will the therapist say or not say with clients (Bugental, 1999). Determining one's pou sto requires in-depth self-reflection to uncover one's "needs, impulses, and values" (Bugental, 1999, p. 93). Having a clear understanding of one's role as therapist creates a foundation from which one can approach the client. When the pou sto is solidly in place, the various interventions and techniques used by the therapist naturally create a cohesive structure within which both therapist and client can safely and productively work together. Based on Bugental's description, I am defining pou sto here as the foundation of the therapist's presence that is grounded in theory and formed through careful, honest, and deep self-reflection.

Bugental (1999) listed the central tenets of an existential-humanistic pou sto as: (a) the therapeutic hour is a microcosm of clients' life and represents how they operate in their life, (b) the job of the therapist is to notice how and reflect back to clients their approach to living, rather than advise, and (c) there is value in attending to the present, living moment in the therapy session with clients. The focus on presence in the living moment, a central principle in existential-humanistic theory, also reminds the therapist to maintain some flexibility. While the structure of the pou sto is essential, operating from a rigid standpoint may at times be counter to what is therapeutic. A therapist firmly rooted in a pou sto will know when moments of flexibility are needed (Bugental, 1999).

Bugental (Heery & Bugental, 2005) also presented the existential-humanistic pou sto as a list of 10 commandments:

1. Be there.
2. Insist that the client be there.
3. Listen and hear . . . more than you talk.
4. Don't let the words obscure the music.
5. When you do talk, keep it brief and uncluttered.
6. Always monitor the alliance.
7. Fit whatever you do to the context of the moment.

8. Don't ask for what can't be said.
9. Insist that the client be there.
10. Be there yourself. (p. 292)

In addition to the commandments listed above, Heery (Heery & Bugental, 2005), a long-time student of Bugental, added that the pou sto also contains the therapist's beliefs about each particular client. For example, when she worked with a woman diagnosed with cancer, Heery added two more beliefs to her pou sto: that her client had the "ability and resources within herself to face [her] diagnosis" (p. 293) and that, at times, the client will "try [Heery's] my belief with resistance and self-doubts" (p. 293).

Although not named as such, the importance of the therapist's pou sto is clearly addressed within other theoretical orientations. Buechler (2010), a psychoanalyst, spoke in her article on suffering about the importance of therapists reflecting on their attitudes about intense emotions, as these attitudes have an impact on the therapist's clinical approach. Buechler identified three main attitudes one can take in regards to suffering: (a) pain is a symptom and actions should be taken to reduce or remove the impact of the symptom, including prescribing medications; (b) as suffering is part of the human condition, the individual needs to learn to accept the burden of suffering; and (c) suffering provides insight and wisdom and the suffering of the patient (used in psychoanalysis verses client used in existential-humanistic model) should be mined for the self-knowledge it can provide.

The therapist's attitude toward suffering impacts how the therapist interprets the defenses of the patient. Buechler (2010) asks,

> With every word we utter, or do not utter, in treatment, we are taking a position about consciousness, defenses, and, more generally, emotional well-being . . . When is that omission a product of our cowardice, and when is it a product of our wisdom? (p. 339)

For these reasons, it is vital for therapists to be aware of their attitude towards suffering, as well as other intense emotional expressions. When the attitude of the therapist is to alleviate suffering, the therapist is more likely to delay interpreting the patient's defenses. In that way, the defenses of the patient remain unchallenged and the patient is more likely to avoid experiences of pain and suffering. When the attitude is that suffering is inevitable and needs to be accepted as a part of life, the therapist is more likely to interpret defenses earlier in the therapy. In this case, the defenses of the patient may be challenged before the patient is ready to deal with what had been previously avoided. It also brings up a potential conflict if the patient wants to continue using defenses. When the belief is that suffering leads to wisdom, the therapist is more likely not to focus on defenses at all, but to look at how pain and suffering serve as a "humanizing function" (Buechler, 2010, p. 351) for the patient.

In his article, *The Death of Psychoanalysis and Depth Therapy*, Firestone (2002) addressed the fall in popularity of psychotherapy. Firestone saw the decline as due to a general cultural tendency towards avoidance of uncomfortable feelings, including pain and suffering, and that therapists can play into this tendency in their work—"Societal forces combined with individuals' resistance have effectively extinguished this unique form of inquiry and conspired to shut it down as a source of insight and illumination" (p. 229). The therapist's defenses can keep the presenting problems of clients from being seen as potential for positive change, so the therapist will work to return clients to their previous state of equilibrium. A client may then lose the feelings of depression or anxiety, but has also lost an opportunity for growth in the effort of the therapist to avoid uncomfortable feelings. "Any attempt to support dishonest defenses or misperceptions that temporarily reduce a person's discomfort does a serious injustice to both the client and the therapist in the long run" (Firestone, 2002, p. 229).

Both Buechler and Firestone, although not naming it as such, spoke to the pou sto of the therapist. Their articles articulated the importance of being clear about the assumptions, beliefs, and ideas the therapist has, as that is the place the individual operates from when working with clients. As described up to this point, the value of the pou sto is that it creates a foundation from which to build the structure of the therapeutic alliance with the client. Other important aspects of the pou sto include identifying transference and countertransference in the therapeutic relationship and helping the therapist to maintain self-care.

When therapists operate from the foundation of a well thought out pou sto, they have very clear guidelines about how to interact with and respond to the client. The guidelines of the pou sto also make it easier for the therapist to identify moments of transference that occur in the therapy, as the therapist feels a pull to interact or respond to the client in a way not supported by the pou sto (Bugental, 1999). The reverse is also true—when the therapist notices a personal desire to interact or respond to the client in ways counter to the pou sto, countertransference is indicated (Bugental, 1999).

In the same way that a well thought out pou sto aids in highlighting moments of transference and countertransference, it also aids the therapist in maintaining self-care (Sapienza & Bugental, 2000). Self-care is especially vital for mental health care professionals, who most often care for individuals experiencing high levels of distress. Due to this, therapists are at high risk of developing compassion fatigue, stress-related psychological problems (e.g., depression, emotional exhaustion, anxiety, psychological isolation, and reduced self-esteem), and job burnout (Shapiro, Brown, & Biegel, 2007). The pou sto is based in part on the careful, honest, and deep self-reflection of the therapist, which makes the pou sto a reflection of the therapist's self, not just the therapist's theoretical orientation. Maintaining connection to the pou sto is a way for the therapist to maintain connection to the self, and maintaining connection to oneself is what allows for a sense of "aliveness" (Sapienza & Bugental, 2000, p. 458) to flourish within the therapist. Recognition of deviations from self and aliveness is possible because of the structure created by the pou sto: When firm guidelines are in place, it is easier to see when they are not followed. When therapists are fully connected to a sense of their own aliveness, it is very difficult to develop compassion fatigue, stress-related psychological problems, or job burnout. In cases of self-care, the pou sto is the "place from which we stand as a foundation and ground that we call up or remember when we are out of tune" (Sapienza & Bugental, 2000, p. 458).

Thus far, we can see the importance of having a well thought out pou sto: It leads to the development of consistent guidelines from which to operate therapeutically, it aids in the identification of transference and countertransference issues, and it helps the therapist remain connected to a sense of aliveness, thereby contributing to self-care. The remainder of this chapter will focus on my perspective of the pou sto, from both a personal and a professional standpoint.

The concept of the pou sto held an immediate fascination for me. Most of my life has been marked, both unconsciously and consciously, by a desire to feel firmly anchored in a sense of myself. It is my tendency to feel like a piece of dandelion fluff, constantly drifting from one place to the next, dependent on the whims of the environment rather than my own agency: a reflection of the emotional and physical environments in which I was raised. The struggle of finding an anchor within is reflected in my 12-year therapy history. After being introduced to the concept of the pou sto, it dawned on me that I have been searching diligently for my own personal pou sto: a foundation within from which to build guidelines of self. When I approach the concept of the pou sto from a personal, rather than a professional, point of view, I can see that the pou sto also provides a sense of permission. A pou sto gives me permission to pick a place to stand and also gives me permission to say that this place is important to me.

When thinking back over my therapy history, I can see how my therapy was impacted by this lack of grounding within myself, or a personal pou sto. The clearest example is seen in my work with my last therapist. Some therapy sessions consisted of sharing a dream with my therapist; eventually I noticed our pattern of doing dream work. I would share my dream and then immediately sit back and wait for my therapist to tell me what it meant. Although my therapist started dream work by having me put my own meaning on the dream images, the sessions always ended with her sharing her interpretation of what the dream meant. What developed was dependence on her to provide meaning for my dreams, and as an extension of that, my life, rather than independence and self-agency to provide meaning for myself. In this case, the more directive pou sto of my therapist impacted my ability to develop my personal pou sto.

My professional experience has also been impacted by a lack of a well thought out pou sto. When I first started working with clients, I very easily got caught up in wondering what to do next or if what I was doing was right. In those moments, I effectively removed myself from being present to the client and no longer heard the "music" (Heery & Bugental, 2005, p. 295) of the client's words. This experience of losing contact with clients was due in part to my lack of a pou sto. I was not firmly grounded in a theoretical orientation or was consciously aware of my beliefs of my role as therapist. I lacked the support provided by the structure of a strong pou sto.

A vivid example of the impact of my lack of pou sto can be seen in my work with William. William was a bright, intelligent young man originally sent to counseling for classroom behavior problems and low academic performance. Although relatively young, he clearly saw how social inequalities impacted his life and the choices available to him. William's classroom behavior and grades improved after our work together, but in spite of that, I developed a sense of despair that I could not change the circumstances of his life: I could not change the way his family members related to him, his socio-economic status, his housing situation, or the traumas resulting from these realities. My sense of despair led to the development of secondary trauma and job burnout. With William, my lack of pou sto impacted my sense of competency as a therapist, my ability to identify the countertransference that was obviously occurring, and my ability to care for myself. At the end of my work with William and the other children at my practicum site, I had serious doubts as to whether or not I wanted to continue with clinical work.

My work with later clients as a pre-doctoral intern reflects the presence of a more established pou sto. By the time I entered my internship, I was more firmly rooted in my theoretical orientation, had established much more realistic beliefs about what I could accomplish as a therapist, and was much more adept at recognizing and working with my countertransference. A clear example of my more developed pou sto may be seen in my work with Phoebe, with whom I worked for about the same amount of time as I did with William. Much of my early work with Phoebe consisted of observing and pointing out her feelings of rage and anger, as well as her tendency to dismiss the validity of her feelings and thoughts. Her personal beliefs, including one about the pointlessness and futility of anger, originally kept her from recognizing and valuing her feelings. Slowly, Phoebe and I explored her beliefs, and Phoebe allowed herself to let go of those that no longer served her and to develop new ones. By the end of our work together, Phoebe was able to recognize the importance of her anger and value her feelings and thoughts in general. Over the course of our work, Phoebe shared the details of her many traumatic experiences, but because of the structure provided by my pou sto, I was able to maintain a continuous presence with her. I was also able to recognize my numerous moments of countertransference and maintain an empathic connection to her without experiencing secondary trauma.

Although many of my instructors and supervisors had spoken of the importance of having a theoretical orientation from which to base my clinical work, it was not until I learned about the pou sto that my role as a therapist crystalized into true understanding. Effective therapeutic interaction requires not just knowledge of theory, but the therapist's knowledge and awareness of self. My value as a clinician is based as much in who I am as a person as it is in what I know about psychology, the two blending together to create my unique pou sto.

References

Bugental, J. F. T. (1999). *Psychotherapy isn't what you think*. Phoenix, AZ: Zeig, Tucker & Co., Inc.

Buechler, S. (2010). No pain, no gain? Suffering and the analysis of defense. *Contemporary Analysis, 46*(3), 334-354

Firestone, R. W. (2002). The death of psychoanalysis and depth therapy. *Psychotherapy: Theory/Research/Practice/Training, 39*(3), 223-232. doi: 10.1037/0033-3204.39.3.223

Fisher, D. (1909). Common sense and attitudes. *The Journal of Philosophy, Psychology and Scientific Methods, 6*, 316-323

Heery, M., & Bugental, J. F. T (2005). Listening to the listener: An existential-humanistic approach to psychotherapy with psychotherapists. In J. D. Geller, J. C. Norcross, & D. E. Orlinsky (Eds.), *The psychotherapist's own psychotherapy: Patient and clinician perspectives* (pp. 282-296). New York, NY: Oxford University Press.

Sapienza, B. G., & Bugental, J. F. T. (2000). Keeping our instruments fine-ly tuned: An existential-humanistic perspective. *Professional Psychology: Research and Practice, 31*(4), 458-460. doi: 10.1037//0735-7028.31.4.458

Shapiro, S. L., Brown, K. W., & Biegel, G. M. (2007). Teaching self-care to caregivers: Effects of Mindfulness-Based Stress Reduction on the mental health of therapists in training. *Training and Education in Professional Psychology, 1*(2), 105-115. doi: 10.1037/1931-3918.1.2.105

11

Resistance:
Of Spacesuits and Turtle Shells

Steve Fehl

BARTLET: My family is off limits.

BRUNO: Sir . . . your candor about a terrible illness was off limits. Your regimen of self-medication was off limits. Due respect, you've used up your off limits.

BARTLET: I'll decide when I've used them up. You don't poll where my family goes, am I making myself clear?

BRUNO: Mh-huhmm . . . Sometimes I have a difficulty talking to people who don't race sailboats.

BARTLET: What?

BRUNO: I have difficulty sometimes talking to people who don't race sailboats. When I was a teenager, I crewed Larchmont to Nassau on a 58-foot sloop called Cantice. There was a little piece of kelp that was stuck to the hull, and even though it was little, you don't want anything stuck to the hull. So, I take a boat hook on a pole and I stick it in the water and I try to get the kelp off, when seven guys start screaming at me, right? 'Cause now the pole is causing more drag than the kelp was. See, what you gotta' do is you gotta' drop it in and let the water lift it out in a windmill motion. Drop it in, and let the water take it by the kelp and lift it out. In and out. In and out, till you got it. The voters aren't choosing a plumber, Mr. President. They are choosing a president. And if you don't think that your family should matter, my suggestion to you is to get out of professional politics. And if you think that I'm going to miss even one opportunity to pick up half-a-mile boat speed, you're absolutely out of your mind. When it costs us nothing, when we give up nothing? You're out of your mind! (Sorkin & Abner, 2001)

I AM A TURTLE. I first learned this about myself attending a workshop dealing with codependent relationships. The turtle shell is my "space suit" (Bugental, 1999, p. 109). I define myself as a turtle to others, emphasizing the importance of pulling into my shell whenever I feel threatened, or at times just uncomfortable. The image of pulling into my shell and waiting there quietly and peacefully until I believe the threat is gone has provided me great comfort, as well as a sense of safety and security. However, more recently, I have learned that pulling into my shell and staying there can also be resistance. I am learning that pulling into my shell removes me from the moment, disrupts connections, stagnates my growth, and sometimes destroys relationships. So my image of comfort, safety, and security is also my tool for resisting experiencing the moment, genuine relationships, and personal growth.

Like President Bartlet in the scene quoted earlier, I want to engage when and how I want to engage. I do not desire, nor do I appreciate, someone else suggesting that I need to re-examine my turtle-like existence. However, in honest self-evaluation, my first response to any situation—positive or negative—is to resist, to close up, to pull in, and to shut out the situation. Like President Bartlet, I need a Bruno Gianelli to help me see how my turtle shell is not just a safe haven, but a fortress of resistance as well.

They enter the building day after day: their heads down, their shoulders drooped, looking defeated, overwhelmed, and depressed.

Some come from homes costing hundreds of thousands of dollars and others come from having spent the night under a bridge with nothing but a blanket. What brings them together day after day is the need for work. Some are out of work for just a couple of days or weeks, others for several months, and still some have not worked in years.

As these desperate job seekers sit down at a computer, attend a workshop or support group offered by this local Workforce Center, they bring with them their pain, their frustration, their hurt, and their anger. At every opportunity, one by one, they share their dashed dreams and their fading hopes. Sometimes they almost shout that they have never had to look for work before or have never had to do a job search this way before. They don't know who to be upset at or whom to be angry with, all they know is that they want—no—they need a job.

I understand the resistance so many of these job seekers express. Their resistance makes sense to me. I even get that they do not know what or whom they are resisting. I get that they just feel the need to resist. Often I have nothing to say but, "I get that it is hard," and sit with them in their anger, frustration, and desperation.

I was struck by this sense of resistance most recently as I was doing some hypnotherapeutic work related to my past relationships. In the hypnotic state, I confronted some of the pain and rejection that are such a familiar part of my connection with my parents. But after the hypnosis, as I worked on my assignments, this deep resentment grew and welled up within me. My jaw and gut wanted to scream, "I shouldn't have to do this! I shouldn't have to convince myself that I am worthwhile or valuable or lovable!" I wanted to face my father and mother, as well as others, and scream at them, "I gave you all I am! I made myself vulnerable to you, and you rejected me!"

It is so much more familiar and comfortable to simply pull back into my shell and lie still in the midst of an open, unprotected beach. It is easier to pretend I am a rock and ignore the fears, the feelings, and the anxiety.

I am used to waiting for the high tide to come along and sweep me—shell and all—back into the familiar waters of remoteness and distorted light. In these great waters, I can move about weightlessly, believing I am swift, strong, and brave.

She is 33 years old and a single mother of two children. She has a master's degree and a steady job where she receives accolades for her work ethic and creativity. Her friends and family regularly tell her how beautiful she is and what an amazing person she is to them. Yet the ache inside is unbearable and so she takes an unfolded paper clip and runs the sharp edge along her arm. After a few minutes, the edge of the paper clip no longer works and the internal pain becomes even more intense. So, she takes a razor blade and with each pass over her arm presses harder. Now the physical pain overcomes the internal ache and she experiences an escape from the angst that is her constant companion. As she slips into this dissociation from reality, she acknowledges to herself that she should not be doing this, but the physical pain is such a distraction and relief from the anguish of her existence. However, as she relishes these moments she also notices blood oozing from the cuts in her arm and she stops; now the escape turns to panic that someone might notice the marks she has just created and the inner torment begins anew.

The ways in which we define ourselves and our world are both enabling and restricting. (Bugental, 1999, p. 126)

While I understand the resistance of my clients and I acknowledge my own resistance to growth, I also recognize the danger of resistance. Resistance is normal, natural, and predictable, as an old therapist friend of mine use to say, but that does not make it good. The struggle is discerning when resistance is helpful and protective and when it is dangerous and damaging.

The question that needs deep exploration in the existential-humanistic psychotherapy model is how does the resistance serve you? (Bugental, 1999).

In my personal journey, I have resisted real connection and intimacy because I experienced these as a threat. This resistance creates confusion: withdrawing from moments and relationships that are good and positive, while at the same time being vulnerable and open with people and circumstances where I am rejected and alienated. Moreover, I often feel awkward and inept in social settings, as well as with my efforts in establishing intimate, caring relationships.

In this morass of bewilderment, in my role as a psychotherapist, I am to walk alongside my clients as they resist new perspectives, new insights, and new ways of relating to their world. The challenge is helping them discern when resistance is healthy and when resistance is detrimental and damaging. Here is where the words of Bruno Gianelli become so significant, "Drop it in, and let the water take it by the kelp and lift it out. In and out. In and out, till you got it" (Sorkin & Abner, 2001). This means working with the resistance, embracing the resistance as an integral part of myself, as well as that of my clients. Acknowledging, even accepting, that the resistance empowers the individual to drop the resistance, as they are ready. In other words, allow the therapeutic process to work and utilize the flow of the process to remove the resistance—"In and out. In and out, till you got it" (Sorkin & Abner, 2001).

"I don't know, Steve," he replied, as he covers his face with his hands to hide the tears. "I have never had to do anything this hard in my life," he continues, the tears flowing quietly down his cheeks into his black-gray beard. "I know," I respond softly and simply.

Eric is the classic Colorado cowboy. His skin is weathered and tan from being in seasons of wind and sun, of hot and cold. His hands are filled with the calluses of years of riding rodeo, mending fences, and more bar fights than he can count. However, throughout all the years of roaming the Rocky Mountains, Eric has never faced a battle like the one he is in now. Eric is battling for his marriage and he does not know if he can share his feelings with his wife. Eric has lived most of his life with the belief that you strike first, strike hard, and keep striking until your opponent surrenders. But that approach is not working in his marriage. His wife is withdrawing, not fighting back, and not challenging him. She is meekly withdrawing, and he doesn't know what he needs to do or even if he can do it. "Steve, talking about my feelings and letting her see me cry makes me feel weak, and I don't want to be weak with her."

Work with the resistance is one of the most reliable distinguishing characteristics of deeper, more life-changing psychotherapy. (Bugental, 1999, p. 146)

As I work on my own resistance and become more deeply aware of my various resistance patterns, I can choose resistances that actually serve me in my life now, not be tied to resistance patterns from my past that no longer serve me. Yes, resistances form patterns that are a resistance that repeats itself over and over. These patterns need identification and naming in order for a new choice of being to be made. I am deeply informed by my experience of my resistance pattern of the turtle, how it serves and does not serve me so I can choose new ways of coming out of my shell and connecting to others. It is essential to identify those moments of resistance patterns in the psychotherapy process. When resistance patterns are consistently identified by the psychotherapist and client and then named in the moment of the resistance, the deeper work of psychotherapy in the existential-humanistic model takes place. The naming of the resistance gives leverage to the psychotherapist and client's work with the pattern for the present and future sessions. Once named, these patterns can be tagged as they are repeated in psychotherapy: bringing to bear the responsibility of making new choices, which is the essential work of the existential-humanistic model of psychotherapy (Heery & Bugental, 2005). These present moments of the client's resistance are where change happens. This process of identifying, naming, and working through the client's resistance patterns is the work of dropping the pole in the water and allowing the flow of the water to move the pole across the kelp in order to remove it from the hull of the boat. In and out, in and out until the resistance is gone, creating space for a different perspective with a different resistance that will better serve the client now.

References

Bugental, J. F. T. (1999). *Psychotherapy isn't what you think*. Phoenix, AZ: Zeig, Tucker & Co., Inc.

Heery, M. & Bugental, J. F. T. (2005). Meaning and transformation. In E. van Deurzen & C. Arnold-Baker (Eds.), *Existential perspectives on human issues* (pp. 253-264). New York, NY: Palgrave Macmillan.

Sorkin, A. & Abner, A. (Writers), & Barclay, P. (Director). (2001). The Indians in the lobby [Television series episode]. In A. Sorkin & J. Wells (Producers), *The west wing*. Burbank, CA: Warner Brothers Television.

12

⌒

And Life Goes On

Barbara F. Strouzas

Care is a particular type of intentionality shown especially in psychotherapy. It means to wish someone well; and if the therapist doesn't experience this within himself, or doesn't have the belief that what happens to the patient matters, woe unto the therapy.

—May, *Love and Will*, 1969, p. 292

HOW IMPORTANT IS MY INTENTIONALITY in relationship to myself and to others? Who do I want to be in the world? How do I want to live? How do I want to make a difference with those I touch? It is not out there, it is in here where I am, where I stand, what I believe, and who I am.

I have struggled with writing—my own resistance to be structured, to sit down and to write. I am out of the school mode, and I do not want to take the time to write. However, wanting and not wanting are irrelevant. I will write. Time presented itself and here I sit, writing. Actually, when I think about it, it feels good to have the space to explore my thoughts and feelings on where I am and where I am going. However, to just simply state that I have struggled, resisted writing, may not be accurate. This writing represents a culmination of the meaning and the application of the more than two-year training experiences from being a part of Unearthing the Moment.

The resistance is how we protect our self-and-world construct systems, but it is also true that it is those systems themselves that protect us from disaster, from formlessness. (Bugental, 1999, p. 128)

My writing, knowingly or unknowingly, represents something quite deep to me. Have I received what I hoped for when I started? Have I received more than I realize? Am I allowing myself to let go and to grow?

I started this training for myself, my needs, and my growth as a psychotherapist and as a human being. I started with a hope of discovering a sense of rejuvenation. I wanted something that would take me outside the structure of 50-minute hours and treatment plans: something I could connect to on a personal level. I wanted a place where I could explore who I am, not just what I do. I wanted a place where I could fully be me and give myself the opportunity to touch my fears and insecurities in order to allow the process of change.

When we think of the therapeutic interview as the site in which the client must reexamine, and very likely revise, significant parts of how she identifies herself and the way she is in the world, it should be obvious that a measure of ambivalence is to be expected. That very well intentioned reexamination must in some measure call into question a client's way of being in the world. (Bugental, 1999, p. 129)

When I received the flier for the training, I was so excited to have an opportunity to work with Dr. Bugental. I met Dr. Bugental and Dr. Heery (Myrtle) at The Evolution of Psychotherapy conference almost 10 years ago. What a gentle and present man. For me, his workshop made the conference, and I left with a good feeling about the time I had spent with him. Everyone has a technique, but Jim had a way of being. I jumped at the chance to spend time with him in training. Unknowingly, I became an Unearther.

Everything happens for a reason—such as, out of a list of 300 names, mine was one of the 30 Myrtle selected to send fliers to for the training—and while I did not know why or what the outcome would bring, I did trust the journey. Unearthing the Moment was a wonderful experience of being. Each training session gave me a renewed sense of peace in myself and the work I do with individuals. Each time reconnected me to the whole of a group of people in search of and in discovery of more—more than what we knew, more than what we are or what we do. It is a journey of growth and of stretching ourselves as therapists and as individuals.

> Life, at its best, is a flowering, changing process in which nothing is fixed. (Rogers, 1961, p. 27)

For me, Unearthing the Moment has been a process of changing from what I knew to what I know, constantly developing and becoming something more. It has been a series of encounters of letting go of how I am and opening up to who I am. It has been a series of changes for me. While some changes are known, some are unknown. I need to allow myself to be open to life's possibilities. I am neither who I was, nor who I shall be. Time is, and I am in time. All I can do is be present to this moment and the possibilities it will bring.

Being open to the moment is such an integral part of change. It has been a part of my change. I have noticed for clients, more can take place in one moment than in an entire series of 50-minute hours. In session I sometimes feel stuck, almost disconnected from the person(s) before me. This feeling seems to be strongest when I am focusing on the expectations of a contract or outcome, and not on the individual. My thoughts stray away from the now between us. I feel obligated to meet contractual requirements. I feel it is up to me to make sure the individuals who come for psychotherapy focus on the issues expressed in their contract, as though I have the ability to make them talk about what I think is important. Even more compelling, I want them to get something out of psychotherapy. I want them to grow and to become the person they can be. I know these are my wants and my goals for psychotherapy, and they may not be the individual's goals. I know I need to keep my desires and the desires of the person separate. I also know I am human and subject to these feelings as they arise. Allowing myself to acknowledge and to accept them as present without judgment helps me to come back to the moment. I am able to use these feelings to remind myself to stop, to sit back, and to relax, and, of course, to clarify with clients their goals.

Identities of the following case vignettes are disguised for confidentiality and provide insight into how the use of the present can successfully be applied to teenagers who are challenged.

A few years ago I was working with a young man, about 16 years old, in a gang and on probation. He was polite but guarded. He came to psychotherapy because he was told to attend. Psychotherapy was not his choice, as he saw it. He did not need psychotherapy, and yet, here he was in psychotherapy. He had already completed his court-ordered anger management class, and his probation officer wanted him to do some individual psychotherapy. "I've already done what the judge said. This is a waste of time." Every week I tried to build rapport and to give him the opportunity to talk about whatever he wanted. After all, I thought, what could it hurt to "do a little psychotherapy"? Well, I was wrong. The more I tried, the more he resisted. The more frustrated he became, the more frustrated I became. However, as I stopped trying and started being present to his resistance, things shifted. At first there was plenty of silence. He would ask if he could leave, stating, "This is boring. There's no point." He knew he could leave, but I would have to report back to his probation officer. He never left. He came every week on time and never missed a session. I would notice his cooperation, his way of participating in psychotherapy. As I let go of what I needed to occur and allowed him to express his frustration, we talked a little. He opened up a little. It took me awhile to let go of my expectations and to allow his needs to come first. I finally said, "Okay, you've met your court requirement. How do we convince your probation officer that you do not need to be here?" That helped. We finally were on the same page of working toward his goals.

When I finally accepted his goals were not a reflection of my ability to "help" him, then my fear of him not participating in sessions moved aside and he did participate. I finally heard him and let go of my self-imposed expectation of a perceived outcome, which gave him space to be. I offered him a space where his resistance was not met with the force of my resistance. He was given a chance to see his resistance as a way that he stood up for himself. After about seven weeks, his probation officer was satisfied with his progress and he could end psychotherapy.

My clients know what they want to talk about and what is of value to them. They have a sense of what they need. When I let go of my expectations and allow myself to be present to the now between us—tone of voice, breathing, what is happening in the moment—then I can easily connect with their needs. Allowing what is present to guide us is my compass for our work. It is that moment of accepting what is that brings into being the discovery of greater potential for the client.

Another example, a 15-year-old Hispanic male was referred for anger management. He had been acting out at school, and his principal suggested psychotherapy would be helpful. Sam had recently moved in with his aunt and uncle because his mother had reported him for domestic violence. When I met him, he was a calm and respectful young man. We spent six sessions together (the recommended number allowed by the school district). Sam was in such pain and grief over the loss of his family. He wanted to hate his mother, but his heart would not allow it. She was an addict and had tried to beat Sam and his younger siblings. Sam tried to protect them from their mother and got punished. While the school district thought he should better control his anger, Sam knew what he needed—someone to listen and to believe in him. He needed to confirm he was a good person and not a "bad boy."

We never did discuss any anger management skills, but he did get what he needed. Sam and I connected because he could be himself without expectation of who others thought he should be. We allowed ourselves to be in the moment, aware of the now. Sam touched a sense of himself. It is amazing to be present when a person gains a sense of his own worth. Sam is a reminder for me that people know what they need. Sometimes just providing space to be with each other as human beings, without expectation or working toward a set outcome, gives someone the permission to explore and to discover who he/she is.

For me, teenagers come to psychotherapy sometimes mandated or not, for a reason which may not be the reason that initially helped them through the door. Known or unknown, they come in search of a connection to whatever has brought them to today, brought them to now, just like Sam. I do not believe we are here to be alone. It is our interconnectedness that binds us across age, gender, and race. Humankind is connected. We need each other to survive and to thrive. We learn and we grow in relationship with one another. As we have often heard, "No man is an island." It is our differences that separate us, but it is our similarities, our human condition of existence, that bind us.

Connection is defined by Webster's Dictionary as meaning "a joining or being joined; a relation; association; specifically, the relation between things that depend on, involve, or follow each other" (Connection, 1966, p. 311). I started the Unearthing trainings looking for something to touch me, to inspire me to continue being and becoming in resonance with whom God (a word, for me, which adds spiritual depth and meaning to my life) intends me to be. I started with the hope I would find a connection to continue the work I began with my psychotherapist and mentor, Reverend Fr. George Vlahos, Ph.D. (Fr. George). Fr. George was a Greek Orthodox Priest and received his Doctorate in Psychology in Vienna where he trained under Viktor Frankl (Frankl, 1959). Their story is long and will be elaborated in another paper. I started psychotherapy with Fr. George when I was 21 years old and continued on and off for more than 15 years. He and I would do marathon sessions lasting six to eight hours, well outside the structure of the 50-minute hour. Structure provides form and parameters, which are important. However, formlessness can at times open up the unknown within. I would come away feeling challenged and rejuvenated, ready to take care of myself personally and excited about my vocation. Fr. George was the catalyst behind my becoming a psychotherapist. He helped open me to myself, which helped deepen my presence and develop practical skills.

I never entered psychotherapy with the intent to find a vocation. I entered like anyone else, to ease my internal struggle. My journey with Fr. George led me to myself, to see my potential, to be open to whom God needed me to be. With Fr. George I realized my gifts and fears, those fears that are a part of my world construct, which contribute to how I see myself and how I am in relation with others. However, I am not only my fears. I am my abilities. Fr. George held me in that space of uncertainty where I resisted change but came to realize that letting go meant giving up what kept me from fully being me.

We need to feel a stability within our own being. The self-and-world construct system provides a core for that stability. When psychotherapy

> calls into question some aspects of an individual's construct system, that person will almost certainly—overly or covertly—resist that therapy . . . resistance serves not only an oppositional but also a protective function. (Bugental, 1999, pp. 128 & 129)

For me, psychotherapy was never about doing but about being. Fr. George encouraged me to grow and to see my potential as a human being. Our time together was about being with one another, experiencing the moments between us. As our relationship grew, I felt the gift of the human experience: the acceptance of another person for who he/she is and the ability to trust in order to open the process of exploring one's inner self. This experience of the actual gave me something I have longed for ever since. Our time together ended when Fr. George developed Alzheimer's. I lost my physical connection to the person I most trusted. In a sense, I lost part of a connection to me. I started the trainings to reconnect to something in me, something I knew was there. I was looking for that sense of rejuvenation I felt with Fr. George. I was looking for something that would allow me to let go and to honor our time together so I could continue to grow into who I will be. I can hold what I know and allow myself to move forward. I can hold our connection in a place where I can touch it whenever I need to feel his presence.

Learning to be aware of and allowing myself to be in the moment has given me a feeling of connection outside of what I know. When I am in the moment, aware of the now, I feel most connected to Fr. George. I am able to let go of my expectations and control and just be. I open to the feeling of being a part of what is present, surrounding and filling me. In the moment I feel calm and connected to God. In the moment I am not alone but a part of what is. With clients that feeling of being in the now is where we connect. Staying present to their experience is giving them the space in which to touch what is in them.

With Fr. George I discovered my worth as a child of God, a larger sense of my being, and as an embodied human being. I am worthy of God's love just because I am, not because of anything I do. I discovered I am a psychotherapist. For me, being a psychotherapist is not separate from me as an individual. Being a psychotherapist is not a job but a vocation. It is what I am supposed to be doing with my life. It is a part of who I am, not what I am.

When I enter the psychotherapeutic space between client and therapist, I am who I am. I do not check myself at the door and walk in a different person. My values, beliefs, and experiences are part of me in relationship to others.

I remain totally open to each client's search for spiritual potential and the language he/she chooses for his/her spiritual journey. The whole of me is connected to the process because I am genuine with people in psychotherapy. Being real and being me helps to create trust between us. With trust comes connection to the actual and to potential yet to be lived. That being said, I hold clear boundaries with my clients concerning my personal belief in God and the use of the word God in psychotherapy.

Through the expression and exploration of one's self, individuals can better understand how their experiences have come together to form their value systems and their view of the world. They can better know where they are stuck in the process of change, and better understand what is holding them back from growth. Through psychotherapy people can discover themselves and challenge how they are in the world, their world construct, which is what I did in my psychotherapy. Through connection to another, in this case a psychotherapist, they allow themselves the opportunity to look at how they are with others and themselves, and consider what contributes to and detracts from their lives. Through my connection with Fr. George, I found my way of being in the world challenged. He gently but firmly pushed me to look at my own issues in order to grow and to be honest with myself. He allowed me time and space to discover what held me back, hold it, and let it go. He taught me that if I could face my fears and insecurities, I could blossom and grow. I learned to let go of what I thought were my limits and expectations, and accept what is and be deeply happy. I now accept me for who I am, not for who others need me to be. I am more fully who God made me to be. I am worthy of His love. I do still have doubts, and my fears and insecurities creep up, but I acknowledge them and do not allow them to guide my life. I am better prepared to be with people on their journey of self-discovery because I am more aware of my own evolving process.

People are so precious—a gift from God. Taking care to be with them in psychotherapy as they journey toward a greater awareness of self is an honor.

> Care . . . is a state composed of the recognition of another, a fellow human being like one's self with the pain or joy of the other; of guilt, pity, and the awareness that we all stand on the base of a common humanity from which we all stem. (May, 1969, p. 289)

A mother holds her child's hand while learning to cross the street; a father holds the back of his daughter's bicycle for support as she attempts to ride a two-wheeler. If we could be fulfilled by doing life alone, we would. We would separate and disconnect from one another, but we do not. We reach out for connection to one another. Even alone in our homes we seek others through chat rooms, tweeting, and online dating. We love and hate and argue and debate with one another. We push and challenge those around us to agree and to accept us for who we are and what we believe. We look for understanding from others in order to acknowledge our existence.

A while ago a young woman came to see me. She was shy and very nervous. She had felt so alone for so long that she was uncomfortable being in a room with another person. For weeks she danced around the issue that brought her to therapy. She would talk about feeling uncomfortable around people, scared to say or do the wrong thing. She would talk about parts of her childhood and how disconnected she felt from how her family saw her and from whom they needed her to be. It took months before she could say, "I think I'm a man. Isn't that weird? "No," I said. "Aren't you shocked?" Again I said, "No." Without going into every detail of her therapy, she was looking for what she had not received from her family. She was looking for acceptance. Her intention was to find a way to connect with another in order to find her connection to herself.

People desire connection with those in their lives and with themselves. People who frequent a favorite restaurant or coffee house, where a "Good morning, John/Jane" brings a sense of connection, find comfort in the familiar. The man who sits working on his laptop in a local coffee house rather than in his office; the mother who brings her children to the park to play with other children; and the woman who sits outside an ice cream store smiling at passersby are all choosing to be in a public area with others. Even with our desire for connection we are separate. All these examples are ways we try to reach out to others and attempt to break down our barriers. We all have barriers as a form of protection and as a way of being in the world. These walls provide a sense of safety from our fears, the unknown, and each other. However, they serve to keep us unfulfilled as individuals and as humankind. They keep us disconnected. One way to challenge these barriers safely, even for just 50 minutes, is in psychotherapy. Psychotherapy is a launching pad to breaking down those walls and to expanding our way of being in the world. The success of psychotherapy is taking our ability to connect with the psychotherapist and expanding it to others in our daily lives.

I have to take what I learned from Fr. George and apply it to other settings in order to continue my journey. I have to take my connection and feeling safe with him and expand it to life in order to enhance my journey for myself and for others. It is a responsibility that I choose. Unearthing the Moment is the continuation of my evolving process. I begin each training with a nervous excitement of what will be. I have been surprised by my openness and willingness to be fully who I am, lowering my defenses in order to connect with others and myself. Some of the role-plays have taken me off guard because, unknowingly, I am in the moment and what is inside comes out. It is amazing to feel the power of the actual—my feelings, my grief, and my loss are present whether or not I consciously acknowledge them. For me, each experience holds new insight into my search for connection and my acceptance of life as it is.

Sometimes, I do not like life as it is. I have no control over some parts of life and that can, at times, anger me. What I want and need is gone. Who I trusted is unavailable. I am scared to go it alone, to trust myself, and to let go. Yet that is what I do. I could choose complacency, but that is not an option for me. I would be living a lie and being less than who I am. These choices are always there. I am not alone as I make these choices. I continue to feel and to use my connection to Fr. George as I continue to choose authenticity in the moment. His words are in my thoughts and his love is in my heart. My faith in God gives me a greater meaning in my service to others, gives me strength to let go of what was and to continue my journey with curiosity and gratitude for what is.

It was not until an exercise at one of the Unearthing Trainings, when Dr. Heery said, "She is grieving," that I understood. I am going to a place I have consciously avoided facing. Even while writing now I avoided approaching the truth. However, my body and soul knew what I had to do. One night I was struggling with words, dancing around my own feelings, and I got sick. I had to pull away from the writing and relax. It was not until later that night, when the house was quiet and I was feeling better that I came back to the computer. Finally, I was connected to the actual within me. I typed and I cried. I dropped my barriers that were protecting me and sat with my feelings. In Greek we say, "E oura ena kala," meaning, "The hour is good." The time has begun for me to move forward in my life, knowing everything will go as it should. I think my fear is that by moving forward I am leaving behind my time with Fr. George. I am not honoring our journey together. How wrong am I? All along I have been writing about my connection to Fr. George, and now that is a part of me, inspiring me. I am not dishonoring our work or our time together. I am sharing it and allowing it to be with me as I continue to grow.

So what is my intentionality? Is it to learn a better way to do psychotherapy? No. Many people can learn a technique and apply it. One is either a psychotherapist or not. My intentionality is to become more than I am. It is to be open to myself and to connect with the parts of me that are blocked by my fears. It is to let go of what holds me from fully being who I am and to connect with others, in the moment, aware of the now between us.

Did I find what I was looking for? No, because I was looking for what I had with Fr. George, and that is unrealistic. However, I did find something else. I found a connection with individuals who add to and enhance my memories of Fr. George. I found a place where I can share myself and be myself. I knew, when this process started, good or bad, something would come out of these trainings. I just needed to trust the journey, God, and myself. I just need to be open to the possibilities as I was open with Fr. George. As usual, the outcome is never something I could have designed. The people God has brought to me are a precious gift I get to receive every time we are together. I am humbled by our experiences and grateful for their presence in my life.

In conclusion, I offer an unpublished poem by Fr. George (1972). It states so eloquently how I feel and what I believe.

Let me be the person I can,
then I'll become more than I am.
But if you expect too much of me,
how can I become what I can be?
When I have acted in ways we both hate,
show me, in your way, that it's not too late.
Help me to feel worthy of new birth,
and, in my way, I'll raise my self-worth.

References

Bugental, J. F. T. (1999). *Psychotherapy isn't what you think.* Phoenix, AZ: Zeig, Tucker & Co., Inc.

Connection. (1966). *Webster's new world dictionary of the American language* (college ed.). Cleveland, OH: The World Publishing Company.

Frankl, V. (1959). *Man's search for meaning.* New York, NY: Washington Square Press.

May, R. (1969). *Love and will.* New York, NY: W. W. Norton & Co., Inc.

Rogers, C. R. (1961). *On becoming a person.* Boston, MA: Houghton Mifflin Co.

Vlahos, G. A. (1972). *Man's inner cries.* Unpublished manuscript.

13

⌒

Trust the Path

Mary Jane Hooper

SINCE THE BEGINNING OF TIME, man has been searching for spiritual meaning. In a mysterious way, the labyrinth, an archetypal form found all over the world, has for thousands of years assisted man in that quest. Whether walked or traced with fingertips, the labyrinth is a powerful tool for reflection leading to a deeper knowledge of the self. It has sparked the imagination of mankind for more than 4,000 years. In the form of a spiral, the labyrinth path is perpetually turning in on itself.

The labyrinth has been used as a spiritual tool and is found in almost all cultures and religions. The origin of labyrinths remains a mystery. The earliest references to the term *labyrinth* suggest a stone structure. The labyrinth design invites a pattern of movement following many turns traversing the entire inner space to the center.

Dr. Lauren Artress (1995), a psychotherapist and Canon Pastor of Grace Cathedral in San Francisco, CA, rediscovered the power of the labyrinth in her search for a spiritual tool to help people in their quest for a deeper connection to God. Following a visit to Chartres Cathedral in France in 1991, where she was struck by the beauty and mystery of the labyrinth built into the floor of the nave, Dr. Artress brought the idea back to her church. After researching the significance of the pattern, she formed the worldwide labyrinth project in

1994. Since that time, thousands of labyrinths have been built in this country and used for worship, healing, and growth.

All of the great religions recognize life as a journey, a path one must walk to discover whom one really is, the true self capable of developing wisdom to respond to the world with compassion. The task is what Lauren Artress (1995), in *Walking the Sacred Path*, called the "substance of the soul." The Buddhists call it the path of enlightenment, and the Hindus describe it as seeking freedom. In the Christian tradition, union with God through self-knowledge is desired.

Thomas Merton (1999), a Catholic monk otherwise known as Father Louis of Gethsemani, often said that the easiest way to come to God is through our own center. As we pass through our own center, we move into the center of God. The labyrinth form leads us into the center and back out again. Once in the center, the stillness allows us to reflect upon our own path as we continue on the journey of our life.

To walk the sacred path of the labyrinth is to discover the sacred space within and to awaken feelings through symbols and archetypal forms. The form of the labyrinth invites us to trust the path and to take the next step. The 11-circuit labyrinth of Chartres Cathedral in France, the most famous of all labyrinths, meanders through four quadrants of a circle, at times approaching the center only to move far away from it, until we finally come upon the central rosette in the center. Alone at the center, one is invited into a deeper presence within oneself, elicited by the stillness following a rhythmic movement of the path leading into the center.

Standing at the entrance of the labyrinth, one realizes there are only two choices to make: to enter and to take the next step. There is one path in, and it leads to the center. The center is a place to pause, reflect, and stay open to what presents itself. It is virtually impossible to control or manipulate the experience; it becomes a path of surrender. Thomas Merton (1999) in his prayer, "Thoughts in Solitude," describes his experience in learning to surrender:

> My Lord God, I have no idea where I am going, I do not see the road ahead of me. I cannot know for certain where it will end. Nor do I really know myself, and the fact that I think I am following your will

does not mean that I am actually doing so. But I believe that the desire to please you does in fact please you. And I hope I have that desire in all that I am doing. I hope that I will never do anything apart from that desire. . . . Therefore will I trust you always though I may seem to be lost and in the shadow of death. I will not fear, for you are ever with me, and you will never leave me to face my perils alone. (p. 79)

The early Christians used the labyrinth as a metaphor, a path that would lead them to God. They looked upon this earthly existence as preparation for the next life, the eternal Kingdom of God. The number of stones in the labyrinth path built into the floor of Chartres Cathedral are the same number as the number of days that an infant spends in its mother's womb. Man develops in the mother's womb before being born on earth. These early Christians also believed that man develops in the earth's womb before being born in heaven. Birth symbolism is implicit in the narrow passages suggesting a return to the womb or a regression to the embryo. Cultures that live close to the land recognize the labyrinth form in nature. The Native American Hopi tradition sees the labyrinth as a symbol for the earth's continuous birthing process.

The revival of the labyrinth in modern times in many ways captures the essence of this medieval quest for meaning in one's life. The death and rebirth aspect of the labyrinth occurs at the center and symbolizes the transition from one way of being or knowing into another form. It is evident in the constant change of direction, reminiscent of the swinging sensation of a pendulum. A constant change in direction from the left, against perceived solar movement, represents death; to the right, moving with the sun represents life. The path away from a previous existence moves one toward death.

At first glance, it looks like a perilous undertaking. But, unlike mazes, labyrinths have only one path into the center and back out again. This is quite like the experience of entering into psychotherapy. Clients may envision the journey as a perilous undertaking. As they begin to confront the world that threatens them, they realize that this great mystery called life is meant to be lived. Dr. Myrtle Heery (n.d.) points out in her paper, *Soul and Intentionality*, that:

The soul is that aspect of beingness that temporarily manifests and inhabits a physical body. The soul uses that body to act in the physical world, dealing with all the perceived limitations of time, space and physical embodiment that we experience here. After death the soul soars like a bird, if you will, flying free once again after its tenure in the world of form. (p. 1)

Even physiological death may be understood as a transition into a new existence.

Like entering the labyrinth, the decision to enter psychotherapy requires a trust in something unknown and unseen. Clients follow the path of their inner guidance. There is nothing to figure out and thus later control; instead, the process is one of being with oneself, listening in a way that requires presence.

It may be like experiencing-centered psychotherapy described by noted psychologist James Bugental (1999) in his book, *Psychotherapy Isn't What You Think*. Both the labyrinth and psychotherapy require courage. Bugental orients psychotherapy to what is actually present. Helping clients appreciate the present moment must assume that clients can find grounding in their center.

Many of the larger-than-life questions about our presence and purpose on this journey called life are spiritual ones. Connection with spirit can be found as one embarks on the journey of the labyrinth and on the journey of psychotherapy. The form of the labyrinth and the form of the therapeutic hour, one visible and the other invisible, both create a wondrous container to enter into presence, leading participants into the source of their being and guiding them home again.

Entering psychotherapy or a labyrinth is like a portal that clients enter, knowing on some level change will occur and they will not be the same person as the one who entered. Clients find meaning in the twists and turns of their own lives, and the path is a metaphor for the life journey. The present moment prepares us for the next moment, a frontier still unexplored. What is important is to find presence and take the next step.

Bugental's (1999) model of psychotherapy identifies three aspects of presence.

- **Accessibility**, where one allows what happens in a situation to affect oneself.
- **Expressiveness**, where one allows oneself to be genuinely known and requires a commitment to put forth some effort.
- **Immersion**, when one has greater access to the preconscious, opening the possibility for unconscious matters to be expressed, leading to a level of intimacy.

In the center of the labyrinth, a crucial experience happens that requires presence. It is at this center, where perception is so fundamental, that one is required to make a change in direction of 180 degrees. Death and rebirth occur at the center, as one dissociates from the past by turning 180 degrees in a direction that allows one to make a new beginning.

As one walks the labyrinth, one is open to whatever lessons or gifts the labyrinth may hold. An important part of the labyrinth experience is to reflect on the experience afterwards. In group settings, a facilitator will process the group's experience by inviting participants to observe how they are feeling and if they were present each step of the way. Questions often arise. Were there obstacles to entering into the stillness? Can their intentions be brought out into the world? Can they relate to their environment in a more open way?

The metaphors within the labyrinth are shaped by our experience and our imagination. The journey to the center demands a basic change in direction. It is a change in direction of 180 degrees, creating an immediate disassociation from the past. To leave the center the person must first turn around and return by the very path by which one entered.

The way of transformation invites one to take a risk so one may endure all of life's lessons and pass courageously through it. The labyrinth offers therapists a tool to help clients enter new frontiers of their life through presence. The therapeutic relationship, like the form of the labyrinth, provides a safe container for this intimate journey.

References

Artress, L. (1995). *Walking a sacred path: Rediscovering the labyrinth as a spiritual practice.* New York, NY: Berkeley Publishing Group.

Bugental, J. F. T. (1999). *Psychotherapy isn't what you think.* Phoenix, AZ: Zeig, Tucker & Co., Inc.

Heery, M. (n.d.). *Soul and intentionality.* Unpublished manuscript. 1-8.

Merton, T. (1999). *Thoughts in solitude.* New York, NY: Farrar, Straus and Giroux.

14

A Journey Toward Authenticity

David Schulkin

I DIP MY HAND INTO THE COLD WATER, feeling it pass through my fingers as I use its resistance to propel myself forward. My arms, used to knowing what to do after more than 20 years of surfing, get me from the edge of the shore, past the turbulent rows of white water, out to the lineup, where I want to be. There I wait, and feel the level of the ocean rise and fall in a rhythm much slower than my everyday pace of life. I contemplate the waves of energy that are moving though the sea and pause to consider which one I would like to attempt to flow with. Timing and positioning are critical.

In a last-minute decision, I turn and paddle my surfboard toward the shore. As the energy catches up with me, I can feel the wave lift me up and thrust me forward. Now I am part of the wave, moving with an ever-changing wall of water. The board under my feet feels like an extension of my body as I fluidly turn and adapt to the constantly shifting environment. Swiftly swooping on the surface of the water, I intuitively make split-second decisions and micro-adjustments to stay attuned to the most powerful part of the wave. I am fully aware and present in order to flow with my surroundings, but also because I know these fleeting moments where I am actually riding the wave will not last forever. Soon the energy dissipates and I use the last remaining speed I have to turn off the back of the wave and coast to a stop in calm water.

My union with the wave has passed. I am once again a human being on a board, paddling back out to the lineup to get into the best position to catch the next wave that rolls my way.

I have been surfing for a majority of my life, and I have been a therapist since 2008. My perspective on surfing, my work as a psychotherapist, even my daily interactions with others have all been positively influenced by Dr. Jim Bugental's existential-humanistic model of psychotherapy (Bugental, 1999), which has propelled me on my journey toward authenticity. Ever since I started down the road to becoming a psychotherapist and even before, it has been a goal of mine to have authentic interactions with the people around me. In order to achieve authentic interactions, I have to be alert to and aware of the continually changing present moment. More than any other psychotherapy model, the existential-humanistic model describes, acknowledges, and embraces the present moment.

Embracing authenticity is an act of embracing uncertainty (Heery & Bugental, n.d.). There is no way of knowing exactly what is going to happen or what the next moment will bring. I can only observe what is happening right now and make choices based on those observations. As a lifelong surfer, I can't help but relate this directly to my experiences in the ocean. When I first catch a wave, I have an idea of what that wave might do, but the reality is I don't really know. So when I am riding a wave, I am living fully, using my intuition and interacting with what is happening in the moment, just as the existential-humanistic model encourages me to seize the present moment and make the most of what I have right now, since it is all there is.

The Existential-Humanistic Model in Surfing

At the core of the existential-humanistic model are four qualities that are proposed to exist universally, which are called the *four givens*. I can relate my experience of riding waves to each of these four givens, which are: Embodiment, Choice, Finitude, and A Part of/Apart From (Heery & Bugental, 2005). Embodiment is illustrated by the fact that it is essential to have a physically fit, flexible body in order to be able to interact with waves. For example, I need strong arms in order to paddle, a well-developed kinesthetic sense in order to balance on the board as it skims through the water, and my other senses at work in harmony in order to accurately interpret the wave energy that comes my way.

Choice is evident because I am presented with choices at every turn. I have to choose where to enter the ocean, where to wait for waves, and which ones to paddle for once I am out there. I also have to make immediate choices while I am actually riding a wave, such as shifting my weight onto my back foot or deciding when to execute a turn at the base of a steep wave.

Finitude is readily apparent because each wave only has a finite amount of time before it hits the beach and disappears, and my mark on that wave—the line that I draw as I surf across the wave's face—is also transitory. And A Part of/Apart From is clear because I feel part of the wave and part of my board in the moments when we are all flowing together seamlessly. However, when the ride is over, and the wave has passed, both wave and board feel separate and more distinct from me. I go back to being a person paddling a board on flat water.

The Existential-Humanistic Model in Therapy

Outside of the ocean, I also apply the existential-humanistic model in my work as a therapist in private practice. The four givens are always present during a therapy session. In terms of embodiment, when clients come into the room, I am already picking up cues about their situation from the way they hold their body; for example, how they move through the room, or how they sit in a chair. Are they hunched over, or fidgety? Do they sit uncomfortably on the edge of the couch, or do they walk with confidence and feel comfortable in their body when they sit? And whether they are aware of it or not, my clients are making assumptions about me and how I hold my body, too.

As therapist and client, we are working within the confines of finitude. We both know our interaction, our time together, is limited. We only have a little less than an hour to forge and deepen an alliance where change can occur. But our time is not just limited to the 50-minute hour—our time is limited on this earth. The existential-humanistic model asks that we acknowledge the central truth of finitude when working with clients in psychotherapy.

Then there is the next given: choice. I have to make the choice of what to respond to and when, while taking into careful consideration which words to use. This capacity to choose is deeply related to my capacity to be mindful in the moment of what is actually going on at the process level, that which is not necessarily being said. This is an exercise in using the same mindful presence I have developed when waiting for a wave. In any given therapy session, I strive to be attuned to my client and compassionately reflect back the unspoken process or underlying meaning behind his or her words.

As a therapist, I am not a blank slate; I am, in fact, growing with my client. I am affected by him or her, just as he or she is affected by me. The psychotherapeutic relationship involves mutual activation of intentionality for both healer and healed, therapist and client. (Heery, n.d.). When a client is working on a particular issue, it can prompt me to reexamine that issue more closely in my own life. The ripples of influence travel from psychotherapist to client and client to psychotherapist. In this model, I allow my clients to deeply affect me, which is one of the great ripples of this work for me.

The Existential-Humanistic Model and Authenticity

What originally attracted me to the existential-humanistic model was not a book or article, but a person. I seek out people who are skillful at authentic communication so that I can learn to be more skillful at authentic communication myself. One of those people is Dr. Myrtle Heery, who is the instructor of the "Unearthing the Moment" therapist trainings I have attended regularly over the past five years, where powerful and authentic interactions continue to inspire me. Just as ripples of water interact with each other as they travel over the surface of the ocean, I am affected by Myrtle and her trainings, and I carry that influence with me as I go on and affect other people in my life. Ultimately, this is all we can do: be influenced by and influence other people—in the most positive way we can—and thus create potentially limitless ripples of influence.

Heery wrote: "The soul is that aspect of beingness that temporarily manifests and inhabits a physical body. The soul uses that body to act in the physical world, dealing with all the perceived limitations of time, space, and physical embodiment that we experience here" (n.d.). This is how we can relate the existential-humanistic model to everyday life. We are all consciousnesses walking around within the confines of our bodies, which is embodiment. We are constantly interacting with each other, just as I interact with my clients or with the waves, and our interactions are often much more subtle and complex than they may appear on the physical level.

We have a choice of how to interact, and this choice has a profound effect on everything and everybody around us. This is a central tenet of my spiritual belief system—that all our actions, large and small, are interwoven with the actions of others and can influence and affect others who may be near or far from us in time or space. This belief is derived from the principle that all matter is made up of vibrating molecules, including the piece of paper you are holding in your hand, or the computer screen that is illuminating these words. These molecules are sending out vibrations—sometimes in the form of light or sound moving though the air, and sometimes in the form of energy moving though the ocean.

When humans interact with one another, we send out vibrations—like sounds from our vocal cords—but also more subtle vibrations that cannot be perceived with just the ears or eyes, such as feelings, ideas, and emotions. Sometimes these vibrations are harmonious and resonate with each other, for example when I am interacting with a very good friend and we buzz like tuning forks: a part of. Sometimes these vibrations are dissonant, for example when I have a disagreement with someone and it sounds like a jangled orchestra: apart from.

We are all sending out energetic or vibrational waves that are interacting with each other all the time, whether we are aware of them or not. It is my belief that these waves of energy affect the people around me, and that those people in turn make their own waves. When I die, my physical being stops being able to affect the lives of others, but the waves I have made are still bouncing around and affecting the people who knew me or knew of me. And in that way, my time on earth is finite, but my effect on my environment is potentially infinite.

The Existential-Humanistic Model in Daily Life

My exposure to the existential-humanistic model through years of classes and trainings has influenced my personal life and how I interact with my friends and family. For example, in the past few years, I have tried to be much more attuned to the more subtle micro-waves of communication that are being conveyed. In my work as a psychotherapist and in my everyday life, I am trying to be more aware of the meta-messages that are not only transmitted by sight or sound—the messages that are being conveyed beneath the content.

For many of my clients, friends or family, the underlying message they are expressing can be louder than their actual words. Two such examples of underlying messages a person may be giving me are, "Nothing ever works out for me!" or "Can you tell how smart I am?"

I listen to the process, because often that is where the deeper connection lies waiting, similar to waiting for just the right wave to ride. And just as it is a powerful experience to catch a wave, it is also powerful to hear and reflect back underlying messages to anyone in my life.

In my work as a psychotherapist and in my personal life, I want to synchronize the meta-messages of "I care about you and hear what you are saying," both verbally and nonverbally. I want my words and actions to reflect the nonverbal messages I am sending, because when those are in line, it is possible to achieve a much more genuine and authentic mode of communication.

I have been working consistently on my own authentic communication in the last few years. In doing this, I have become more aware of situations where I am not as authentic as I could be, where I might be saying one thing while simultaneously conveying something else totally contradictory.

An example of this contradictory communication in my own life is when my wife sometimes talks for me. She teaches writing at the university level and words come effortlessly to her, while I am somewhat dyslexic. So when I can't find the right word to say, she often steps in. I have noticed that when she talks for me, I often don't use words to say I want to talk. Instead, I often silently wait for her to notice that she was talking for me, and then hand me the proverbial microphone.

Now I am starting to speak up more, and if I notice my wife is talking for me, I just start talking and pick up the thread of the conversation in whatever story she's telling—so I speak, in order to claim my own voice.

Conclusion

When I enter the ocean, when I am actually sliding on the dynamic liquid surface of a wave, I tap into the power of the combination of presence and interaction. When the wave gets steep, I crouch low and gently glide my fingers over the wave face. When the wave becomes slower, I look back, turning my body and then my board towards a steeper section of the wave face, enabling me to stay connected to the intensity of the pocket, or the steepest part of the wave. I exist wholly in the present. I am conscious of the energy that exists within me while simultaneously being attentive and responding to the energy that is immediately affecting me.

And that is ultimately the goal: to have that awareness and presence both within and without, to be present with the four givens: Embodiment, Choice, Finitude, and A Part of/Apart From, and to find the activities that keep you present and in touch with authenticity. In my life surfing is a way for me to revisit and reclaim this authenticity that has become increasingly important in my communication, work, and relationships.

Hopefully some ripples from this chapter inspire you to find and engage with activities that you find authentic and meaningful. I also hope that as you read these words, you are somehow influenced or inspired by them. And in this dynamic ocean of influence, you will go on to affect other people in the infinite web of interconnection that we are all a part of.

References

Bugental, J. F. T. (1999). *Psychotherapy isn't what you think.* Phoenix, AZ. Zeig, Tucker & Co., Inc.

Heery, M. & Bugental, J. F. T. (2005). Listening to the listener: An existential-humanistic approach to psychotherapy with psychotherapists. In J. D. Geller, J. C. Norcross, & D. E. Orlinsky (Eds.), *The Psychotherapist's own psychotherapy: Patient and clinician perspectives* (282-296). New York, NY: Oxford University Press.

Heery, M. & Bugental, J. F. T. (n.d.). *The paradox of authenticity.* Unpublished manuscript.

Heery, M. (n.d.). *Soul and intentionality.* Unpublished manuscript.

15

⌣

Existential Presence Within a Foreign Culture: Reflections From Travels in Israel and Palestine

Sarah Burdge

EXISTENTIAL-HUMANISTIC PSYCHOTHERAPY, as a modality, aims to assist therapists in guiding clients in how to be fully and deeply present with the authentic moment as it arises. Additionally, concepts taken from this modality are also alive within any intentional relational context including the cross-cultural research context that will be explored in this chapter. It is within these types of authentic moments that existential and transpersonal experiences assist the birth of insights. Aspects of experience that can arise within these authentic moments can include thoughts, sensations, emotions, memories, and intuitions—as well as transpersonal experiences. Transpersonal experiences in this context are those that transcend an individual's isolated internal experience. Examples of transpersonal experiences that may arise in authentic therapeutic moments include awareness of the experience of another even when no words are spoken, experiences of deeply attuning with another's experience, or any number of experiences of attunement to individuals or phenomenon beyond one's individual self within the relational context. As exemplified by the religious and social leaders whom I interviewed during my travels in Israel, culture intimately informs how these experiences unfold.

This experience of transcending one's self or attuning to another's experience can be done more readily with individuals who are similar to each other. For example, parents who know their child intimately can more easily attune to the child's experience. A psychotherapist who lives in the same community and is of the same cultural origin, gender, age, etc. of a client can more easily attune to that client than if the client is essentially different in any number of these and other ways. So how might transpersonal existential moments be different between individuals of different cultures? As the field of western psychology matures, and as more research is done regarding psychological differences of humans across various cultures, it is becoming increasingly clear that the experience of humanness is vastly different for humans living in different locations and within different cultures around the globe. According to Sweder (1991),

> In the language of cultural psychology there are no pure psychological laws. . . . There are intentional persons reacting to, and directing their behavior with respect to, their own descriptions and mental representations of things; and there are intentional worlds, which are the realities we constitute, embody, and materialize out of our descriptions and representations of things. (p. 99)

In other words, we cannot assume that individuals who were born and developed psychologically in significantly different cultural contexts will have similar psychological structures or relational experiences. Thus, when traveling to and living within different cultural contexts our existential relational moments will be strongly influenced by the different contexts and psyches of the people we interact with. As a therapist and researcher, it is a deeply challenging process to develop and evolve levels of self-awareness that allow for, both observations of differing experience in relation to a culturally different other, as well as shared/attuned moments.

Research and Travels in a Foreign Culture—
Developing My Pou Sto

For my Ph.D. dissertation research I chose to research how religious practice influenced peace-oriented social activism. I performed my research in Israel based on the long-standing cultural and religious conflicts in that region of the world. In order to perform this research, I needed to travel and live in Israel for months at a time. Although the main focus of my travels and experiences in Israel was my research project, this experience of cultural emersion, also deeply informed my evolution as a therapist as it developed my awareness of differences in the moment-to-moment unfolding of human connection within an unfamiliar context. What follows are some reflections from my travels.

After spending three months in Israel, a country I had only briefly visited once in the past, I found myself both fatigued and aware of many layers of myself in a new and unfamiliar way. I was in Israel primarily to perform some initial research towards my dissertation study of peace activists working to bring peace to the current conflict using spiritual and/or religious practices and awareness. However, the complexity of all I was undertaking in my journey propelled me to realize that I was also there to explore myself spiritually, to stretch myself to subjectively experience living and being in another culture rather than just "visiting." I felt with all my senses the earth and culture at this spot on the planet that is so full of history, both profoundly beautiful and filled with violence. It is the earth in that vicinity that has given birth to all three major monotheistic religions, has birthed thousands of prophets, and has ached with the pain of thousands of years of human conflict. To be fully present to all that is occurring at any given moment is truly a transpersonal experience and in this complex culture this required of me new levels of psychological observation and the development of new therapeutic and intuitive senses.

During my time there I met with roughly a dozen well-known and respected social activists who were strongly connected to spiritual or religious beliefs and practices as part of their active work towards peace. They came from either Jewish or Arab culture. They came from many religious backgrounds, including Jewish, Greek Catholic, Sufi, Buddhist, Christian, and Druze. They were all deeply committed to creating peace in their region of the world and were actively involved in creating their vision of this peace within their communities and the surrounding region. I was blessed with opportunities to watch these leaders work and to have private dialogues with most of them.

Although these dialogues were not therapeutic, I used my skills as a clinician in being fully present to all they presented to me. I found that being present in the living moment with these individuals required a deepening of existential awareness within me that was similar to what is necessary in many clinical encounters I have experienced within my own culture.

As in any clinical encounter, I needed to find my *pou sto* (Bugental, 1999), or internal grounding and perspective through which to be present with the interviewee. Being truly present to all my possible thoughts, feelings, and sensations in such an unfamiliar setting could lead to a feeling of chaos when attempting to conduct a research interview. Thus, having my own pou sto solid helped capture what I was experiencing during my interviews. This pou sto needed to include my knowledge of the culture as well as my finely tuned awareness of what was unfolding in my moment-to-moment interactions with the people I met. It also needed to include my desire to notice the emotional, somatic, and spiritual ways that the activists were presenting while discussing the interview topic. However, I discovered that a pou sto is partially based on assumed shared experiences of reality. It implies that I understand the "other's" inner experience, as well as her or his needs, wants, and desires. My deepening into a pou sto that is appropriate for a given person depends on my own inner process of connecting with myself and on my intuitive guidance leading me to a place where I can truly receive and observe the other.

This place of receiving the other has many dimensions within it. These dimensions range from something as simple as the unspoken agreement about the meaning of body language to a dimension as complex as how my client or interviewee and I experience our personal sense of self. For an example of the first, in both Israeli and Arab cultures, when speaking with another woman about important matters it is normal to be very close physically, even touching. For me to stay aligned with a chosen pou sto of relational awareness and cultural respect would mean molding myself to these unfamiliar styles of interaction. Thus, when my own inner impulse may be to back away from such close proximity to another woman, I would need to notice the impulse and let the other woman determine the "correct" distance. For an example of the latter dimension, I as an American experiencing myself as an independent entity with many degrees of freedom of choice of action and belief. Arab culture is much more communal and collective, and most decisions about personal actions are made according to community norms and community sensitivities. As an example of this, on two occasions I had the honor of visiting and interviewing Arab activists in their home villages. In both cases it was assumed that I would meet the entire extended families and eat a meal with them after our dialogue. To leave before this would have been an insult. My awareness of these cultural norms demanded of me that I hold a different pou sto within when interviewing these individuals. I needed to have some knowledge of their culture and have more channels of perception open to how their subjective experience may dramatically differ from mine, as well as holding awareness of my goal in meeting with them.

Resistance Within a Culturally Unfamiliar Context

As I observed my subjective experience during these interviews, I was aware of more levels of resistance within my own psyche to what was unfolding in the actual moment than I normally encounter in my clinical interactions. Part of this resistance seemed to stem from my ego-self feeling itself in the unfamiliar territory of interacting with a person of a foreign culture and thus struggling to find its normal balance. Even with my intentionality to be aware of my inner experience and meet it with equanimity, I experienced frequent fear in the face of unknown or unfamiliar types of interactions. To be increasingly open to the subjective experience of one from another culture, I found I needed to continually surrender my own expectations or identity structures. This meant attending to my fear so that I had enough inner space to be present and grounded throughout my interactions with the activists. If I did not set my intention on this self-care and surrender then I could immediately perceive an intuitive distance between my interviewee and myself. Fear created an immediate defensive barrier between me and what was unfolding in the relational field. I was called again and again to open to their experience regardless of how unfamiliar or fearful it felt. Thankfully, in most cases I was able to notice this ego contraction and choose intentionally to breathe, notice, and remain open. At the exact millisecond that I felt myself contract when confronted with the difference of another person, I could often choose to open my heart and remain in respect and curiosity about the other. This meant being fully present with the existential unknown of how our culturally different psyches would interact in the coming moments.

Self-and-World Constructs and Culture

As mentioned above, the experience of maintaining this relational presence as a therapist within my own culture is an easier task. In a clinical situation when faced with a client expressing an experience or viewpoint that differs from my own, I choose to not judge and am openly curious about them and can usually do this without resistance or fear. However, as two people living, and in most cases, born in the same culture we have a fundamental familiarity with our collective cultural consciousness and an unspoken agreement about many values and ways of being. Another way of conceptualizing this is that many aspects of our self-and-world constructs (Bugental, 1999) are similar in a clinical situation with a client from my own culture. Bugental defines a self-construct as maps for conducting our lives and as "constructions of our awareness [that] are only partially conscious, but they give us a sense of identity, continuity and purpose" (p. 117). "The self-and-world construct system provides ways of coping with the openness of possibility" (Bugental, p. 121). These constructs are like the skeletal infrastructure of our psyches. We often can't observe them easily through our day-to-day experience, but they deeply inform our perceptions and understandings of our experiences. When I choose to open myself to truly receive another person from another culture, especially when I am physically located within the other's culture, we may have little or no overlap in our self-and-world construct and thus the task of truly meeting in the moment together requires a wider perspective of awareness.

For example, I had the honor of witnessing the first-time meeting of a well-known Orthodox Rabbi who is actively involved in the peace movement and a well-known Sufi Sheikh who is actively involved in teaching inner peace.

As I listened to the Rabbi and Sheikh greet each other, and converse over a period of about three hours, I was fascinated by how different their ways of communicating were than my own and then each other's. It was only after hours of reflection that I realized that the Rabbi asked short concise questions politely, attentively, and with curiosity of the Sheikh. The Sheikh answered all questions with long stories, within which there were no direct answers. Occasionally the Sheikh would pause after a story and offer a question to the Rabbi. The Rabbi answered all questions attentively, directly, and concisely. However, I could feel and intuit from my place in the room that they both were successfully efforting to be truly loving, open, and accepting of the other. They were holding mutual pou sto's of respect and openness to learn from the other. Even if their words may have never fully met, it appears that their hearts did and they left each other's presence with hugs and handshakes and clear love for the other. It appears as if they were able to find a ground or pou sto within and still shape-shift their receptivity to receive the other. If one were to simply capture their words and from these alone discern whether these men were truly attuning and meeting the moment together, the answer may have been negative. It took awareness of the transpersonal field between all of us present, openness to nuance and the strong presence in the moment to correctly "track" their eventual deep, heart-felt connection. The grace and ease at which they did this is an example for all therapists.

I have found the environment within which a therapeutic or interview encounter is taking place to be profoundly impactful in our dialogue efforts. In my experiences in Israel I was the foreigner making the effort to be subjectively present with myself, but from within a foreign matrix. The forces of the collective consciousness surrounding me were unfamiliar as were the customs and differing subjective realities of those I interviewed. I found that my reaction to that environment, on a very transpersonal level, was to feel exhausted after every encounter with people. It was as if my psyche was being asked to reshape itself to fit the mold of the collective consciousness that I was embedded within. The forces of the collective consciousness are not asking my permission or even pointing out the rules; the invisible transpersonal forces just exist. Although I, and the individuals I encountered were all human, we had vastly different ways of reacting to and understanding the world. My deeply embedded world construct was being constantly challenged just in being physically present with another from this foreign culture.

Self-and-World Constructs and the Spiritual Dimension

The common language that I found we could all speak transcended physical and verbal language and was more from the heart. I found that we could most easily meet when both an interviewee and I widened our awareness to include the spiritual dimension. Often there was a silent knowing, devoid of words or explanations that arose when we realized we were speaking from this place. Usually the entrance into this type of meeting occurred via a shared spiritual practice. This took the form of a moment of shared prayer, a moment of silence or an active engagement in spiritual practices such as a Sufi Zikr or a Jewish Religious service. After jointly EXPERIENCING the transpersonal together, we both would often notice and acknowledge that beyond our individual cultures, we held a common vision of the power of a Divine force nourishing and leading us all. For example, I had the blessing on several occasions to join an interfaith group of Jewish, Christian, and Muslim individuals in a Sufi Zikr in a small Mosque in the Old City of Jerusalem. One of the activists I met during my travels was the resident Sheikh, and his vision of the path to peace was to have community members of all faiths participate in each other's religious rituals as a way to build community. Words cannot describe how powerful it was to be standing in a very diverse group of 40–50 individuals in Jerusalem and be chanting together words from all of our faiths and to feel the presence of a spiritual force joining us all together. When we spoke afterwards of how this spiritual place may be the place of collective peace, we reached a place of common knowing. We found an experiential way to join our inner experiences together. There are deep implications for these experiences. Beyond all our profound cultural differences and differences in the very roots of our psyches, we may have a place of meeting that is not in the personal but rather in the spiritual. This may be what is being touched in deeply authentic existential therapeutic moments. I am left pondering how a person from any culture can truly receive, understand, and experience the other from a differing culture without a strong spiritual sense of self, in whatever form that may take. It is from this spiritual place that we are all created and a matrix within which, at our deepest core, we all live.

As I left the presence of my interviewee's and returned to solitude in my hotel, I often felt increasing levels of loneliness. This feeling was partially explained by the more obvious reality of missing the friends and family at home that I have not seen for months. However, there was a deeper aspect to this loneliness. I experienced it as an existential level loneliness for the presence of those with the same or similar self-and-world constructs and collective consciousness. At some deep intuitive level I, or the "I" within me as defined by my culture of origin, is detached from its fellow "I's." When I sat in deep presence with myself, my psyche felt like an island or a lost sheep. I felt the tug of desire to be in the presence of familiar "I's." That experience crystalized two insights for me. First, as a clinician working within my own culture with an individual from another culture, I realized that my client may be experiencing this same loneliness. Even if I am able to be fully present with a client's subjective experience, I am still within my familiar matrix and the client is not. The client may be experiencing some form of his or her own fear or confusion around being in unfamiliar psychic territory, surrounded by a different collective consciousness than his or her native one. I imagine that the only way to truly meet the client in this situation would be if we could both step out of or transcend the surrounding matrix. Entering into existential authentic presence in the moment through some form of transpersonal practice together, quite possibly, may allow us to join together beyond our world constructs. However, since this is not always possible, I may be able to fall back on my own experiential knowing of what this loneliness feels like. Second, I can remember how easy it was to desire separation from a different culture than my own. I experienced that truly opening to another culture and its experience of reality requires a loosening of my internal grip on my cultural perspectives. The therapeutic challenge is to be a traveler with my clients in understanding their self-and-world constructs enough to be able to journey together through their psyche. An existential level of loneliness is, most likely, not a desired state for people within most cultures. My bridging of this relational gap in our shared experience of the moment in a therapeutic setting with an eye out for this loneliness can create an alliance that may not be present without my own inner experiences from travels in a different culture.

Conclusion

From a distance I am aware that when I am immersed in the field of a familiar culture there is a sense of safety and comfort, like a key in a lock. I feel connected to my culture in ways that I was not aware of previous to my experiences in Israel. At the same time I am deeply drawn to truly experience the reality of others living within different cultures. This feels to me like the same dichotomy within me that the planet is currently struggling with. Does our survival depend on us all becoming the same, globalized consciousness or does our survival depend on learning how to tolerate, respect, and feel comfortable with radically different psyches within our world community? Transpersonal practices such as meditation, prayer, and ritual may be one of the keys to evolving humans of all cultures to understand how to be fully in the moment and present with what is unfolding without fear or unintentional actions of violence or judgment.

My experiences with the many peace activists I met in Israel not only pushed me to grow in my understanding of my own psyche but also deepened my understanding of some of the basic premises of existential-humanistic psychotherapy. To be truly present with a therapeutic pou sto, as well as be truly connected with the authentic experience unfolding in the moment in the therapy room, involves being mindful of our self-and-world constructs and how they are informing our contact with the moment and with the client. To be truly present as a psychotherapist also involves being present with my ego-self as well as my transpersonal-self as they both allow me access to different aspects of my client and our relational experience. Experiences of deeply attuned connection with individuals from other cultures allow for the possibility of a deepening of contact with the present moment and make space for a relational authenticity that can set the stage for transformative psychotherapy.

References

Bugental, J. F. T. (1999). *Psychotherapy isn't what you think*. Phoenix, AZ: Zeig, Tucker & Co., Inc.

Sweder, R. A. (1991). *Thinking through cultures: Expeditions in cultural psychology*. Cambridge, MA: Harvard University Press.

16

Existential and Spiritual Themes in Disaster Relief Work

Mark C. Yang

LIKE MANY OTHER mental health professionals around the world, in the aftermath of the devastating earthquake in Sichuan, China, in May of 2009, a number of the students and faculty from the Alliant International University's Clinical Psychology Psy.D. program in Hong Kong desperately wanted to utilize our training and expertise and be of some assistance to the survivors of the earthquake. The images we had seen through the media moved our hearts. Yet, we were very much unsure as to what we could offer. All of us lacked experience with disaster relief work. Nevertheless, we just knew that there must be something we could offer from our training.

Eventually, we made contact with Dr. Yang You Chuan and Dr. Deng Hong from Huashi Hospital in the City of Chengdu in Sichuan, China, who introduced us to a wonderfully dedicated team of volunteers who have been committed to helping the victims of the disaster. Through them, we learned much about our limitations, our naiveté, and what it means to serve the survivors of the earthquake. In the process, we have become friends.

What we've discovered is a parallel journey. We learned that just as the volunteers had to go and establish trusting relationships with the survivors before learning more about their needs, we—the students and faculty from Hong Kong—needed to do the same in terms of establishing the same trusting relationships with the volunteers first before we could begin to find out how best to serve. How often have we been taught in our clinical psychology program of the importance of doing a proper assessment? It was important that we find out what exactly are the needs of the volunteers and the survivors, lest we end up serving ourselves and in the process, adding to the burden of the volunteers. We found out that this took time. We found out that we had to be patient. We needed to have a long-term perspective. We very quickly found out that given our geographical separation, our lack of consistent availability, and finally, our inability to speak the local dialect, there was very little we could do to help the survivors of the earthquake. It was a time of some despair.

Yet, as we faced and sat with this despair, an opportunity presented itself to us! It became clear that our mission is the same as that of the volunteers. When I asked a committed group leader of the volunteers what help I could offer to him, I was thinking in terms of material and professional assistance. I was humbled by his response. He shared with me that the most important things he offers to the survivors are intangible. He travels weekly, three hours each way, to offer the survivors support, companionship/presence, and a listening ear. It became clear to me that this is exactly our role as volunteers. While there is little that we could offer directly to the survivors, we could take the same supportive and companionship role to the volunteers as they serve the survivors. The group leader reminded me of the most important fundamental healing factors in therapy. He shared with me that it is important for the survivors to know that they are not alone and have not been forgotten. This is the message that the students and I wanted to bring to the volunteers as they toiled anonymously week to week. We wanted them to know that they are not alone and that we honor and support the work that they do.

This chapter is the result of our collaboration. We, in the mental health field, constantly remind caretakers of the importance of self-care. Ironically, sometimes we forget our own message. Thus, the students and I thought it important for us to organize and initiate a weekend retreat for the volunteers to simply come together for a time of relaxation, recharge, and sharing. Loosely based on the work of Victor Frankl (1959) and logotherapy, we prepared two simple questions for reflection: How has the earthquake changed your life? And how has the earthquake changed and/or enhanced your worldview?

Presuming that the volunteers might be more comfortable talking about the changes and impact of the earthquake upon the survivors' lives, we were intentional in asking the volunteers to think about the earthquake's impact upon their own lives. This is consistent with the theme of self-care. We did not want an "out there" search for impersonal answers, but rather an "in here" search for personal meaning. We believed that such personal meanings discovered will ultimately lead to renewal and transformation.

> Searching is a process of transformation from inside, facilitating transition and psychological shifts inwardly by which the individual moves the process of living from one stage of life to the next, forming patterns of beginnings and endings. These patterns become conscious and choiceful to the individual through the searching process lived in psychotherapy. (Heery & Bugental, 2005, p. 254)

Or, in the words of Nietzsche, "He who has a why to live for can bear almost any how" (Frankl, 1959. p. 12). We believed that helping the volunteers to reflect upon their "whys" would help them to endure their "hows" leading to renewal.

What I present here are the themes that emerged from our weekend of sharing. What I remember most from the weekend is the amount of deep laughter that we shared. I've learned that in the face of tragedy, if we choose to heroically confront the suffering, what often emerges is a deeper sense of meaning and awe. It is entirely appropriate that laughter be the result. I wish you could have been there with us that weekend. This was not possible. Instead, what I can share with you through this chapter are the lessons that I learned from the volunteers that weekend.

Letting Go and Living in the Moment

A basic existential belief is that life and death are interdependent; they exist simultaneously, not consecutively. The rural survivors, being much closer to the land, perhaps closer to existence, being around life and death all the time with the birth, raising, and slaughter of livestock are much more accepting of life and the impermanence of life. A number of the volunteers shared that they were impressed with how the survivors so quickly came to accept this truth. I believe that the acceptance of this fundamental tenet that life and death are interdependent is critical to the well-being and spiritual growth of the survivors.

The wisdom of such a paradoxical view is expressed in these timeless quotes from the following philosophers and psychologists:

Seneca: "No man enjoys the true taste of life but he who is willing and ready to quit it." (Montaigne, 1965, p. 61)
Saint Augustine: "It is only in the face of death that man's self is born." (Montaigne, 1965, p. 63)
Irvin Yalom (2002): "Although the physicality of death destroys man, the idea of death saves him" (p. 126). [In other words, the physical earthquake destroyed many lives, yet the earthquake also saved and improved many lives.]

The earthquake is an excellent reminder of the existential given that people are thrown into groundlessness, a concept advanced by Martin Heidegger (1962). Indeed the very ground that we walk and live on both gives and takes away life. Often, we talk figuratively about being shaken to our foundations. The earthquake serves as a powerful, undeniable, and literal reminder that indeed even our very basic foundation of living our everyday lives must not be taken for granted. Life and death are simultaneous, not distinct nor consecutive. In order for the survivors to recover and even thrive, they must come to some form of acceptance that the earthquake is not an anomaly but an existential, everyday fact of life. Awareness and acceptance of this fact and the terrible consequences of the earthquake are things that we all must confront, and out of this confrontation can come tremendous growth.

The growth that can result from this confrontation is that we live more authentically and live more in the moment. Martin Heidegger (1962) believed that there are two fundamental modes of existing in the world: (1) a state of forgetfulness of being or (2) a state of mindfulness of being.

> **Forgetfulness of Being**: Living in the world of things. Heidegger refers to this as "inauthentic" living. Unaware, fleeing, tranquilized, avoiding choice. Everyday living.
>
> **Mindfulness**: One marvels not about the way things are, but that they are. Authentic, responsible for choice, awareness, transcendent. One embraces one's possibilities and limits; one faces absolute freedom and nothingness—and is anxious in the face of them [note: not absence of anxiety]. (Yalom, 1980, p. 31)

The letting go I heard from a number of the volunteers points to this type of living. One volunteer talked about letting go of perfection (related to the forgiveness of herself and others). How she no longer waits until she's attained some self-prescribed goal before rewarding herself with living. She was always striving and striving, always not quite good enough. She knew intellectually that she needed to let go, but her work with the survivors and the confrontations with the fragility of life impelled her with the courage to live in the present. Another volunteer talked similarly about living a slower pace of life internally. About simply enjoying walks in the park with her daughter. Prior to the earthquake, she had always been too busy to take these walks and did not take the time to enjoy what was around her. But her work with the survivors helped her to enter into an Ontological Way of Being (from the Greek ontos meaning "existence" or "being") where one remains mindful of being, not only mindful of the fragility of being, but mindful too of one's responsibility for one's own being (Heidegger, 1962). This is a state where one wonders not about why things are the way they are, but that they are. From another perspective, both of these volunteers and others became aware of the Buddhist concept of detachment—don't cling to things, because everything is impermanent. Which paradoxically does not mean that you don't let the experience penetrate you; on the contrary, you let it penetrate you fully. That is how one can finally detach. Finally, from the existential perspective, the volunteers' work reminded me that existence/life cannot be postponed.

Putting Things in Perspective—Wonderment and Awe

In becoming more aware of our impermanence, we also gain a deeper appreciation of perspective. This came across in a number of ways in the sharing of the volunteers. First of all, a few of the Christian volunteers shared readily about how they recognized their limitations in the face of all the destruction and all the need. They readily recognized their insignificance in the presence of the Almighty God. They recognized that though they had numerous questions, they were limited in their understanding as to the reason for all this suffering. This reminded me of an analogy offered by Victor Frankl (1959) in his book *Man's Search for Meaning*:

> A question is asked whether an ape which was being used to develop poliomyelitis serum, and for this reason punctured again and again, would ever be able to grasp the meaning of its suffering. The answer is obvious. With its limited intelligence, it could not enter into the world of man, i.e., the only world in which the meaning of its suffering would be understandable.
>
> And what about man? Are you sure that the human world is a terminal point in the evolution of the cosmos? Is it not conceivable that there is still another dimension, a world beyond man's world: a world in which the question of an ultimate meaning of human suffering would find an answer?
>
> This ultimate meaning necessarily exceeds and surpasses the finite intellectual capacities of man. What is demanded of man is not, as some existential philosophers teach, to endure the meaninglessness of life, but rather to bear his incapacity to grasp its unconditional meaningfulness in rational terms. (p. 99)

What Frankl is proposing reminds me of the Taoist perspective of submitting to the Tao. Submitting to a hidden order of things. There seems to be a hidden order of things regarding life and death that some of the survivors implicitly knew. They were able to move on without being tormented by the never-ending question of "Why?"

I can also imagine the Christian volunteers understanding the following advice given by a Hasidic sage: "When a man suffers, he ought not to say, 'That's bad! That's bad!' Nothing God imposes on man is bad. But it is all right to say, 'That's bitter! That's bitter!' For among medicines there are some that are made with bitter herbs."

Whether you agree with the Christian or Hasidic tradition of surrender to the Almighty, there was undeniably a theme of surrender in the sharing of the volunteers. The main form of this surrender was asking the very real question of "What can I do in the midst of such overwhelming need?" In the form of a statement, it becomes, "I see my insignificance next to such overwhelming need." This naturally begs the questions, "What can I offer? What difference does it make if I go (to serve as a volunteer) this week or not?"

Heroic Nihilism

The opposite approach to surrender is defiance, as characterized by Albert Camus. Camus (1955) went through a period in his thinking, which started with nihilism and ended with what he called heroic nihilism. The volunteers from both Chengdu and Hong Kong went through a similar process when we were confronted with our limitations. Camus' "new vision posits that we can construct a new life meaning by cherishing our 'nights of despair,' by facing the very vortex of meaninglessness and arriving at a posture of "heroic nihilism. . . . The values of heroic nihilism consist of courage, prideful rebellion, fraternal solidarity, love, and secular saintliness" (Yalom, 1980, pp. 427-428).

A human being, Camus believed, can attain full stature only by living with dignity in the face of absurdity. The world's indifference can be transcended by rebellion, a prideful rebellion against one's condition. So in the face of such insurmountable suffering and need, Camus would admonish the survivors and all of us volunteers to persist to exist. Why should we continue to go? Because transcendence awaits us upon facing this despair. Camus (n.d.) writes, "In the depth of winter, I finally learned that within me there lay an invincible summer."

The volunteers that we shared the weekend with were all invincible heroes. They transcended their ordinary lives by persisting to serve the survivors week after week. Out of the thousands of volunteers, they have persisted in their service. Their number is a testament to their persistence and invincibility. Their invincibility results from their consistent self-inquiry as to "Why should I go?" Or even simply, "Do I want to go?" and deciding to go nevertheless!

Finally, in terms of transcendence and putting things in perspective, I am reminded of the teaching by Irvin Yalom (1980) that altitude gives us perspective, which helps to reduce anxiety. It's about all of us coming to some sort of perspective, whether it's submitting to a higher order to things, a stance characterized by heroic nihilism, or surrendering to a higher power with awe. The ontological mindfulness evident in the lives and sharing of the volunteers testifies to such transcendence.

References

Camus, A. (1955). *The myth of Sisyphus and other essays*. New York, NY: Alfred A. Knopf.

Camus, A. (n.d.). Quotes. Retrieved January 9, 2010, from http://www.quotationspage.com/quotes/Albert_Camus.

Frankl, V. (1959). *Man's search for meaning*. New York, NY: Pocket Books.

Heery, M. & Bugental, J. F. T. (2005). Meaning and Transformation. In E. van Deurzen & C. Arnold-Baker (Eds.*), Existential perspectives on human issues* (pp. 253-264). New York, NY: Palgrave Macmillan.

Heidegger, M. (1962). *Being and time*. New York, NY: Harper & Row.

Montaigne, M. E. (1965). *The complete essays of Montaigne* (Ed. & Trans., D. Frame). Stanford, CA: Stanford University Press.

Yalom, I. D. (1980). *Existential psychotherapy*. New York, NY: Basic Books Publishers Inc.

Yalom, I. D. (2002). *The gift of therapy*. New York, NY: HarperCollins.

17

Presence in Existential-Humanistic Psychotherapy and in the Shamanic Journey

Sandra Harner

WHAT COMES TO MIND when you hear the word "presence"? In the common vernacular, it can mean a physical form is at a given place. The form is objective, tangible, and manifest. Presence can also imply a quality of close relationship or a heightened state of awareness. In this use, it is a subjective experience of here and now. Presence also can refer to "something (as a spirit) felt or believed to be present" (Mish, 1993, p. 921), or, more specifically, "a divine or supernatural spirit felt to be present" (Presence, 1996). Presence, as a state where the material and the invisible meet, can transcend the boundaries of each, retrieve us from isolation, and enliven us.

Bugental (1987, 1978) describes presence as the level of openness to influence and willingness to disclose subjective experience in the psychotherapy session. He considers it essential for psychotherapy. Four of his rules of ten for therapists specifically refer to presence (Bugental, 1990). Two are so important that he repeats them: "Be there!" (p. 133) and "Insist that the client be there" (p.133) Further, two underlying assumptions from Bugental's existential-humanistic perspective directly address presence in the therapist's work. One is that therapists maintain full presence to the client's experience in the moment. Another is that therapists closely attend to "clients' immediate inner flow of experience" (Bugental, 1995, pp. 18-19). In shamanism, an ancient way of healing and knowledge, the presence of spirits is a core assumption.

Just as much of the objective world goes on beyond our direct knowledge, especially in these days of vast communication technologies and networks, so our subjective inner worlds are largely imperceptible to ourselves and to those outside of us. For all our resources, comprehension of the exigencies of our lives remains fairly limited. Presence extends our modest capabilities to attend to the subjective and objective realms.

As individuals, each of us plays out the drama within our own limitations. Opportunities arise that offer the possibility of enlarging our scope of experience. To what degree are we present? Seeing the opportunity as an opening, an invitation to see with a wider vision, is rejected by some and welcomed by others. A person might well question if it is an illusion, an imposter, or the "real thing." Presence is our friend; time, its companion. Because of time, we are often forced to make choices. Even choosing not to choose becomes a choice, by default, for living continues. Change is ceaseless. In moments of choice we may come to see ourselves, and the living force around us, more fully.

Existential-humanistic psychotherapy and shamanic practice open new possibilities of choice and discovery through the use of "presence." Although they have different starting points, emphases and some critical basic assumptions, they both share some fundamental principles and urge us into the unknown. Consistent with our culture, which prizes the "objective," mainstream psychology generally assumes an objective, materialistic stance that emphasizes the *inner* life of the self. It largely considers altered states of consciousness to be inner experiences, psychological manifestations of the mind-brain interface and social-behavioral influences. For shamanism, on the other hand, the altered state of consciousness is a defining experience undertaken deliberately in order to access sources of wisdom and help in another, *outer*, reality of spirits. Both shamanism and existential-humanistic psychotherapy are partnerships in lived experience. Few choose either; both require presence.

Psychotherapy usually takes place in a normal waking state of consciousness for both therapist and client. Of course, hypnotherapy, sonic-driving, or drug-facilitated therapy (such as with sodium pentothal, entheogens, LSD, MDMA or other substances), are exceptions. The results are framed as *inner* experiences of the person requesting help. The psychotherapist's role in existential-humanistic psychotherapy is largely that of guide and companion with "technical knowledge . . . so thoroughly incorporated as to be implicit in the therapist's whole way of being" (Bugental, 1978, p. 33).

Bugental (1978) effectively uses the concept of "journey" with traveler and guide as an analogy by which to describe the psychotherapy process from the perspective of his existential-humanistic approach. In it, the relationship between the therapist and client is prominent. They pursue their mutual objective imbedded in presence and communication, employing such tools as working with resistance, the actual moment, searching and exploring, and intentionality (Bugental, 1978; 1999). Responsibility for choices and their consequences, for actualizing the lessons learned, rests with psychotherapy client.

The shamanic journey is undertaken in an altered consciousness that the shaman enters in order to experience a reality based on shamanic methods and direct knowledge obtained while in that state, also understood as the Shamanic State of Consciousness (M. Harner, 1990). The shaman is in an altered state of consciousness during the journey and the client remains in an ordinary state of consciousness. This process is a primary tool of discovery demanding full presence of the shaman who may provide access to direct spiritual healing and who conveys to the client the information obtained in the course of the journey. It is the client's choice to act or not to act on that information.

In psychotherapy and in the shamanic journey, there are missions or intentions. Existential-humanistic psychotherapy "seeks to decrease anxiety and pain . . . beyond that important function to evoke the potentialities that are latent within each of us" (Bugental, 1978, p. 15). For the existential-humanistic psychotherapist, the goal is to provide access to the mystery that is the client, to potentiate the client's healthful growth, and to support the client's developing autonomy. The psychotherapist must remain disciplined and true to his or her own experience with acute awareness of the unique needs of the client. The degree to which the client is willing to engage, moving to action, is critical to the process.

A primary goal of the shaman, also, is to ease or empower the lives of their clients. The shamanic practitioner is traditionally at the service of those in the community, for purposes of healing, divination, and psychopomp services, even healing the dead. In the shamanic journey, healing and help come from another reality *outside* of the person. It is as real as the more familiar objective, consensus reality of the senses. It is a private reality, however. Its specific details are not available for objective validation by others. Those who enter this alternate reality discover a world rarely glimpsed in daily life. The triad—shamanic practitioner, client, and spirits—is the necessary complement of active forces, each with its own role. Three-party communication is the structure. It requires presence, in the fullest sense of the word, with courage, discipline and attention to the details of the journey as well as the client's needs.

Likewise in existential-humanistic psychotherapy one enters an unknown, privileged realm. Presence in both the therapist and the client are required on this journey that, as it progresses, is likely to be challenged to adapt to change. The therapist is present to the client and the client is present to his or her own felt experience in the moment and available to engage with the therapist. The client has the responsibility of acquainting himself or herself with his or her own inner world, of exploring it and searching for that which is meaningful to him or her. The therapist acts as guide and refuge, if need be, as the client discovers an amazing world that resides within. In individual psychotherapy, the dyad or two-party communication is the usual operant model. In both systems, the seeker may complete the journey (shamanic or in psychotherapy) with increased knowledge; there are discoveries beyond the initial, specified purpose. It is also the journeyer who chooses how to act in daily life after the journey.

Harner Shamanic Counseling (M. Harner, 1988) is a contemporary adaptation of shamanic methods, principles, and practices. It is a hybrid system developed for teaching skills to individuals so that they may journey on their own behalf and work autonomously. It is based on core shamanic universals or near-universals that occur cross-culturally. Journeying to solve problems oneself, and seek answers to personal questions, draws on some of the themes discussed previously that apply to both shamanic practice and to existential-humanistic psychotherapy. Intention and intentionality are critical as the person clarifies the question of most pertinent current concern that will be the purpose of the journey. The journeyer must determine what is most important personally at this moment. During the journey, the person must be present to the experience without resistance. The journeyer must choose to bring into action the information gathered in the journey.

In the training process, the shamanic counselor is a teacher of method, a coach and a mentor, prescribing a series of five specific preliminary journeys for the trainee to practice in order to become acquainted with a personal map of the journey territories and resources. In order, they are (a) Journey to the Lower World to meet a waiting animal; (b) Journey to the Lower World to the same animal and ask an important question; (c) Journey to the Upper World to a tutelary spirit; (d) Journey to the Upper World to meet that Teacher and ask an important question; and (e) Journey to the Upper World (or Lower World) and ask how to implement one of the answers given in the second or fourth journey. In the context of preparing the trainee for each new journey's tasks, the shamanic counselor provides instruction on how to journey to the Upper and Lower Worlds, maintain presence, and ask questions; and gives feedback on the trainee's adherence to the methodology; and supports the client's autonomy in interpreting the content of the journeys. The "real" counselors of content are those the trainee meets in the journeys. The training process, itself, needs presence on the part of both trainee/journeyer and the counselor. For an example of Harner Shamanic Counseling journeys by one individual over an extended period of time see *Ema's Odyssey* (S. Harner, 2014).

The fundamentals of the shamanic journey and existential-humanistic psychotherapy share some common elements, such as presence, the quality discussed here; intention; and a collaborative relationship with client autonomy as a goal. The shamanic journey and existential-humanistic psychotherapy differ significantly in the states of consciousness involved and in the necessity of acknowledging spirits as an integral part of the shamanic system.

With extensive training and experience in both shamanic journeying and existential-humanistic psychotherapy, I have come to the conclusion, at this time, that each has its distinct place. While the shamanic journey *can* provide practice in developing skills for presence, so can many other practices.

To use the shamanic journey or other shamanic practices as vehicles by which to hone proficiency in presence does an injustice to both psychotherapy and shamanism. Both systems provide valuable, often closely parallel, legitimate means for helping others live more fully. Each system is internally consistent. The most obvious disparity lies in the secular nature of psychology and the sacred or spiritual nature of shamanism. Yet there are points of cross-over and continuity between them. They address human needs in different ways that may or may not be reconcilable for given individuals.

Is shamanism psychotherapy? I think not, although research indicates the journey's positive psychological effect (S. Harner, 1995, 2001, 2003, 2004; Harner & Harner, 2000; Harner & Tryon, 1992, 1996, 1997). Is psychotherapy shamanism? Likewise, I think not. My position on possibly integrating them into one service is a work in progress. Bugental's (1978) concern about the wide array and levels of preparation brought to the public in the name of therapy remains pertinent to this discussion:

> I know that many kinds of experiences can be *therapeutic*, but I feel that a distinction needs to be made as to what is truly *therapy*. To be sure, there are many legitimately trained, fully credentialed bunglers in this work, but that does not equate to saying that just anyone should set up shop to be a therapist. If one, no matter what her or his education, intends to offer psychotherapy, that person should in respect for human dignity seek preparation that is thorough and meaningful. (p. 146)

Psychology as a field is becoming increasingly sensitive to the importance of spiritual aspects of life and is making some early responses to biological, psychological, and spiritual connections. For example, the DSM IV has a diagnostic category for spiritual problems and an appendix with culture-bound syndromes steeped in spiritual explanations. With growing recognition of indigenous healing practices, medical students are increasingly being exposed to folk remedies and traditional, spiritual healing modalities. How complementary, alternative, and native practices will eventually integrate with conventional medical practice remains to be seen. Those who would also offer such specialties need thorough training, preparation, and direct experience. Fully integrating the spiritual into psychotherapy practice is a courageous and relatively pioneering practice with fruitful potential (Heery, n.d.). Exciting possibilities of change are emerging.

In the face of changing paradigms, it is important to remain open to the potentialities they offer, while recognizing our responsibilities to respect individual differences and provide the services requested and expected; to know the limits of our scope of practice and our training; to honor community standards of practice, as well as the law and ethics for that practice. Genuine communication relies on tolerance of differences and acknowledgment of shared interests. The secular, in psychotherapy, and the sacred, in shamanism, unite through a common word—presence. Perhaps more than a happy accident of semantics underpins these various meanings.

References

Bugental, J. F. T. (1978). *Psychotherapy and process: The fundamentals of an existential-humanistic approach.* New York, NY: McGraw-Hill.

Bugental, J. F. T. (1987) *The art of the psychotherapist: How to develop the skills that take psychotherapy beyond science* New York, NY: W. W. Norton.

Bugental, J. F. T. (1990). Ten commandments for therapists. *Psychotherapy, 27,* 133.

Bugental, J. F. T. (1995) What is distinctive about this existential-humanistic perspective in psychotherapy. *The Saybrook Perspective,* 18-19.

Bugental, J. F. T. (1999). *Psychotherapy isn't what you think.* Phoenix, AZ: Zeig, Tucker & Co., Inc.

Harner, M. (1988). Shamanic counseling. In G. Doore (Ed.), *Shaman's path: Healing, personal growth, & empowerment* (pp. 179-187). Boston, MA: Shambala.

Harner, M. (1990). *The way of the shaman* (10th anniversary ed.). San Francisco, CA: Harper San Francisco.

Harner, M., & Harner, S. (2000). Core practices in the shamanic treatment of illness. *Shamanism, 13*(1-2), 19-30.

Harner, S. (1995). *Immune and affect response to shamanic drumming.* Unpublished doctoral dissertation, Fordham University.

Harner, S. (2001). Shamanic journeying and health research. *Shamanism, 14*(1), 19-22.

Harner, S. (2003). Shamanic journeying and immune response. *Shamanism, 16*(2), 9-13.

Harner, S. (2004). Shamanic journeying and psychological responses. *Shamanism, 17*(2), 16-23.

Harner, S. (2014). *Ema's odyssey.* Berkeley, CA: North Atlantic Books.

Harner, S., & Tryon, W. (1992). Effects of shamanic drumming on salivary immunoglobulin A, salivary immunoglobulin M, anxiety, and well-being. In J. Pentikainen & M. Hoppal (Eds.), *Proceedings of the International Association of Historians of Religion* (pp. 196-204). Helsinki, Finland: Finnish Literature Society.

Harner, S., & Tryon, W. (1996). Psychological and immunological responses to shamanic journeying with drumming. *Shaman, 4*(1-2), 89-97.

Harner, S., & Tryon, W. (1997). Therapeutic effects of shamanism. *Shamanism, 9*(1), 27-28.

Heery, M. (n.d.). *Soul and intentionality.* Unpublished manuscript.

Mish, F. C. (Ed.). (1993). *Merriam Webster's collegiate dictionary* (Xth ed.). Springfield, MA: Merriam-Webster.

Presence. (1996). *Webster's new universal unabridged dictionary.* New York, NY: Barnes & Noble.

18

Dream Work in the Here and Now

Cynthia S. Sauln

I AM A DREAM WORKER. I keep a written record of dreams that I remember, and many of the dreams have informed my waking life actions. My dreams have led me to continue my life journey in new and amazing ways, including leaving a long career in another field in 2006 to go back to school and pursue a Ph.D. in Clinical Psychology. Dreams are sacred to me. They are often mysterious, connected to my Source of inspiration, and seem to carry a spiritual message. I have also learned firsthand that they "always come in the service of health and wholeness" (Taylor, 2009, p. 10). They sometimes provide understanding of complex situations in waking life and, no matter how confusing, scary, or seemingly unconnected to my waking life they may be at first glance, it is possible to use the dream as a signpost and a tool for growth.

Dream researchers and theorists, based on the work of Carl Jung, have advanced the understanding that dreams speak a universal language of metaphor and symbols, and reflect our unconscious needs, desires, conflicts, and spiritual understanding. Dreaming cultures throughout the world and throughout history have used dreams to contact ancestors, as visions for the future, and to bring healing to the dreamer or often, to the larger community. According to Bulkeley (2008), dream images and symbolism have been the basis for healing, rites of passage, vocational choices, problem solving, and personal transformation across nearly every civilization in recorded history.

My Own Dream

As I thought of how dreams work for me, it made sense to use a personal example as a metaphor for my experience of existential-humanistic psychotherapy principles and how I apply it in my practice of psychotherapy. I had the following dream near the end of the first Unearthing the Moment training series in 2011, when I was struggling to complete a paper as the final course requirement.

> I am standing in a room, wearing a T-shirt with a low neckline that bares the front of my chest. Dr. Heery (Myrtle) is standing there, looking in my eyes intently, and insistently saying in her inimitable Southern drawl, "Presence, I'm talking about presence here," and I wonder, "What does she mean?" The word presence is stuck in my mind, and I notice the word "Presence" is written on my bare chest. I am startled by how vividly it is scrawled there—and then Myrtle says to me, "Are you listening?" and I wake up. (Sauln, 2011)

The night before this dream occurred, I was thinking about the required paper. When I awoke from the dream, I thought the dream was telling me something about the paper, and in particular, about the concept of presence as the essential tool for the therapeutic relationship. However, as I began writing and connecting with articles by other therapists, I found myself worrying that I had nothing to write about presence that had not already been said by someone else. This worry about writing was not a new state for me; I often experienced difficulty digging down into what I really wanted to say on paper. The worry and anxiety continued as I sorted through the reading I had done pertaining to the theoretical framework, considering and discarding ideas, but the dream continued to stick with me and distract my efforts. I was confused, and wondered why the dream had occurred. I pondered how this dream might connect to living in the here and now and the essay I was writing. This was an instance where confusion could be helpful—in the words of Bugental (1999):

"Confusion is your friend. It means you're not using your familiar habits, and so there is an opportunity for you to see and react freshly" (p. 107). I decided to pay attention to the distracting dream and use it.

With that in mind, after thinking about my intention for the essay, I saw the message from the dream in a different light. I was reminded that dreams are sacred territory for me and how, in the past, they had delivered a message to me. I was reminded of Myrtle's concept of a "soul call," as in "the soul leaves messages on my inner answering machine" (Heery, n.d.). Perhaps this dream was a soul call, asking me a question, leaving me a message on my inner answering machine—"Am I fully present to my own inner experiencing, am I listening deeply and embodying the beliefs that are foundational to this way of therapy, or am I just thinking about it?" Searching began, which according to Bugental (1999), is the energized process, guided by concern that will lead to enriched living (p. 63), and which in this case, hopefully would result in a deeper knowing of my answers to these questions. So, instead of the course I originally started on with my final essay, I stopped and began to work with the dream in the present moment. For this process I used the form of dream work Yalom (1980) describes as taking responsibility for all parts of the dream—"which is aimed to maximize the individual's appreciation of his or her own authorship of the dream" (p. 248). Recognizing I was the author of the dream fit quite nicely with the existential-humanistic point of view. I had a choice to notice and work with my immediate inner experiencing (confusion, not-knowing, conflicting emotions); I needed to take responsibility for each of the elements of the dream and what they might mean for me (not my therapist or someone else's interpretation). I had to trust that in some way this dream explication was exactly what was needed to write the paper.

As I began, I was amused by the idea that all of the elements of this theoretical framework might be present within the dream. I decided some playfulness might be helpful to begin reassembling the elements in a way that would decode the meaning. I sat at my computer, closed my eyes, thought about the dream, and laughed out loud at the image presented to me—what could be more symbolic for embodied presence than having the word tattooed across my chest? "OK, no problem," I thought, and felt this would be easy. I began to unfold the dream by thinking about how the existential givens and the concepts in Bugental (1999) related to me in my dream in that moment.

Searching and Concern

In the dream, I was the client baring my chest (my heart/my soul) to Myrtle, the therapist. She asked the question, "Are you listening?" which may mean I was listening to content, but not more deeply for my own inner experiencing. She was not telling me what to do or paying attention to what I was saying, she was asking me the question so that I would listen more deeply to myself. "Am I listening?" I repeated this phrase over and over again—what does it mean? What is the message for me? The more I pondered, the more I connected with my anxiety. How do I take this information and communicate the meaning, while using the anxiety about not knowing to fuel my writing when it was so uncomfortable? As I sat, I became more connected with my feelings of ineptitude, my questioning, my anxiety over wondering if this is what was expected, was this good enough, how does this fit, and I realized this experience was a lot like what my clients are going through. They sit with me, stuck in not knowing and confusion—sometimes they want me to help, or to do it for them, or to pay attention to the story instead of the experience of being in relationship. I say to them (and to myself in this moment), "Sit with the confusion, stay in the not-knowing, just keep asking the question, and wait to see what comes up as you hit the core of the inner experience that comes with the questioning, not the words that come with the thinking." But right now, when it was my turn, it was not so easy. My bare chest in the dream was my vulnerability in this moment, my fear of exposure, the question, "What if I am not good enough or seem foolish?" I experienced that by sitting with these thoughts and wondering what else there was in this dream for me.

Pou Sto

The concept of *pou sto* is central to the existential-humanistic psychotherapist's engagement with his or her client. Bugental (1999) described pou sto as "a place from which to exert power, a place to ground one's work, and a base of operations" (p. 85). Perhaps the image of Myrtle in the dream emphatically saying, "Presence, I'm talking about presence here," was actually a reminder that she always stands very firmly in relation to the other, and her appearing in the dream with me was a reminder of this key concept and a message that my presence in this dyad was a place to stand as well. Although I was exposed in the dream and questioning, I realized I was also standing quite firmly, looking directly at her. When I asked the question, "Who are you to me?" I realized I am both of us; I am a part of and apart from—the vulnerable one and the authority, the client and the therapist, the student and the teacher. I remembered the perspective of being a pilgrim on this journey with a client, which relieves me of having to know the exact direction we will go in or the need to have the answers to all questions. I was also reminded of the necessity of balancing the subjective and the objective, "to keep alive to the possibilities, opportunities, and threats they present; and to learn wisely to balance their competing impulses" (Bugental, 1999, p. 156). In the dream, Myrtle spoke to me to get my attention—she was aware I needed the reminder. Then I wondered if Myrtle was actually saying presents, (as in, "I'm talking about presents here") meaning gifts, or a way of saying that being here, being alive in each moment is full of gifts. Struggling was a gift too—the anxiety compelled me to keep wondering, to keep looking for meaning. This somehow blended into thinking about finitude—I will not always be here, all I have is this present moment, and I am grateful for life, this dream, and the struggle of learning to be a psychotherapist and all it brings.

This example may sound self-indulgent, but I am still touched by considering the gifts that might have been in the dream. Dream work is a place to stand in my practice of psychotherapy. In my willingness to struggle with the messages in the dream, I deepened my own understanding. I gained the learning in a way that was very personal and unique to me: "Just listen. Be present. Go deeper."

Dream Work With Others

My personal experience with my dreams has also supported my desire to work with dreams in clinical practice with adults and children. I have found that adults spontaneously will present a dream or nightmare in therapy that is representative of their waking life struggles or concerns, but the material or meaning may not be consciously available until they speak the dream out loud. If the dream is a nightmare, it may be particularly difficult to get past the fear or distress to find the meaning; the client's inclination is often to push the dream away. Using a similar approach to the earlier description of working with my own dream, I ask the dreamer to tell the dream in the present tense. Then I ask him or her to tell it again, this time looking at the associations between the parts of the dream, and allowing the mystery of the dream to unfold. This creates, for the two of us, the opportunity to work together to help the dreamer explore the meaning of the various symbols, people, and activities represented in the dream. There is a context for the dream with the background information about the dreamer's life, but the final meaning and interpretation always rests with the dreamer, not the therapist. This has proven to be a way for me to strengthen my alliance with the client, as well as provide a different way for the dreamer to look within to find answers and healing. Crook, Lyon, and Hill (2004) conducted a study of 65 therapy clients who were asked about their reactions to working with dreams in therapy. The clients completed measures about their attitudes towards dreams, dream activities, and recall scales, and a session evaluation form. They were also asked to complete information about the most recent dream brought to counseling, the meaning they gave the dream after the session, and how much counseling time was spent on the dream. Not surprisingly, summary results were that clients found that spending more time working with their dreams in therapy was very helpful to them.

Working with children and their dreams has been particularly intriguing for me. Children often express their curiosity about life and their view of sacred things in voices different than adults might use. In clinical and non-clinical settings, children and adolescents have spontaneously presented their dreams to me and after discussing them, have offered explanations and interpretations that seemed wise beyond their age. I have found the insight expressed through the discussion of the dream material to be useful in making sense of difficulties and developmental changes in their waking life, as well as providing clues to their spiritual understanding. My conversations with them in therapy about their dream life led me to conduct a study of children's dreams for my doctoral research. In 2012, over the course of five months, I interviewed 32 English-speaking children ages 6–12 who were not previously known to me, about dreams they identified as meaningful. I collected 73 dreams, nightmares, and drawings from them. Although the design and intent of the study was not to conduct therapy or provide spiritual direction to the children who participated, there were confirmations that working with their dreams could be therapeutic and could provide insights to the children about their waking life experience.

Asking a child to share his or her dreams, listening and clarifying the dream, rather than interpreting it for him or her, seemed to repeatedly lead to some level of understanding for the child about the experience. The dream often seemed to have the characteristic of creating a way to connect with a child that was indirect, meaning that rather than querying a child about his or her daily experiences or problems, talking about the dream first offered a unique opportunity to enable him or her to share more deeply than he or she might have with a stranger asking direct questions. In the research, there were many wonderful examples of dream stories and conversations rich with unexpected gems of meaning from the child who told the dream; in every meeting, the dream story was an avenue into a deeper conversation with the child. It was an important part of the process to be aware and alert to following the child's lead and to be authentically present to the experience in the moment. Marya, a 9-year-old girl in the study, was one example:

> Although enthusiastic at first about being interviewed concerning her dreams; she had a hard time sitting still, focusing on the questions, and an even more challenging time finishing the questionnaires. She asked to finish several times, ran out of the room and back in again before finally sitting down. Her hyperactivity was frustrating and I wondered if this was helpful, especially since the interview brought up times in the last year when Marya had difficult nightmares about a tragic death in her family. However, the importance of listening became apparent when Marya offered these comments late in the interview.

C: So it sounds like you have good dreams and lots of bad dreams too—you have some pretty scary dreams.

M: Yeah, when I grow up I probably want to do this too. I want to hear kid's dreams.

C: You want to hear kid's dreams? Is there anything else you want to tell me about the dreams in particular?

M: No.

C: I can see that they really have an effect on you. You remember them.

M: My family really cares about us, but it's been crazy and it's all that sort of stuff—there is no one to listen to the dreams. (Sauln, 2013, pp. 138-139)

Children often see and express the sacred in the ordinary experiences of their daily lives, including their dreams. Being present with them and listening to their stories offered the opportunity to listen to their spiritual awareness in a way that might not have been possible in a structured conversation. Findings from the qualitative and quantitative results showed evidence of children's spiritual awareness in all domains, reflecting their spirituality in the areas of awareness-sensing, value-sensing, and mystery-sensing. In addition, the findings showed correlations between some of the dreams, meaning making, and spiritual understanding. I continue to work with the dreams and nightmares of children and adolescents to help them discover the messages, meanings, and insight that can guide them through their waking life issues and challenges.

Conclusion

There is so much to learn about practicing existential-humanistic psychotherapy, but the dream mentioned earlier in this chapter meant to me that I have to quit thinking and doing so much, that I need to attend to my own experience, and be fully present with the other. I have to step into the mystery of the numinous, the dream, and listen for the soul call:

Soul is not a tangible entity but a construct that points to the spiritual dimension of the human being. . . . In Western culture we tend to believe that thinking can open every door, unlock every secret. Thus, we know little about the world of the soul where cognition is dethroned and imaginal processes are more important. As a result, we often mistake the menu for the meal and delude ourselves that we understand once we have an abstract definition in place. Yet unless our knowledge of the soul is rooted in personal experience, our abstract definitions simply hang in space, devoid of meaning and rooted in nothing. (Elkins, 2005, p. 137)

Or as Myrtle Heery says, "Psychotherapy is a process whereby the individual's soul speaks and is responded to" (Heery, 2002, p. 13). I believe that the rich and imaginal world of dreams is a way to allow the soul to speak and if I am my authentic self with my clients, sensitively attending to the moment, then it is likely that working with their dreams will surprise me and allow me to respond and be helpful in ways that I cannot always know. If I am learning, listening, and encouraging the other to be with the inner experience in the moment, and keep calling attention to it, what needs to be shown will come into awareness.

References

Bugental, J. F. T. (1999). *Psychotherapy isn't what you think*. Phoenix, AZ: Zieg, Tucker & Co., Inc.

Bulkeley, K. (2008). *Dreaming in the world's religions: A comparative history*. New York, NY: University Press

Crook Lyon, R. E., & Hill, C. E. (2004). *Client reactions to working with dreams in psychotherapy. Dreaming, 14*(4), 207-219.

Elkins, D. N. (2005). A humanistic approach to spiritually oriented psycho-therapy. In L. Sperry & E. P. Shafranske (Eds.), *Spiritually oriented psycho-therapy* (pp. 131-152). Washington, DC: APA.

Heery, M. (2002). Inside the soul of Russian and American psychotherapy trainings. *Journal of Humanistic Psychology, 42*(3), 89-101.

Heery, M. (n.d.). *Soul and intentionality*. (Made available by the author, January 2010).

Saulin, C. S. (2011). The power of the dream in the here and now, *Unearthing the Moment XIV.* Petaluma, CA: International Institute for Humanistic Studies.

Sauln, C. S. (2013). *In my dreams I am the hero I wish to be: A mixed-methods study of children's dreams, meaning making, and spiritual awareness.* (Doctoral dissertation). Available from ProQuest Dissertations database.

Taylor, J. (2009). *The wisdom of your dreams: Using dreams to tap into your unconscious and transform your life.* New York, NY: Penguin.

Yalom, I. D. (1980). *Existential psychotherapy.* New York, NY: Basic Books.

19

A Balance of the Selves

Pamela Cronin

USING JAMES F. T. BUGENTAL'S EXISTENTIAL-HUMANISTIC therapeutic approach between therapist and client is the basis for this chapter. The structure of the model presented is designed by this therapist to assist the client in accessing parts of the self in the present moment, both in the therapeutic setting and in everyday life. Incorporating Dr. Bugental's theories and drawing from his lifelong experience and commitment to his work as a gifted psychologist and teacher has played an important role in the therapeutic setting for this writer. His significant writings, research and demonstrations of the importance of this model and his contributions to humanity, especially the mental health communities, are extraordinary. As a member of the therapeutic community, it is an honor to have participated with him as a student of his work, and a privilege to recognize that his dedication to this work will long continue to flourish and influence people worldwide.

Being in the present moment, therapist with client, and capturing an instant of connectedness at whatever psychological level available in that moment can create and solidify a bond whereby client and therapist recognize in that instant they are there together, trusting the process in a moment of truth and acceptance. At times verbal communication permits a client to know that the therapist is fully present, and that she is listening, hearing, seeing, sensing and feeling as the client communicates her thoughts and feelings. Non-verbal communication is of equal importance. The therapist nods acknowledgement, she feels and looks interested and involved with what the client says, and together they hold the space of being there, trusting the process in the present moment.

Thoughts and feelings from different aspects of self abound in the moment for most children and adults who have the ability to freely associate and communicate with whatever entity speaks to them in the moment. During the course of life we sometimes consciously recognize that several aspects of self are present, accepted, and acknowledged in that moment as we talk with them. Over time they may become our friends, guides and participants in accomplishing our dreams. Alternatively they may remain unconscious, feel dismissed, invalidated or negated depending on the individual's level of differentiation and acceptance of self. When a solid balance between self, reason, and emotion exists, through negotiation a satisfactory outcome will emerge for the individual consciously or unconsciously. This was demonstrated by Carl G. Jung when he addressed his voices and their interactions with him (C. Jung, 1961).

> Once, while I was in my laboratory and reflecting again upon these questions, the devil whispered to me that I would be justified in publishing my conclusions without mentioning Freud. After all, I had worked out my experiments long before I understood his work. But then I heard the voice of my second personality: "If you do a thing like that, as if you had no knowledge of Freud, it would be a piece of trickery. You cannot build your life upon a lie." With that, the question was settled. From then on I became an open partisan of Freud's and fought for him. (p. 148)

As this model unfolded in my work, it became a tool with which to identify and communicate with other aspects of self who were speaking initially to children and later adults who were present, feeling and thinking in the moment in the therapeutic setting. It became clear that when some children spoke in different voices as though answering each other, these entities were real for them. My work to develop a way of bringing these parts of self to conscious awareness and to recognize, understand, and know how they influence life in the present moment began to emerge. By utilizing and weaving some of the concepts developed by James Bugental, Patient Patterns for Presenting Concerns, (Bugental, 1987), into the moment when working with some children and adult clients it became evident that parts of the patterns fit, and the client slipped naturally into the role or fantasy of listening to the different parts of self.

The following is a map of the objective and subjective functions developed by Bugental (1987):

Patterns Objectifying the Concern
Naming
Describing
Valuing
Patterns Tending Toward Objectification
Associating Functionally
Associated Causally or Analytically
Detailing History or Life Events
Patterns Tending Toward Subjectivity
Bodily Awareness and Associating
Describing Dreams and Fantasies
Emotional Association
Recognition in Process
Largely Subjective Patterns
Spontaneous Fantasy
Free Association
Concern Guided Searching
(p. 150)

Historically the objective and subjective world was given a map through Freud's concept of Id, Ego and Super Ego unveiling. Later these constructs were expanded with the understanding of Inner Child, Solid Self, and Critical Voice. These commonly accepted and recognized concepts of self are further transformed into a collaborative model created to simplify and give life and voice to the individual as she begins to refer to her thoughts and feelings as they appear in the therapeutic setting. (Throughout this chapter, I have chosen to use "she" when referring to the client and the different parts of self.)

Lucia Capacchione, an art therapist and psychologist, addresses those parts of us through art and writing with her clients. She wrote of the historical perspectives of the parts of selves saying, "The concept of the Inner Child is not new. It actually has roots in mythology and fairy tales" (Capacchione, 1991, p. 19). "In this century, psychologist C. G. Jung and mythologist Joseph Campbell have shown us that these myths and legends have widespread appeal because they illustrate universal human experiences" (Capacchione, 1991, p. 20).

> Jung saw the child as an archetype, a universal symbol existing within the collective unconscious. In his essay "The Psychology of the Child Archetype," he wrote: It is . . . not surprising that so many of the mythological saviours are child gods. This agrees exactly with our experience of the psychology of the individual, which shows that the "child" paves the way for a future change of personality. In the individuation process, it anticipates the figure that comes from the synthesis of conscious and unconscious elements in the personality. It is therefore a symbol which unites the opposites; a mediator, bringer of healing, that is, one who makes whole. Because it has this meaning, the child motif is capable of numerous transformations. . . . I have called this wholeness that transcends consciousness the "self." The goal of the individuation process is the synthesis of the self. (Capacchione, 1991, p. 20)

Since the 1960s the Inner Child has become a popular theme in psychology. The Inner Child is that part of us who feels like a child and may cause us to behave in a childlike or childish way. Hugh Missildine wrote about it in his groundbreaking book, *Your Inner Child of the Past*. The child state is also an important aspect of Transactional Analysis, which was developed by Eric Berne in the sixties and popularized in the seventies. Berne presented us with a picture of the inner world made up of a parent self, a child self, and an adult self. The parent self sets out the rules and regulations (the shoulds and the oughts). The child self feels and reacts. The adult thinks, makes decisions and solves problems. (Capacchione, 1991, p. 21)

The individual mirroring a solid sense of who she is reflects a well differentiated sense of being. Fredda Herz Brown recognizes that families are the primary influence in our lives (Herz Brown, 1991).

Through the course of our lives we interact in many systems. However, it is the first system with which we interact, our family of origin, that has the most powerful and persistent influence on how we think and feel about ourselves and how we interact with others. It is this system that has the most powerful impact, both positive and negative, on our future relationships. The family system is driven by emotional forces; in part that is why it is so important to the development of a sense of self. (p. 5)

It becomes more important then to bring to conscious awareness that we have the ability to develop tools and skills quite early and instinctively begin to trust that the developed, differentiated self knows how to cope with life as it happens in the present moment. When the client is asked about a movement, a look, or a feeling happening at that time, she is introduced to the notion that some part of her is directing what is being said or felt. In my work I have seen an imagery map for this subjective world and invited into the room and addressed the **Unicorn, Angel** and **Dragon** (Cronin, 2003). Further refining this concept has proved effective for me especially with children and individuals who are spontaneously inclined to allow the fantasy that thoughts and feelings have a name and relate to other parts within the psyche. James Bugental cautions the therapist about the use of spontaneous fantasy in the therapeutic moment (Bugental, 1987).

Word of caution. Two sorts of circumstances are contraindicative for the use of spontaneous imagery: First, patients with poor ego structure, in the midst of extreme anxiety or depression or confronting extra therapeutic crises, are generally not well served by this suspension of usual objective-coping processes.

The second group of patients with whom one must use discretion in encouraging spontaneous imagery are usually effectively functioning people who plunge gladly into the pool of fantasy and can scarcely be lured out. I do not mean that they are autistic. I mean they readily find imagery and fantasy which they tell extensively and in therapist-entangling detail. A whole therapeutic hour can pass in this way; rich pictorial and dramatic vistas are presented, and very little genuine therapeutic inquiry occurs. With such patients, after a maximum of ten minutes of such material, it is well to call for consideration of what the imagery is expressing. This may lead to discovery that a resistive function is being served under the guise of subjective exploration. (p. 165)

With the caution fully in hand, I have witnessed the use of imagination in the moment as a powerful force in psychotherapy. Definitions of Unicorn, Angel, and Dragon follow and it is important to share the power of this imagery in my psychotherapy practice. A partnership develops in the subjective world through the use of these images. It is interesting and exciting to observe a client putting not only Angel or Dragon in communication with each other, verbally, nonverbally and physically, but to see how Unicorn is somehow brought into the core task of assisting Angel and Dragon to negotiate with Unicorn and access awareness and the subjective reality that they do in fact at times unconsciously operate in the world supported, controlled or victimized by these inner entities. When the client learns to check in with these "partners," Unicorn begins to look toward creating a balance within the psyche. Developing a strategy where one becomes more consciously aware of what thoughts and feelings are present as situations evolve helps the individual hold on to a sense of being true to oneself more frequently in the "now" moment. The notion that within Unicorn two other entities, Angel and Dragon reside, helps reframe the emotional association that determines how healthfully we live mentally, emotionally, spiritually and physically. This is a key to unlocking the door to the psyche's internal structure in this process.

Recognizing that along a broad spectrum of learned behavior, human imperfections tend to lead to erroneous core beliefs. These beliefs create imbalances between the emotional, mental and sense of who Unicorn is. Based upon conscious and unconscious information passed from generation to generation, these core beliefs settle in and resist change especially if there is a loss of control throughout a child's developmental stages. Donald W. Winnicott coined the term *good-enough mother* (1990, p. 57). He believed that whatever the environmental conditions are, the most crucial one is maternal care. "At first it is the mother herself who is the facilitating environment" (Winnicott, 1990, p. 85). "The infant will grow and succeed in the maturational process if there is a facilitating environment" (Winnicott, 1990, p. 239).

Winnicott addressed the steps leading to the development of the True Self and the False Self, writing the following:

> The infant gradually develops the capacity to conjure up what is actually available, and the good-enough mother has to keep providing this kind of experience, which feeds the infant's sense of narcissistic omnipotence. The infant then can serenely enjoy the illusion of omnipotent creativity and control. Not only is there the physical experience of physical satisfaction, but also an emotional union and the beginning of a belief in reality as something about which one can have illusions. The final steps can now be taken, the gradual letting go of omnipotence and the gradual disillusioning of the infant when it comes to recognize the illusory element and establishes contact with reality. (Winnicott, 1992, p. 163)

> Through the infant's impulses (met and confirmed by the mother) the infant discovers the environment and the Not-me world and the establishment of the Me. (Winnicott, 1992, p. 216)

> The caring mother must also protect the infant from complications and impingements from the world that the infant cannot understand. If the environment is not safe, the infant may respond with compliance. This compliance could lead to the isolation of the infant from its own spontaneous and life-giving core. (Winnicott, 1992, p. 171)

> The false self develops at the earliest stage of object relations when there is not good-enough mothering, when the mother does not meet and implement the omnipotence of the infant. Should the infant's gesture be repeatedly missed, the mother substitutes her own gesture, which is met by the infant's compliance.

The literature supports the notion that a conscious balance between the aspects of self permit the individual to function in a more fluid way while simultaneously living rather than surviving in the moment experiences. In a perfect world, the connection between all aspects of self would operate as a beautifully crafted Swiss timepiece. In human terms, however, life is less than balanced and is often chaotic. (Winnicott, 1990, p. 145)

Definition of Terms

"She" represents both he/she as individuals throughout this chapter. The Latin word anima refers to spirit and animus represents the soul (Jung, 1960, p. 345). In the most basic sense they describe the female characteristics in men representing the archetype anima, and the male characteristics in women representing the archetype animus. Carl G. Jung wrote the following:

No man is so entirely masculine that he has nothing feminine in him. The fact is, rather, that very masculine men have—carefully guarded and hidden—a very soft emotional life, often incorrectly described as "feminine." A man counts it a virtue to repress his feminine traits as much as possible, just as a woman, at least until recently, considered it unbecoming to be "mannish." (Jung, 1959, p. 158)

As civilization develops, the bisexual primordial being turns into a symbol of the unity of personality, a symbol of the self, where the war of opposites finds peace. In this way the primordial being becomes the distant goal of man's self-development, having been from the very beginning a projection of his unconscious wholeness. Wholeness consists in the union of the conscious and the unconscious personality. Just as every individual derives from masculine and feminine genes, and the sex is determined by the predominance of the corresponding genes, so in the psyche it is only the conscious mind, in a man, that has the masculine sign, while the unconscious is by nature feminine. The reverse is true in the case of a woman. All I have done in my anima theory is to rediscover and reformulate this fact. It had long been known. (Jung, 1959, p. 175)

The entities that speak during the therapeutic hour may at times be more masculine than feminine in the client. Confusion may occur when an individual has been raised to deny or resist any opposite feelings, thoughts and behaviors that are considered inappropriate for a girl or a boy to have, and these feelings may be repressed or denied. In the therapeutic setting, the masculine and feminine aspects of self are recognized, validated and invited to present as they interact with each other during our "in-the-moment" process. They are encouraged to acknowledge and value the role they play in the individual's life.

Ego—Self—Unicorn

Unicorn may represent the solid and resilient part of the self that is guided through life's stages with enlightenment and a sense of freedom to choose what is best for the whole person living in the present moment. On the opposite end of the spectrum, Unicorn may manifest as a survivor who dodges the obstacles and landmines of life without ever realizing that there is a way to live in the moment rather than survive the drama and journey of being in "alert" mode at all times.

When Unicorn inside the child is taught from the beginning that honoring and respecting the essence of self is invaluable, she begins to sort through and solve the formidable issues presented during the course of life. Unicorn is the protector of the individual's heart and soul. In a perfect world, she seeks knowledge in order to move toward the light from the shadows and asks to live with love and joy in the moment presented. She is the guide of trust, intuition, perception and the nucleus of inner strength. Unicorn is the mentor of Angel and Dragon and she listens to them with respect, love, honor and care. Her goal is to acknowledge their needs and assist them in understanding available solutions and choices so that when decisions are made, they bring satisfaction and closure in a mutually beneficial way to all aspects of self and the situation presented. In an imperfect world, for Unicorn, survival is a need that comes from the darkest places of self, the place that precludes a view into the possibility of living "in the moment."

Id—Inner Child—Angel

The concept of an in the moment Angel presents the client with the notion that within Unicorn resides a solid entity that understands her value, thrives with resilience, gives and receives unconditional positive regard, has a strong sense of esteem, and a focused awareness and consciousness of life and living in the now. She understands that Unicorn listens to what she has to say and knows that she can rely on and trust that Unicorn is on her side even if she makes a mistake. In this position Angel represents the feeling parts of herself that depict autonomy and the ability to accept that she is willing to trust the process of life in the present moment. Angel believes in what she knows she feels, and if she begins to experience discomfort either emotionally or physically, a warning flag goes up, and she addresses the feelings in the now moment. She senses the reality of what is being presented and processes her feelings in a balanced way that incorporates the ability to seek clarification and understanding of the issues. If she has misinterpreted the information received she has an innate ability to reinterpret the data and continue the emotional communication without flight-fright responses and elevated cortisol levels as though she is being threatened or attacked. Angel has the ability to move fluidly from moment to moment. She processes, clarifies, and communicates feelings of love, joy, sadness, and anger. She experiences her strengths and flaws without the fear of abandonment, rejection or the loss of love because of that which she is or is not to another. Angel and Unicorn are good friends and are confident that they are able to negotiate with and be there for each other in the moment. They cooperate and share their intuitive and perceptive parts for the balance of the self.

At the opposite end of the spectrum Angel's feelings reside in a place of fear, distrust, pain, and vigilance with little understanding of what self-respect or esteem entail. This Angel has been taught that her thoughts and feelings are invalid or less than those of another. She is made to feel guilty or ashamed and develops erroneous core beliefs that she is unworthy of enjoying love, happiness, safety, and self care. She lives in the shadows of darkness; her essence feels denied, unacknowledged, devalued, and dismissed. She is depressed and in despair. She becomes a saboteur of all the good she deserves in the present moment. Much of the sabotage is unconscious albeit some behavior is acted out consciously. Based upon her learned behavior, Angel may choose to assist or destroy Unicorn on the way to life. She may try to please others at the expense of herself, only to feel resentment and anger when she discovers that pseudo Angel is never real or present for her when needed. She feels empty and alone. In reality for most individuals Angel lies somewhere between the opposites depending upon the level of resilience and the unique ability of the child to live and or survive life.

Super-Ego—Critical Voice—Dragon

Dragon is the protective and objective part of self that has supported living and or survival. An autonomous Unicorn leads Dragon to assist in the decision making process and shares information in a mutually beneficial and respectful way. Dragon recognizes that it is her role to alert, discuss and process with Unicorn and Angel any pending danger, unsolved issues, or hidden agendas. She has learned about life and how to cope with what is presented at any given moment. In a perfect psyche, this Dragon, like Angel, listens to the safe and happy Unicorn and knows that life is good in the present moment. The secure and valued child within understands boundaries and social rules and recognizes the need for reasonable discipline when warranted. Dragon reasons, analyzes and recognizes that when her behavior is acceptable or unacceptable at a social or self respecting level, rewards or consequences become an appropriate self monitored result. A balance between Unicorn, Angel and Dragon exists and the entities within work in unison negotiating without blaming, shaming or punishing any aspect of self. The ability for concern guided searching prevails.

It follows then that if Unicorn lives in a pseudo sense of self, both Angel and Dragon will develop survival tools that preclude reasonable connection and communication between the three entities. Conflicts develop between the critical mental prowess of Dragon and the emotional acting out feelings of Angel. Unicorn in this stance is dictated to and controlled by Dragon who takes over running the show because she feels she is the one most qualified to make the decisions for all. Angel feels unprotected and distrusts Unicorn for not hearing her so she pulls on Unicorn, polarized from Dragon. Unhealthy choices are often made by unconscious default or an inability to cope with the emotional associating within this framework.

Some art from the Middle Ages depicts women with long leashes loosely attached to their wrists, gently cascading down beautiful gowns onto the jewel studded collars of dragons lying peacefully at their feet. Other works of art portray dragons with fire flaming from their nostrils as they ferociously pull the women in the direction the dragons wish to go. The dragons are clearly in charge of what is happening and the women appear to be out of control. This visual application of Dragon applies to individuals whose lives have not had balance between the spectrums of life. When Unicorn has had to fight for survival, Dragon learns to become the essential critic and an over controlling entity who claims Angel and Unicorn as victims. A no win cycle begins for all concerned.

In the therapeutic process it becomes evident to the client that the ongoing thoughts within are now being consciously addressed in the moment. The therapist listens and when appropriate asks the client who is speaking. Frequently children will quickly assimilate who is directing whom and are clear that they want Dragon, Angel and Unicorn to work together. Adults also begin to examine why they continue to respond in the same way to old patterns of learned behavior. Practicing using the tools of listening to Unicorn is further expanded by asking the client to choose three items that represent Unicorn, Angel and Dragon. These items may include beloved stuffed animals, pillows, blankets, toys, jewelry or other items of sentimental value. When issues surface, the client selects a time and place where she may hold, talk with, and hear what the different parts of self are thinking and feeling. The purpose is to bring the parts of self to reality via the senses and actualizing the inner experience through dialogue. Valuing what each part of self has to contribute prevents either Angel or Dragon from over-riding or invalidating each other.

When there is recognition that being authentic in the moment with Unicorn, that it is appropriate to value, nurture and love all aspects of self unconditionally, a sense of relief and knowing begins to emerge. In that moment, there is for her unification with Angel, Unicorn and Dragon and she knows that whatever decision she makes, it is through conscious choice rather than old unconscious reactions. The essential choice for her becomes whether or not to move into the present and live, moment-by-moment, now.

References

Bugental, J. F. T. (1987). *The art of the psychotherapist*. New York, NY: Norton & Co.

Capacchione, L. (1991). *Recovery of your inner child*. New York, NY: Simon & Schuster.

Cronin, P. (2003). A balance of the selves. Unpublished Manuscript.

Herz Brown, F. (1991). *Reweaving the family tapestry: Multigenerational approach to families*. New York, NY: Norton & Co.

Jung, C. G. (1960). *The structure & dynamics of the psyche*. MI: Pantheon Books.

Jung, C. G. (1959). *The archetypes & the collective unconsciousness*. New York, NY: Bollingen Foundation, Inc.

Jung, C. G. (1961). *Memories, dreams, and reflections*. New York, NY: Random House.

Winnicott, D. W. (1992). *Collected papers: Through paediatrics to psycho-analysis*. Sussex, England: Routledge.

Winnicott, D. W. (1990). *The maturational processes and the facilitating environment: Studies in the theory of emotional development*. London, England: Karnac Books.

20

⌣

Art Therapy: An Existential Approach

Michael Barbee

(Art) alone knows how to turn these nauseous thoughts about the
horror or absurdity of existence into notions with which one can live.

—Nietzsche, *The Birth of Tragedy*, 1967, p. 48

I HAVE BEEN FASCINATED BY THE ROLE OF ART in creating mean-
ing since my first clinical experience in a state psychiatric hospital in Georgia
over 25 years ago. I watched severely disturbed patients create spontaneous
works of art in an attempt to make meaning of their experience and communicate this with me when I began to sit and witness their work. (One of my
greatest lessons that year was to let go of the need to do something for those in
my care and learning to be with them.) Patients labeled as psychotic such as
Cindy, who drew her earthly house and her heavenly house and her intimate
relationship with Jesus, consistently depicted transpersonal and universal
themes of good and evil, the meaning of life and their place, or lack of place,
in the world. I began to look further at the role of creativity in "madness" and
found Prinzhorn's (1972) *Artistry of the Mentally Ill*, a collection of images from
prolific institutionalized artists in Germany near the turn of the last century.
I also discovered the existential psychologists, especially Rollo May (1975,

1985), whose work helped me frame the struggles of human life that Christian theology no longer answered. My clinical supervisor gave me a copy of May's (1985) *My Search for Beauty*, which documented the role of art-making in May's own life and the existential crisis of his young adulthood.

Creativity and the Postmodern Condition

Our creative imagination is the expression of that freedom which defines us as human. (Flynn, 2006, p. 105)

As I moved into training in art therapy, I brought this concern for meaning making and the role art plays in our struggle with existential themes. This link between creation and meaning is given a theoretical foundation in May's (1975) *The Courage to Create*, in which he saw art as a universal therapist providing a way of managing our inner turmoil. The psychologically healthy person is one who overcomes life's dilemma through creative action. Creativity brings together both aspects of what Freud saw as the central themes of life—love and work. "Our passion for form expresses our yearning to make the world adequate to our needs and desires, and to experience ourselves as having significance" (May, 1975, p. 131). The creative act is an encounter in the present moment, which requires a quality of engagement with the environment. This encounter also brings anxiety, and creative individuals are able to live with this anxiety but wrestle with it. The courage involved is the capacity to act in spite of despair. Producing art represents an assertion of the self, a commitment to action, increasing the move toward self-actualization. It involves engagement while encountering the experience of limits. In my work in an inpatient men's unit, my patients found it quite difficult to move out of their isolated and withdrawn experience of depression and engage at all in an art therapy group. They often asked for the most limited and least expressive of media—a small sheet of paper, a pencil with an eraser, and a ruler. Their ability to move out of despair and engage in creation led to increased expression, relating to others, and to articulating their own inner experience.

Art history shows that lasting works of art are those that inspire us to struggle with existential themes and provide a record of humanity's struggle to interpret existence. However, within the field of art therapy, there has been a tendency to attempt to work within the scientific and medical model to somehow legitimize art therapy. The notion of empirically validated forms of treatment emphasized by managed care has resulted in studies that measure, label, and standardize specific techniques and assessment tools. This approach is antithetical to what existential art therapists see as the inherent ability of art to illustrate and transform the existential themes of human life. This function is especially significant in a postmodern age of fragmentation of identity, in which the self is seen as a changing construction which brings together parts of identity from a variety of contexts for use in a given situation (Gergen, 1994). In the men's unit mentioned above, I became interested in and studied my patients' attachment to gender roles they had lost, with a corresponding loss of identity, and the relationship of these losses to an episode of clinical depression (Barbee, 2006).

Art therapists must include multiple perspectives to adapt to the ever-changing realities of the world and engage in a process of co-created meaning, according to Alter-Muri (2007). She rejected narratives that have one meaning or story to tell and refused to accept meta-narratives, universal ideologies, or prescribed meaning for artistic symbols. "Art therapists embracing a postmodernist approach become co-creators with their clients in a life of meaningfulness rather than continuing to act as mere interpreters of the signs and symbols of pathology or the continuum of health in their clients" (Alter-Muri, 2007, p. 84). An existential approach to art therapy addresses these concerns. Men in the art therapy group were increasingly able to use creative expression to envision new sources of meaning and more vital images of who they were or could be, and to engage with others through their visual expression after having so few words to communicate their isolated experience.

Existential Art Therapy Theory and Practice

Art embraces our deepest fears, loneliness, pain and guilt. (Moon, 1990, p. 54)

Two art therapists in particular have served as guides for existential art therapy. Shaun McNiff (1992) advocated for our encountering an image in the form of dialogue. Art products are not seen as clinical data, and there is no correct interpretation. Interpreting destroys presence, creates distance, stops dialogue, and allows us to avoid emptiness and the withholding of meaning. One must be comfortable with ambiguity and multiple meanings. Dialogue evokes new responses and perspectives versus verbal repetition of the same material. My most powerful creative experience was in a weeklong painting workshop with McNiff in which we constantly interacted with our images, inviting them to inform us and guide us. Existential themes of meaning, isolation, and loss became present experiences through the creation of silent dramas, which enacted the visual images.

McNiff saw images as transpersonal guides, with their own separate existence with which we interact, drawing us out of our isolation and limited views of art as projections of ourselves. We change in response to images. "Creation is a collaborative process and an intimate relationship between artists and their materials in which the participants continuously transform one another" (McNiff, 1992, p. 64). Writer Jeannette Winterson (1996) described this encounter with the art in her own environment.

I move gingerly around the paintings I own because I know they are looking at me as closely as I am looking at them. There is a constant exchange of emotion between us . . . the picture on my wall . . . is a living line of movement, a wave of color that repercusses in my body, coloring it, coloring the new present, the future, and even the past, which cannot now be considered outside of the light of the painting. (p. 19)

This process allows openness to opportunities for finding meaning outside ordinary learned responses. Individuals who created photographic narratives of their experience of being transsexual found that interacting with and telling their story through these images both helped articulate a coherent identity over time, as well as move the story along with new insights and understandings which might not be articulated or seen verbally (Barbee, 2002).

Stephen Levine provided a theoretical foundation for this approach in the inherent nature of the arts. "The arts are pathways or methods that take us deeper into ourselves and our experience. As we enter unreservedly into the depth of ourselves, we encounter healing energies and experience the hope of integration" (Levine, 1992, p. 23). Engaging in the imaginative process of creation moves one beyond fantasy, an isolated experience of inner obsessions. He felt that we indulge ourselves in fantasy because our capacity for imagination has been wounded. The arts provide a medium of healing by restoring the ability to imagine. They bring into the living moment past suffering and provide containers in which pain can be held and owned; suffering is thus not avoided, but seen as a gift providing power and vitality. My patient, Janet, spent the first few months of our work together mostly nonverbally, beginning each drawing with a line down the center depicting her split experience of herself and expressing her isolation, suffering, and enmeshment with her adult son. With the drawings as a safe way to engage with me, she gradually became more engaged in the present, with meaningful activities and with those around her, gaining a stronger sense of self and decreasing her suffering. "The use of the arts as a means of healing the soul testifies to the inherent power of men and women to confront the depths of their own pain and to emerge with a sense that life is indeed worth living" (Levine, 1992, p. 7). The use of imagination leads one beyond individual human existence in time to experience the universal.

Bruce Moon (2004) is another art therapist who has formulated a practice of art therapy that is existential in focus. He described the condition of individuals in our current society as experiencing (or avoiding) a condition he refers to as *soul loss*, which is defined as seen in the emptiness, boredom, and longing for meaning with which clients present. The primary focus of existential art therapy is engaging the client in a creative struggle with his or her own existence and humanity's ultimate concerns. The art process makes meaning visible and turns aimless events into meaning-filled experiences. Making art allows one to organize raw materials, work imaginatively with them, and transform them.

Moon's view affirms our inherent healing ability through a positive view of the human capacity to create—people are capable of creative resolution of problems in artistic work that can apply to other areas of life. Art is an arena for engaging with conflicts in the present. Conflict is seen as a theme, a symbol of life in process. This engagement engenders an attitude where particular struggles will not be avoided, but seen as a validation of life. "Creation does not ease, but rather ennobles, pain. It does not cure; it accepts" (Moon, 2004, p. 45). There is an acceptance that suffering and struggle are essential elements of life and are universally experienced; this calls for passionate and active engagement with life as it is. Art utilizes, rather than diminishes, this tension through empowering action.

Moon (2004) felt that we have lost an appreciation for struggle and urged therapists not to be complicit in the devaluing of pain and the temptation to focus on eradicating it found in many treatments. Creating art calls for active engagement with life and enables the structuring of one's inner sense of chaos. It reflects and communicates with others the creation of new meaning. Bart, in his on-again, off-again engagement with treatment, creates profoundly deep and disturbing images of pain and death that contain his experience and draw him out of his isolation through sharing with a non-judgmental psychology intern. Through art making, we are called out of existential isolation to act on the environment, and are given hope of transcending suffering. Art gives the perception that there is some inherent order in the chaos of existence. Images engage with stories beyond the individual. Looking at an empty canvas is a reminder of how alone the artist is, and this emptiness calls for response. Artists are constantly reminded that they must choose, act, and are free to do what they want in their work. Choices made in use of media, color, and composition preclude others and create a record of choices. Mistakes may be transformed through ongoing choices. Meaning is created when this process is witnessed in the context of the relationship. An art therapist's job is to do art with clients, be open to them, honor their pain, and to accompany them on a journey. Moon (1990) practiced art therapy in a studio setting where he worked alongside clients. In this approach, the therapist must be willing to go through the same journey and be familiar with his or her own pain.

Art's Facilitation of Existential Psychotherapy

The client needs an experience, not an explanation. (Fromm-Reichmann, in May, 1983, p. 158)

Art therapy practiced from an existential perspective necessitates moving out of one's isolation into meaningful engagement with the world in the here and now. It affirms one's freedom to create meaning through acting on the environment and provides a record of choices made and one's responsibility for them. The four areas of ultimate concern outlined by Yalom (1980)—death, freedom and responsibility, isolation, and meaninglessness—are encountered in the creative process. The use of art materials and their mastery provide the kind of boundary situations Yalom associated with coming face to face with one's limits and therefore one's mortality—limits of various materials to express what one wishes to convey, limits provided by the boundaries of the page or canvas, and limits of one's ability to manipulate the medium. Art therapy requires that one live one's response-ability in the moment through action; change in the absence of action is theoretically and practically impossible, as Yalom noted. Action is more easily avoidable in talk therapy. The locus of control can only be internal as one acts on the medium at hand. There is no way to displace one's responsibility or avoid autonomous behavior. The finished product is a record of choices made manifest and records the way we have used our freedom. The making of art is a relationship with the world throughout the process and expresses our individuality when we do not rely on stereotyped imagery (Ellingson, 1993).

In making art, one also bridges the gap between oneself and others and facilitates communication of both the personal and the universal, drawing the artist out of the experience of isolation. I have experienced this function of creation over and over in group therapy using art, in which individuals lost in their own internal experience relate to a theme such as trauma, depression, or substance abuse, and become engaged with each others' work, finding common ground while communicating their unique experience with other group members. "It is in sharing that the patient is able to rediscover his own identity, bring honor to his suffering and meaning to his life's journey" (Moon, 1990, p. 27). Finally, meaning is actively created in the living moment when art is brought into being and interacted with. The search for meaning outside oneself as a distraction from the burden of meaning creation cannot be so easily pursued. In art therapy groups, there is an enlivening quality, which is often missing in talk therapy groups.

This view of art therapy is consistent with the process of existential therapy outlined by Bugental (1999). Emphasis is on present experience versus information. There is an immediacy of present awareness through acting, a focus on process rather than product. The temptation to talk about, in order to avoid action, is overcome. Art and its creation can bring concerns into the living moment and present new views. Megan, who years ago, depicted her relationship to a twin sister with Borderline Personality Disorder as enmeshed and suffocating, can now illustrate a healthy self-concept with appropriate separation and boundaries with her sister and others in a moving way, capturing what we have talked through over the years. This example illustrates a principal that is crucial to Bugental's model, as it is our perception of our situation that is often the problem. In offering multiple perspectives, art may assist in allowing the problem itself to change for the client who is invested in fixing it or getting rid of pain. Art reduces isolation and self-centeredness and allows one to relate more effectively with the external world. Autonomous action is required as the artist's concern is mobilized and searching is made manifest visually. Habitual responses are bypassed as clients struggle with unfamiliar media and struggle to communicate through them. New perceptions are created, offering other views than those currently causing suffering to the individual.

As existentially oriented therapists, we know that much of what happens in our work is non-verbal and does not involve the content of the hour, is unexplainable in traditional theories and techniques, and involves the transpersonal and intuitive. We are also comfortable acknowledging that we struggle with the same existential themes of mortality, freedom and responsibility, connection and isolation, and the search for meaning with which our clients struggle. In the supervising of psychology interns in a community clinic with a difficult population whose needs and pathology can seem overwhelming, the use of art has provided rich perspectives and new understandings of clients' experiences and the therapeutic relationship. One intern and I used art in our supervision over a period of two years, in which she was able to find her own visual language for the therapeutic relationship, its dynamics, and changes over time, as well as differences in specific relationships. This experiential approach provided new insights into her own professional identity, her ways of engaging with difficult individuals, and the many complicating influences inside and outside of treatment. Both in our clients' lives and our own personal and professional growth, the art process and product can open out the perceptual process so that new options are illustrated in concrete form, beyond the conscious or that which can be verbalized, and add the advantage of documenting this process. Art making pushes us beyond our comfort with cognitive knowing and explaining, and involves other ways of knowing—intuitive, perceptual, kinesthetic, and sensory.

> Things are not all so comprehensible as one would mostly have us to believe; most events are inexpressible, taking place in a realm which no word has ever entered, and more inexpressible than all else are works of art, mysterious existences, the life of which, while ours passes away, endures. (Rilke, 1934, p. 37)

References

Alter-Muri, S. (2007). Dissolving the Boundaries: Postmodern Art and Art Therapy. *Art Therapy: Journal of the American Art Therapy Association, 24*(2), 82-86.

Barbee, M. (2002). A Visual Narrative Approach to Understanding Transsexual Identity. *Journal of the American Art Therapy Association, 19*(2), 53-62.

Barbee, M. (2006). Men's Roles and Their Experience of Depression. *Art Therapy: Journal of the American Art Therapy Association, 13*(1), 31-36.

Bugental, J. F. T. (1999). *Psychotherapy isn't what you think*. Phoenix, AZ: Zeig, Tucker & Co., Inc.

Ellingson, M. (1993). A philosophy for clinical art therapy. In H. Landgarten & Lubbers, D., (Eds.), *Adult art therapy* (pp. 3-20). Springfield, IL: Charles C. Thomas.

Flynn, T. (2006). *Existentialism: A very short introduction*. New York, NY: Oxford University.

Gergen, K. (1994). *The saturated self: Dilemmas of identity in contemporary life*. New York, NY: Basic Books.

Levine, S. (1992). *Poesis: The language of psychology and the speech the soul*. Toronto, Ontario, Canada: Palmerston Press.

May, R. (1975). *The courage to create*. New York, NY: W. W. Norton.

May, R. (1985). *My search for beauty*. Dallas, TX: Saybrook.

May, R. (1983). *The discovery of being*. New York, NY: Norton.

McNiff, S. (1992). *Art and medicine: Creating a therapy of the imagination*. Boston, MA: Shambhala.

Moon, B. (1990). *Existential art therapy: The canvas mirror*. Springfield, IL: Charles C. Thomas.

Moon, B. (2004). *Art and soul: Reflections on an artistic psychology*. Springfield, IL: Charles C. Thomas.

Nietzsche, F. (1967). *The birth of tragedy* (Kaufmann, W., Trans). New York, NY: Vintage Press. (Original work published 1872)

Prinzhorn, H. (1972). *The artistry of the mentally ill*. New York, NY: Springer-Verlag.

Rilke, R. M. (1934). *Letters to a young poet*. New York, NY: W. W. Norton.

Winterson, J. (1996). *Art objects. Essays on ecstasy and effrontery*. New York, NY: Alfred Knopf.

Yalom, I. D. (1980). *Existential psychotherapy*. New York, NY: Basic Books.

21

⌁

The Therapist's Use of Poetry in Therapy: Deepening Relationship and Understanding Through Creativity

Louis Hoffman

THERAPISTS AND OTHER HEALERS long ago recognized the connection between creativity, madness, and healing (Diamond, 1996; May, 1985). Psychological pain and suffering inspired many of the great artists of history. More recently, therapists began discovering the important role of creativity in the healing process. Initially, therapists focused on assisting clients' usage of the creative process, such as poetry, to facilitate their healing process; however, therapists can also use poetry to facilitate the therapy process. This chapter begins with coverage of the central ethical and pragmatic issues before venturing into four different approaches to using poetry in therapy. In the application portion of the chapter, several poems are included. It is my intent to let the poetry speak itself.

Ethical Issues

The therapist's use of poetry introduces new potential ethical issues. To understand this, we first must address two different ways therapists use poetry in therapy. First, therapists may share poetry of other writers or published poems. Second, therapists may share some of their poetry with their clients. Both usages incur ethical issues.

The most challenging ethical issues are incurred when therapists share their own poetry. When therapists share their own poetry, particularly a poem written about the client or the therapy relationship, they become vulnerable and may be disclosing more to the client than they realize. The therapist risks the possibility that the client may interpret what the therapist does not recognize or want to be known by the client. Additionally, the therapist entails the risk that the client may misinterpret the poem. The sharing of poetry can be a deeply intimate process that can change and deepen the therapy process. For many, poetry is seen as being romantic, and thus sharing poems can elicit erotic transference or feelings or be misinterpreted as having romantic intentions. Therapists must be aware of these possibilities, ready to clarify the misinterpretation of intentions, and alert to the possibility of needing to discuss and clarify boundary issues.

Because of these risks, it is generally prudent to take extra caution when considering sharing a poem with a client. When first using poetry in therapy, it wise for therapists to consult with colleagues, a consultant, or a supervisor prior to sharing the poem. There are at least three factors that should be evaluated by the therapist and, if utilized, be part of the consultation. First, the therapy relationships should be considered. If the client has poor boundaries, is in the midst of difficult transference issues, or likely to misinterpret the poem, then it is likely not in the client's best interest to share the poem. Second, the reasons for wanting to share the poem should be considered. Therapists should examine with their colleague whether the desire to share the poem may be impacted by countertransference issues or the therapist's ego. Finally, the poem should be explored. The author of a poem is often not aware of its full meaning when it is first written. It is important to explore potential undertones of the poem that the therapist may not recognize. Additionally, the therapist should explore how the client could misinterpret the poem.

A second important issue related to the therapist's use of poetry pertains to clinical records. What constitutes documentation of psychotherapy susceptible to subpoena varies from region to region and changes over time. If the poem is shared with the client, then the therapist may also be faced with questioning how to document the use of poetry in the therapy notes. My recommendation is that, if therapists share a copy of a poem they have written with the client, they should offer the client a copy, include a copy in the chart, and include a rationale of why the poem was shared with the client that discusses the potential benefits to the client and therapy process. Additionally, before sharing the poem with the client, the therapist should obtain a written or verbal informed consent that should be documented in the client's chart. Some clients may not wish to hear the therapist's poems. It is important that clients are made aware of the potential ramifications of the therapist sharing poetry and have the opportunity to state they do not wish this to be part of the therapy process.

Sharing poems written by others is less risky and could be seen as an extension of bibliotherapy, which is a common practice in psychotherapy. However, it is important to recognize that poetry is different than recommending other forms of reading. Poems can be more difficult to understand and are more susceptible to different interpretations. As noted previously, some people tend to associate poems closely with romantic intentions and they are often seen as a more intimate form of communication. Thus, even if not the therapist's own poetry, it is wise to be aware of how the client may interpret or misinterpret the implicit messages in sharing poetry.

In summary, while the therapist's usage of poetry may be beneficial for the therapy process, it is important for therapists to be aware of the potential risks involved. Especially when first beginning to incorporate poetry into the therapy process, therapists should seek out supervision or consultation from more experienced therapists. It may be wise to continue consulting with colleagues on a regular basis, even if not in each instance, when incorporating the use of the therapist's poetry into the therapy process.

Pragmatic Issues

Discussion of a few pragmatic issues may help provide a frame for understanding how therapists can successfully utilize poetry. When teaching and presenting on the use of poetry in therapy, it is common for people to respond by stating, "I can't write poetry" or "My poems are not good." As anyone can write poetry, these statements really are more reflective of insecurity about being able to write good poems. From a therapeutic perspective, bad poems, aesthetically speaking, can be good poems. In the context of therapy, healing, and growth, the quality of the poem is, at most, minimally related to the effectiveness of the poem. Additionally, being concerned about the quality of the poem often creates an environment hostile to the creative process. Thus, a foundation for writing poetry in healing and growth contexts must be creating an accepting, nonjudgmental approach to the poetry being produced, regardless of whether it is one's own poems or the poems of others.

Second, it is best to let go of any prejudgments about what a poem should be. For instance, some maintain prejudices that poems must rhyme, have a rhythm, be highly abstract, or have a particular structure (i.e., four-line stanzas). However, there are many different forms of poetry. When people have these prejudices about poems, I generally encourage them to read a few different published poets with different styles and then try to write at least one or two poems from different styles of poetry. Through freeing up conceptions of what a poem is, writers are able to find their own voice and be more creative.

Existential-Humanistic Therapy and Poetry

It is common to see poems quoted in existential-humanistic writing and read in existential-humanistic trainings, yet there is very little that has been written on the use of poetry in existential-humanistic therapy. As Furman (2003) noted, the majority of poetry therapy literature draws upon psychoanalytic thought, and the other therapy modalities are often ignored. Yet, Furman also maintained that poetry therapy can be integrated with many therapy orientations and, in particular, can resonate quite well with existential therapy.

Furman (2003) maintained that poetry works to magnify human experience while also clarifying and bringing meaning, which he notes "could easily be adopted as a manifesto for existential therapists as well" (p. 197). In magnifying experience, poetry does not seek to change or distort one's humanity, but rather to take it in and experience it more deeply. Similarly, poetry generally seeks to describe, not label or pathologize human experience. As such, it fits well with existential approaches to therapy.

Poetry can also be understood as a phenomenological practice. Phenomenology is a descriptive practice in which it is sought to describe and illuminate the fullness of one's experience. Similarly, poetry often is used to describe one's experience. Through the incorporation of symbols and metaphors, poetry is able to capture aspects of one's experience alluded to in other forms of writing.

Poetry can also be understood as connected to the existential-humanistic concepts of authenticity and presence. Bugental (1965) noted,

> A person is authentic in that degree to which his being in the world is unqualifiedly in accord with the givenness of his own nature and of the world. Authenticity is the primary good or value of the existential viewpoint. (p. 32)

Similarly, it could be maintained that a primary good sought in poetry is authenticity. Stated differently, a poem could only be considered good in so far as it is authentic. Presence, though asserted as a primary component of existential-humanistic therapy (Bugental, 1965; Schneider & Krug, 2009), is a difficult construct. Although it is often described in reference to "being fully present," it is more than this simplified understanding of presence. Being fully present may be an aspect of presence, but the concept of presence cannot be fully contained solely in the idea of being fully present. Presence also entails an authentic emotional radiance, in which there is an emotional quality to being with someone. Similarly, poems often carry with them a powerful presence and, at times, reflect the presence of the author.

The Therapist's Use of Poetry

Poems resemble dreams in several ways. Poetry taps the resources of the unconscious, similar to the dream process. This connection to the unconscious is one reason why poetry can be such an effective tool for enhancing the therapy process. However, when the poem is the therapist's own, it must be kept in mind that it is now about the therapist's unconscious instead of the client's. Many therapists restrict using poetry to part of their personal self-exploration for this reason. Writing poetry in the service of self-awareness offers great potential for therapists to increase their healing potential.

Poetry grips many layers of human experience. It stimulates both the conscious and unconscious mind. It encompasses the rational as well as the irrational. It stimulates thought as well as emotion. Poetry is able to hold together and unite the paradoxical nature of human existence. Additionally, poetry is relational in its essence It draws the poet and the reader toward other people, humanity, nature, and the spiritual world. This nature of poetry brings great potential for deepening the therapy and relational processes. Stated differently, poetry brings with it opportunities for healing, understanding, and engaging the whole being in the therapy process, both in the existential-humanistic and transpersonal models of psychotherapy that are the focus of this book.

The next section shifts to the application of poetry to the therapy setting. Four different benefits of the therapist's use of poetry are discussed: (a) poetry to illuminate countertransference and therapist experience, (b) poetry to deepen understanding, (c) poetry to convey empathy and deepen therapy relationships, and (d) poetry for the therapist's healing.

Poetry To Illuminate Countertransference and Therapist Experience

Therapists must remain aware of their own experience of the client as well as potential countertransference to maintain a healthy therapeutic relationship. The intimacy involved in a therapy relationship, especially when engaging in existential-humanistic approaches, stirs many emotions within both the therapist and the client. The complex emotional experience often challenges therapists' ability to decipher what is their own reaction to the client, what is their countertransference, and what may be elicited from the client. Poetry may assist the therapist in clarifying these complex dimensions of the therapy relationship.

The poem that follows was written after a therapy session, as I searched my own experience trying to clarify my emotions from the session.

Searching for Your Freedom
Clutched chest with gasps for breath
Air now a challenging commodity
Shoulders tensed in a v-shaped defense
Your body leans forward, rocking,
You resist
Fighting tears, tears I know could set you free
Fearing losing control, weary from clinging to it
Praying for assurance, wanting just to be held

I am here

Fear keeps a distance,
Protecting your essence deep within
My eyes search you, seeking the hint
Telling me your great fear
I search for that perfect reflection
Just to let you know, I see
You are safe here; there is no shame.

With your tears come mine
I search for that perfect expression
of genuineness, proving I care.
Drawn to caring, pulled by you
Pushing my own fear of no control,
I return to searching . . .
What will set you free?
What will help you be?

Poetry To Deepen Understanding

Using poetry to deepen understanding is a variation and expansion of using
it to understand transference and countertransference. In addition to helping
therapists understand their own emotional and relational experience, poetry
can also assist them in better understanding the process of therapy in general.

The poem below was useful in both helping identify countertransference and relational issues, in addition to working through some personal struggles with the therapy process. This poem, too, was a collage that was long in the making. It began with a particular group therapy session that followed a predictable pattern with one client. I had worked with this client for nearly a year giving little second thought to the approach I was using and was confident of the client's improvement. Finally, one night when the client came in smiling and left crying, I felt forced to question my approach. I followed this process with several clients over a couple of years before writing this poem that brought some closure to the issue.

Ode Unspoken

You came with a story . . . your story
    a precious myth of being
You wore your smile
    placed strategically
    like your hair
    just how you wanted me to see you
I cringed at your claimed happiness
    and did not hesitate
    as I took from your face
    that strategic smile
    so perfectly placed
Tears came
    as the room fell small
    pulling me closer
    my eyes, too, heavy
Through your blurred eyes
    I think I saw
    a brief glimpse of you
    words now, brought you in
    instead of pushing me away
Did I take your smile?
    Steal your happiness?

Or, did I find you at last
    the wounded child
    hidden
    left standing on the curb
    . . . waiting . . .
Did I crush your myth?
    Or offer
    a small piece of life?
Did I evoke pain?
    Instill sorrow in your heart?
    Steal your happiness away?
Or did I offer a bit of me
    an invitation to be seen
    clearly now, as
    compassion broke through
Did the walls crash down
    crushing you
    into a new story
Or did the walls gently melt
    as care outlasted resistance
    and love broke through

Poetry To Convey Empathy and Deepen the Relationship

Poems can also be used to help therapists better understand their clients. When these poems are shared with the client, they often deepen the relationship. This section contains two poems. The first poem was written following an emotional therapy session, when a client was preparing for her mother's death.

Approaching Death

Words cradled in loving arms
In this, the last embrace
Touch fades through rubbery skin
Gray strands run smoothly along fingers

Images of childhood reversed, as
Comfort through the old eyes of a child

The deepest whispers are those not heard
. . . only felt
Presence,
Offering comfort no words could provide
Tenderness,
Eyes softly touching a heart
Freedom,
Life no longer fought for
     . . . as a tired soul released

The wish to say goodbye, now
Not later
Not as harsh wish, merciful
A wish to die when not alone
While fearing the near departure
Mama, say goodbye today
And let me be the warm face
As you "go gently into the dark" embrace

The second poem was chosen to illustrate how poetry can be used to seek empathy in challenging therapeutic contexts. Therapists, especially new therapists, will often describe that angry and erotic transferences or these actual feelings are the most difficult to deal with in the therapeutic relationship. These feelings often are the most difficult emotions to deal with in life in general. Although this poem was not connected with a client, it was written in a situation when I was trying to understand someone's anger directed toward me that did not seem to make sense. In particular, I was working very hard to retain an empathetic and compassionate stance toward this individual who was lashing out at me in a rather extreme manner. This poem came after talking through the conflict with a mutual friend. I told my friend at the end of the conversation that I did not know how much longer I could maintain compassion and empathy.

The poem could easily be interpreted as an angry poem, but in reality anger is just one small aspect of this poem. The emotions present when writing this poem were soft emotions of caring and sadness for my friend, who had become enveloped in anger toward me. After finishing the poem, I was able to return to a place of compassion and empathy for this individual.

In Need of an Enemy
My rage is all I consume
Since this bitter life phase
Enveloped me
My heart of compassion
Seeks healing no more
But a target, any target
That can justify my rage

I have no god
Who can bear its brunt
And the world . . .
Well, the world
It's just too diffuse
I need a man,
Preferably straw
I guess you'll do

Each jarring blow
Confuses, I know
But sets me free
Friendship's just a small price
Cheaper than a pill
Easier than a drink
I am the dominant one, you see
My power over you
Quells the voice
Complaining of my fading

I guess you'll do
My compassionate lamb
I'll rise from invisibility
And regain my power
Strong and vicious enough
So that your tears
Hide mine own

Poetry for the Therapist's Healing and Growth

Finally, therapists can use poetry as part of their own healing process. This final poem is one with many voices, including my own. The poem started to percolate years before it was written, while on a trip to China where several of us from the United States, along with Mark Yang, spent some time with a group of relief workers who had spent the last year helping the victims of the Sichuan earthquake (see Dias, 2011). The relief workers were verging on burn out and compassion fatigue, but nobly persisted despite being questioned by their friends and family as to why they would continue in this difficult work. But there are many other voices woven into this poem of people questioning why they pursued being a therapist when the job involved so much direct and vicarious suffering. My voice, too, is strongly present when, at times, I have wondered why I did not chose an easier path. The poem began to crystalize after reading a quote in Trent Claypool's (2010) dissertation, where Tom Greening spoke of "paying one's existential dues" (p. 110). Yet, it still took a bit of time, with pieces of the poem gradually emerging before the words finally found their way onto paper. The poem continues to keep me grounded by reminding me why I chose this field.

Why I Drink This Cup
Inspired in part by Tom Greening's concept of "existential dues"

Why do I return to this bitter cup?
That so long taints my mouth
Why must I ask these questions
Of existence
That plague my soul

And tarnish my mind
That bring my focus to the tragic
And brings my spirit so low

Why do I return to this bitter cup?
Listening to these sad stories
Of evil and existence gone vile
Visiting places even God left
And would not return
Searching the ground for each tear
Each drop of blood

Why do I return to this bitter cup?
Sitting across the broken hearted
With innocence shattered
And bones crushed by the play
Of the powerful ones
Why do I listen to these stories?
My tears mingling with those
Of the isolated souls

Why do I return to these bitter cups
And drink deeply of this suffering?
I guess I'm just paying my
Existence dues
Taking in the suffering of the world
And polishing my soul with our tears
Weeping for tragedies no world ought bear
I drink the bitterness and share this cup
In hopes that the tears of many
May prevent the need
For the shedding of more
And still
I drink this cup

Conclusion

Poetry is a powerful medium of healing. It is also an underutilized tool of therapeutic action. In my own journey in becoming a therapist and a healing person, few things have been more powerful than poetry. Regularly I notice that I am different with my clients when writing and consuming poetry. When I discontinue this practice, a greater distance gradually seems to come between the individuals I am attempting to offer help to and myself. The same has been true with supervision, teaching, and even leadership roles. For some, other artistic modes, such as painting, may be more helpful. What is important is finding what mode works for you and then pursuing it.

References

Bugental, J. F. T. (1965). *The search for authenticity*. New York, NY: Hold, Rinehart, & Winston.

Claypool, T. (2010). *On becoming an existential psychologist: Journeys of contemporary leaders*. ProQuest, UMI Dissertation Publishing (3412340).

Diamond, S. A. (1996). *Anger, madness, and the daimonic: The psychological genesis of violence, evil, and creativity*. New York, NY: State University of New York Press.

Dias, J. (2011, August 9). *Emerging metaphors: Suffering, coffee, and connoisseurs of pain*. New Existentialist Blog retrieved from http://www.saybrook.edu/newexistentialists/posts/08-09-11.

Furman, R. (2003). Poetry therapy and existential practice. *The Arts in Psychotherapy, 30*, 195-200. doi: 10.1016/S0197-4556(03)00052-2

Schneider, K. & Krug, O. (2009). *Existential-humanistic therapy*. Washington, DC: American Psychological Association

May, R. (1985). *My quest for beauty*. Dallas, TX: Saybrook.

22

$\mathcal{C}\longrightarrow$

Naming the Actual
To Unearth Our Sacred Selves

Deborah Haarstad

THE PROCESS OF NAMING THE ACTUAL in group psychotherapy and bereavement support groups is an effective method for unearthing our sacred selves. Deepening and expanding awareness in the here and now opens participants to a more honest understanding of their true nature and an enlarged view of their potential. Through the creation of a safe environment, where the actual can be named, individuals unearth the inviolable spirit with which they were born.

When I am asked what makes group psychotherapy different from individual psychotherapy, I give a list of the well-known benefits: instilling hope, experiencing universality, offering and receiving help and encouragement, developing social techniques, sharing advice, and trying on new behavior (Yalom, 2005). In response, I am met with the statement, "I could never be in a psychotherapy group. I wouldn't want others making comments or judgments about what I do or say." The unpredictable nature of a psychotherapy group can elicit our deep fear of being exposed in public, of having our flaws named, our values questioned, or our beliefs attacked. Rollo May (1953) claimed, "The great bulk of our anxiety comes when some value we hold essential to our existence as selves is threatened" (p. 41). When a core belief is threatened, one can feel that one's self could likewise be destroyed. It can then be said that the power of naming the actual in a group setting goes to the heart of our existential desire for belonging and our corresponding fear of isolation. Participating in a psychotherapy group is a courageous journey to reveal our sacred selves.

After our first group meeting of "Unearthing the Moment," it became clear to me the focus of our work was to be centered on naming the actual experience in the here and now rather than a strictly didactic format. The ensuing wave of anxiety led me to ask myself, "Why is it so difficult to name others' actions as I see them?" Almost immediately I recalled times when I had asserted myself by naming what I saw happening only to be met with either retaliation or negation, which left me feeling somewhat young and unsupported. Fear of retaliation is one reason Irvin Yalom (2005) referred to process commentary, including naming the actual and reflecting on the meaning of the actual, as a taboo in social behavior, considered rude and impertinent. He stated that process commentary is "indispensable and a common denominator of all effective interactional groups" (p. 150). Before we delve into the effectiveness of naming the actual in a group setting, let us explore the reasons for this taboo.

Throughout our lives, we are socialized in such a way as to discourage naming others' actions when doing so would cause them embarrassment or make them self-conscious. As a result, we are able to act and speak freely, safe in the knowledge that others are not paying too close attention or seeking to control our behavior through their commentary. In fact, when we are met with harsh criticism, it can often evoke early memories and anxieties of having our behavior controlled by parental criticism.

Groups, from small families to large organizations, often have a structure that controls the flow of information. The greater the transparency of information, with inclusion of group participants in decision-making, the better the group sustains the meaning and creative function of the group (Heider, 2005). While more rigid structured groups with a hierarchy of authority in place (e.g., oppressive government), have a greater chance of participants rebelling and dismantling the function and sustainability of the group. Transparent authority and inclusive group participation can lead to equalization of power and leveling of hierarchy.

Transparency in a psychotherapy group leader is an essential ingredient in naming the here and now in the group process. Relationships are deepened, with the leader, the individuals and the group as a whole through the process of naming the actual and reflecting on its meaning (Yalom, 2005).

The use of the actual is instrumental to change and an effective means of meeting a client's goals for treatment in both group and individual psychotherapy. Jim Bugental's (1999) rationale for the emphasis on the actual is "the goal of heightening the client's own immediate and subjective awareness" (p. 23). The therapist shines a light on that which is present but currently unnoticed by the client. Through his experience as a therapist and a consultant to other psychotherapists, Bugental (1999) was convinced that: *Increased awareness in the living moment means increased effectiveness of self-direction and satisfaction in living* (p. 24).

Clients come into therapy often sharing the common goals of seeking relief from suffering, having better relationships with others, and living full or more productive lives. They frequently wish for change, but underneath there is a stronger commitment to avoid change and stay with that which is familiar. The process of naming the actual helps clients gain awareness of this avoidance, this clinging to old behavior, as it emerges within the group process, which is where they have the opportunity to act in a new way. Taking action and having an effect on their environment leads to the feelings of efficacy and empowerment that may have previously been lacking.

The group setting is the ideal environment to explore interpersonal learning through using the here and now with direct feedback. When attention is brought not just to the participants' behavior, but also to how their behavior affects other group members, the participants have a rich opportunity to make choices that could enhance their relationships to others in the group, and have the ripple effect of changing how they relate to others outside the group. A freely interactive group will develop into a social microcosm of the participant members, where they will interact with the group members as they interact with others in their social sphere (Yalom, 2005).

When I lead Spousal Loss Bereavement groups, which are brief psycho-education groups, rather than psychotherapy groups, the first evening is spent discussing challenges, concerns, and goals. The most commonly shared goal by group participants is relief from suffering, followed by a list of the many forms their suffering takes (e.g., sadness, fatigue, isolation, and confusion). As the group progresses, and safety and support are evident, the focus shifts from their physical and mental concerns to more social, spiritual, and interpersonal issues. They begin to speak of deeper concerns: anger over their loss, the feeling that their spirit has been broken, their will to live self-assertively stifled, and tremendous anxiety because of separation from their loved one. When participants courageously admit to strong feelings of anger, or admit their total dependence on their deceased partner for companionship, they are most often met with acceptance and recognition. This acceptance by others opens them up to seeing themselves in a new light. Finding they were not rejected as they had feared, they can now begin to accept these parts of themselves and soften the harsh self-condemnation they had been carrying.

Sometimes instead of showing signs of acceptance, the group or the group leader might act in such a way that triggers a client's fears of rejection, which needs to be monitored and examined for any unsafe aspects by the group leader. The example that follows is disguised to protect confidentiality. In the case of a group participant who was giving an overly lengthy and tedious check-in regarding the details of his week, I interjected stating, "In the interest of time, I need to interrupt you so everyone will have an opportunity to speak." The man became enraged, grabbed his belongings and headed towards the door. I turned to the group and asked them what they were experiencing and how they might feel if he left. Several members stated they would be upset and disappointed if he walked out of the meeting. The clarification of his importance to the group was an opportunity for him to return to his seat and share what he was experiencing at a deeper level. Choosing to focus on the client's actual in-the-moment experiencing, I asked him what was happening. He poured out a story of his brother's serious health issues and his fear of losing another beloved person. The other members were moved from originally feeling frustrated over his verbosity to being touched by his willingness to show vulnerability. Even though we did not specifically discuss the other participants' reaction to his drawn out check-in, he was able to draw his own conclusions. At the next meeting he began by saying, "As a teacher I have a tendency to be long-winded, and I am not accustomed to being interrupted. I will try to be brief but it is not in my nature, so you may have to let me know if I speak too long." Even in this somewhat limited exercise of naming the actual, the client was able to identify his effect on others and seek to make the appropriate changes.

Had the previous incident occurred in a psychotherapy group rather than a brief, psycho-educational group, it would have been an excellent opportunity to the focus on the here-and-now feelings of the group members towards this individual while he was rambling on at length. Learning of the other participants' frustration with him when his discourse runs long would have illuminated both his perception within the group, and the limitations in his relationships outside the group. There are few settings where it is socially sanctioned to comment on the in-the-moment relationship occurring between people. The ability to do so is a truly unique feature of psychotherapy groups and lends power to this format.

When I assess the most effective groups I have attended, I find the common feature is a group leader who is able to steer the conversation away from outside material and focus instead on the relationship with one another as it is occurring in the here and now. It is the responsibility of the group leader to establish an in-the-moment focus early on while shaping the group norms. Bugental (1999) cautioned that these observations require careful and measured input and laid out a three-step sequence, moving from *recognition* ("You sound . . .") through *reflection* ("How often you . . .") to *interpretation* ("Once again you . . .") based on frequently demonstrated patterns (p. 25) This process only works if there have been repeated encounters at each step before you progress to the next. If a *group member* seeks to establish this norm, it can be perceived by the other members as an attempt to elevate him or herself above the others. In the case with my verbose client, it would have been an entirely different situation if another member had chosen to interrupt him and move the group along, and most likely would have been perceived as a play for power.

In individual work, the therapist functions as the sole instigator of change. In a group setting the therapist builds a culture where honesty and spontaneity of expression are the desired norm, which facilitates and permits confrontation, but only after safety and support have been established. Once group cohesiveness is in place, group members can begin to assist the therapist with the task of activating the here and now. This may be done when group members speak directly to one another about how they feel they are being perceived: for example, "I feel I am boring you when I see you yawn while I am speaking." However, the task of interpretation based on a client's behavioral patterns ("Once again you . . .") remains the responsibility of the psychotherapist, as does any illumination of the group process. The group leader is an affected observer who maintains the objectivity needed to hold impressions and content and gives sensitive feedback about patterns of behavior and interactions that have happened over the course of several groups. This storage and sharing of information in the context of the goals of the group is the sole responsibility of the leader, not the responsibility of participants.

Throughout the Unearthing training, I have been increasingly exposed to the process of keeping an in-the-moment focus. I admit that it does not come naturally to me, and I must first master how to think in the here and now. At times I feel rude and pushy when returning to a topic another is resisting. It takes courage to act in a directive manner when the group as a whole is fighting that direction. It also requires empathy, compassion, and the ability to find a less threatening approach while establishing safety and trust. One technique used to soften an inquiry is the use of the conditional phrase *if* ("*If* you were angry right now . . ."). The use of conditional phrases can free up the participants by not insisting they speak in absolutes ("I am angry.") and creates some space from a challenging topic. Another technique used to create opportunities for each member to take responsibility, is to ask questions: i.e., "Is there anyone who has not shared today and would like to?" This question also ensures that each member is given ample opportunity to share during the group.

By consistently bringing the focus from matters outside the psychotherapy group back to what is actually occurring inside, the group leader sets a norm, which will be internalized by the participants and encourage them to set their own limits. There are times when the process is obvious to all, but is too challenging for the members to comment on directly. It is important that the group leader not push some members to speak on an issue they feel too anxious to address. In most cases, the group leader has the greater skill to speak the unspeakable. I am reminded of the first psychotherapy group I attended in my early twenties. After openly commenting on a client's recurrent destructive behavior, psychotherapist Nathaniel Branden noted the stunned reactions of the psychotherapy group members and said, "If you are willing to live it, you need to be willing to hear it said aloud." That was a pivotal juncture for not only the individual originally spoken to, but for the group as a whole. The fact that I still remember this moment, which occurred over 30 years ago, both illustrates and validates Bugental's (1999) rationale for the emphasis on the actual.

This powerful moment of naming the actual was an opening for the group to delve into a deeper conversation of a critically important issue. In the ensuing discussion we were all able to recognize parts of ourselves that were holding us back from acting on our original goals; the awareness and acceptance gained were crucial steps towards transcending our limited self-concepts, and clearing the path to a more benevolent connection to all that exists. Spirit, says Branden (1997), is a summons to rise, to shatter and transcend the boundaries of the familiar (p. 182). In defining spirituality as "pertaining to consciousness and to the needs and development of consciousness," Branden concludes that "whoever commits to awareness and personal growth as a way of life, which entails, among other things, self-awareness and self-examination, is on a spiritual path" (p. 180). Naming the actual in a psychotherapy group is a mindful practice of investigation, meant to discover the best within, and unearth our most sacred self.

References

Branden, N. (1997). *The art of living consciously: The power of awareness to transform everyday life.* New York, NY: Simon & Schuster.

Bugental, J. F. T. (1999). *Psychotherapy isn't what you think.* Phoenix, AZ: Zeig, Tucker & Co., Inc.

Heider, J. (2005). *The tao of leadership: Lao Tzu's tao te ching adapted for a new age.* Atlanta, GA: Humanics Ltd Partners.

May, R. (1953). *Man's search for himself.* New York, NY: W. W. Norton & Company, Inc.

Yalom, I. D. (2005). *The theory and practice of group psychotherapy* (5th ed.). New York, NY: Basic Books.

23

Existential-Humanistic Psychotherapy:
The Personal in the Professional

Daniel B. Wasserman

EXISTENTIAL-HUMANISTIC PSYCHOTHERAPY is a relationship-based, clinical modality of instituting personal change that emphasizes the present moment, the spontaneous flow of human experience, and the systematic study of subjective awareness. Existential-humanistic psychotherapy also references the inevitability of death as a primary—or perhaps the ultimate—source of meaning in an individual's life. The limits of the human lifespan lend special importance to how we use our time while we are alive, while we have life (Bugental, 1965)!

Studying existential-humanistic psychotherapy has been a breath of fresh air in my life, both professionally and personally. After several decades of practicing as a psychologist, I have increasingly found myself feeling worn down. At times, I have felt empty and mechanical, and the work somewhat dull and lacking in depth and intensity. I believe that my condition was caused in part by the demands of a busy practice, with many extremely difficult and challenging clients, as well as from a personal schedule that was overcommitted. These feelings also seemed to stem from frequent battles with health insurance companies for reimbursement, and from the pressures I felt to keep up with the many requirements of state law, ethics standards, and limiting liability exposure.

Beneath these surface factors, however, was something that felt more subtle and, at the same time, more profound and disturbing. My state of malaise seemed to result from experiencing an external demand to conform my treatment methods to the latest institutionally-touted, scientific models. For years, I had endured an encroachment on the psychotherapeutic process by professional medicine, the pharmaceutical industry, and the health insurance industry. These entities seemed determined to redefine emotional and behavioral problems exclusively in biochemical and neurological terms. The universal solution offered from this vantage point consisted of pharmaceuticals and a confining list of talk-therapy approaches.

Sadly, the difficulty I was experiencing as a psychologist was exacerbated by cohorts of my own professional associations who increasingly encouraged that treatment be limited to "manualized" or "evidence-based" treatment protocols. It appeared that my own profession might collude with health insurance companies to ensure that only such specific, and in my experience limited, forms of treatment would qualify for third-party reimbursement. I became frightened that I would no longer be able to make a living practicing my profession as I had known it. I became afraid that such attempts to objectify therapy would ultimately redefine the field that I originally entered because of my excitement about *the human encounter.*

Absence of Vitality: Science and the Subjective Human Experience

An enduring frustration of mine, throughout my graduate education and in later professional life, was what I perceived to be the demand to shoehorn the grandeur, and pathos, of the human experience into models of science that originally were developed for the study of inanimate phenomena (e.g, chemistry, physics, geology). Attempts at conforming psychology to these models overlook the fact that the entity under study, the human being, has *inner awareness* or *subjective experience* that influences observable behavior. Humans, as distinct from inert matter, and presumably from most of the lower species, can reflect on their experiences and choose how to behave.

While still a graduate student 35 years ago, I already had concluded that any science that approaches the study of people without incorporating an investigation of human awareness, is destined to be impoverished and of limited meaning or usefulness. Though such studies may achieve some level of statistical precision, they will inevitably leave out the *essence of what it means to be human*.

Here I am reminded of the philosophical tale of a man who, walking down a street at night, comes upon another man crouching on the pavement under a streetlight, obviously searching. "Lost something?" the first man asks, and offers his help when told by the second man that he has misplaced his keys. After looking for a while and finding nothing, the first man inquires, "Is this where you lost them?" The second man replies, "No. I lost them over there in the dark alley." The first man then asks, "Well, why are you searching for them here?" The second man responds, "Because the light here is better." (Freedman, D. H., 2010). This story captures what I view as the main dilemma of psychology in purporting to become a "real science." In order to emulate the descriptive and predictive order of the physical sciences, research in psychology (and its sub-category, psychotherapy) frequently omits the essence of the human experience: inner consciousness and subjectivity. In my experience, much research on psychotherapy achieves internal validity at the expense of leaving out what would be most *worth* studying.

The result of this omission is a field that exhibits statistical discipline, but lacks heart. Experimental design is allowed to trump meaning. The human spirit is sacrificed for what is measurable and quantifiable. It is as if a musical composer were confined to using only major chords because they are easier to play.

This resonance is similar to a scene in the film *Amadeus* (1984), where an expectant Mozart eagerly awaits the critical reaction of the king to the premier performance of a spectacular opera Mozart has written. His majesty, knowing little about music yet realizing his position requires him to say something, mutters, "It's nice. But it has too many notes. Take out some notes." A horrified Mozart looks on, wondering which notes he would eliminate. Unfortunately, taking out "some of the notes" of subjective human experience often leaves psychotherapy research "a shriveled, desiccated fragment" (Laing, 1967, p. 26) of true human understanding.

How revitalizing it is, then, to encounter existential-humanistic psychotherapy! This approach exults in subjective human experiencing. It explores the contours and textures of the inner realm and helps us to know, in rich detail, its flavors and fragrances. Bugental (1999) a preeminent exponent of this model, says that this psychotherapy isn't *about the subjective*; it is working directly *in the subjective*.

It is my contention that such study is imperative to any meaningful understanding of the human experience, despite the difficulty of its being fitted into objective, scientific models.

Existential-Humanistic Psychotherapy: Therapeutic and Spiritual Connections

Concurrent with my present, two-year course of study in the existential-humanistic psychotherapy, I have made connections with other spiritual and therapeutic influences that I believe carry important thematic overlap with this modality. I have encountered this through the influences of: (a) Transpersonal psychotherapy (Hastings, A., 1991; Walsh & Vaughan, 1993), a model that stems from Transpersonal Psychology, originating in the 1960s as a result of the collaboration of psychologists such as Abraham Maslow and Anthony Sutich (Scotton, Chinen & Battista, 1996); (b) Western Sufism, a brand of spiritual mysticism brought to the West from India by Hazrat Inayat Khan (1982); (c) Nonviolent Communication, a model for interpersonal communication developed by Marshall Rosenberg (1999) and influenced by the work of Carl Rogers (1961); and (d) Fourth-Way Consciousness Studies, a spiritual school brought forth in Russia in the 1800s by G. I. Gurdjieff.

What do all of these schools of thought have in common? Each emphasizes the subjective experience of the individual and stresses the exploration of inner, personal reality as the defining quality of being human. These traditions point toward the essential factor of life existing only in the now. Gurdjieff (1963), for example, propounds that personal freedom can be best (or only) achieved by overcoming conditioned or mechanical reactivity, and by developing a *conscious, spontaneous* life. Other factors of these models include the qualities of taking a non-judgmental stance as a powerful, respectful, responsible, and peaceful basis for communication and growth.

The potency of the immediate moment is strongly emphasized in the transpersonal model of psychotherapy (Scotton, Chinen & Battista, 1996). The transpersonal model leans into and incorporates many spiritual aspects of how a person changes and becomes more whole. The past is gone, and the future has not yet happened. References to both past and future (in thought or conversation) tend to be abstract, conceptual, and judgmental, which might be necessary at times, but is not the force that generates change in an individual. They exist removed from what is being felt at the current juncture. One could say that all we actually have in life is a lengthy series of present moments that pass through the present, from future to past, as we live them and as we proceed along the timeline of our lives.

Encountering the Existential-Humanistic Model

The Actual

Much of what constitutes the problems being addressed in therapy resides in the complex web of thoughts, conjectures, interpretations, and meanings that the client has woven around his or her actual experience. This web sometimes keeps the person distant from the very processes that could resolve the issues and help meet his/her needs. However, speaking and listening in terms of what actually is being experienced in the present moment brings the energy of immediacy into the human interaction. This emphasis upon the flow of ever-present experience brings my clients and me in touch with an *actual* reality, as distinct from thoughts *about* reality. I find this to be an essential component of change, both in my work with therapy clients and in my everyday personal experience.

I feel an instant excitement when attention is called to the immediate experience that either I am having or the client is having. When clients are caught up in their thoughts *about* their problems, they seem disempowered and the conversation feels dead. This pattern frequently is expressed in complicated theorizing about events in the past or about worries they may have about what may happen in the future. It also tends to be voiced in speculation about cause-effect relationships, such as how a current problem may have precedents in the past. This "talking about" has not produced change in the client.

Concepts, beliefs, and judgments are one step removed from experience. A simple, direct question such as, "How do you feel about that right now, in this moment?" can open up an entirely new flow of thoughts, feelings, and perspectives on the issues at hand. In turn, this frequently leads to more energized and creative discussions, to actionable solutions, to useful shifts in viewpoints on reality, and to a felt sense in the client that the problem is on the way to being resolved.

Finitude

Each one of us will simply cease to be. . . . You will be as if you had never existed, which was, however, the way you were before you did exist—and not only you but everything else. Nevertheless, with such an improbable past, "*here we are*" [italics Wasserman].

—Alan Watts, *In My Own* Way, 1972, p. 114

A related aspect of existential-humanistic psychotherapy that I find worthwhile is the emphasis on death as an inevitability that gives urgency to life and to therapy. Simply put, life does not last. That fact, that stark reality, means that we cannot afford to hide out or to waste time. The existential-humanistic model of psychotherapy focuses attention on this perspective and helps both therapist and client use this awareness to an enlivening advantage.

The initial effect of this emphasis is to help the individual to wake up to the intimidating reality that our individual lifespans are finite. This fact governs our existence whether we are aware of it or not. Our life will be over, more or less on a schedule, regardless of whether we choose to be conscious of this reality. Therapy can be the encounter for awakening to this fact.

A second effect of being aware of life's final boundary is to concentrate a person's attention on what most matters now. If life is limited, it is essential to use one's time on what is valuable. It is important to show up for one's life in a conscious way, invigorated by the potentialities of the moment. Someday we will take our last breath, and there will be no more moments. The therapy process with attention to the now, and to making meaning in the now, is what I have found enlivens the process of change that the client is seeking.

My Deliberate Experience

In terms of my personal life, I now utilize what I am learning from the existential-humanistic model to complement spiritual teachings I now receive from the Sufi and Fourth Way lineages (Khan, 1982; Gurdjieff, 1963). Just as in therapy, where I direct my curiosity to the immediate experience of other people with whom I work, I now notice an intensified hunger for concentrating on my own inner experience. I recently attended a weeklong retreat of Sufi practice, followed by a five-day silent Sufi retreat. I undertook the silent retreat to deepen and integrate the understanding and insights gathered in the preceding "loud" camp, one involving chanting, singing, and dancing practices. Excited by these experiences, I now seek an amplified sense of *interiority*, as one of my teachers ably phrased it.

I find myself on a quest to be more aware of my inner experiencing, for personal growth and for spiritual awakening. As often as I can in daily life, I attempt to harness energy from focusing on the present moment and from viewing whatever I think and feel as precious, because it occurs in a moment that never will come again. I take special satisfaction in appreciating *the now*, respecting the knowledge that the flame of my life will one day be extinguished. This awareness makes what happens in any given moment matter all the more, including the therapeutic hours I spend with my clients.

Whereas scientists predominantly study external phenomena (events primarily outside the self), the mystic pursues understanding of internal experience. This includes sensations, perceptions, thoughts, emotions, interpretations, desires, aversions, expectations, and assessments—all of which comprise human awareness. My behavior may be something that a scientist can count and categorize. However, *only I know what I think and feel*.

Studying the constructs in these models helps me to maintain connection to my inner experience. Continued personal development within the existential-humanistic and spiritual models contributes to my ability to articulate my inner experience in a way that others can grasp. This self-growth fundamentally enhances the presence that I bring to the therapeutic relationship, and allows for the vitality of the subjective to remain central to the human encounter.

Ironically, turning inward and being conscious of my life in these ways helps me to connect to a larger perspective on what lies outside myself. I consider this paradox to be quite spiritual. On the surface, it appears that I am very small in the vast expanses of time and space in the infinite cosmos. However, *awareness* is the common element that I share with all beings that have come before me, with all beings with which I presently share this existence, and, I presume, with all beings that will come after I am gone. Underneath all individual differences—physical, cognitive, and emotional—and underneath the very perception that we are separate beings, is the unifying element of *consciousness* itself, which transpersonal psychology has expounded upon since William James (1958) and more recently with Friedman, H. L., & Hartelius, G. (2013).

This awareness, *this deliberate experiencing of life*, appears to be the great connecting force in life. Through it, I can achieve a link with all aspects of the universe, near and far in space and time, thereby leading to *a felt sense of the one being*. With this, I find it possible to move beyond my identification with my individual ego, to have at least fleeting glances of life beyond separation, and to connect with something far greater and larger than my egoic self. Perhaps this is what Jesus meant when he said, "Whosoever believeth in Him may not perish; but may have life everlasting" (John 3:15 Douay-Rheims Version).

The Personal in the Professional

Polster and Polster (1973) report,

One's future welfare often travels in disguise and its blessings are frequently recognized only after extensive turmoil, when finally one may say my divorce or quitting my father's business or even, alas, my heart attack was the best thing that ever happened to me. One of the difficulties in moving out of the familiar is the temptation to close off the full drama of change before its own attractions have a chance to ripen. What is hard to appreciate, when terror shapes a catastrophic gap, is that this blankness can be a fertile void. The fertile void is the existential metaphor for giving up the familiar supports of the present and trusting the momentum of life to produce new opportunities and vistas. The acrobat who swings from one trapeze to the next knows just when he must let go. He gauges his release exquisitely and for a moment he has nothing going for him but his own momentum. Our hearts follow his arc and we love him for risking the unsupported moment. (pp. 120-121)

An important component of personal growth and development consists of being spontaneously available to the uncertainties and possibilities of the present moment. One can stay safe through careful planning and by "nailing down" (limiting) the potentialities of the now. However, it seems that the richest and most profound personal change comes when one enters into the realm of the unknown, where things are uncertain, undefined, and open. Deep growth and development magically lie in a willingness to venture forth and to move forward, particularly when one is unsure of what lies ahead and especially when negative circumstances threaten one's sense of identity and safety. Holding this uncertainty in the moment in the therapeutic hour is part of waking up to change.

As the existential-humanist Bugental (1999) states,

A psychotherapy of the *actual* must confront the endless ambiguity of human existence, the shading of meaning and emotion that words can only incompletely convey, the ambivalences aroused by our addressing the very life structures upon which the client has come to depend, and our own and the client's emotional bond, which we both know must ultimately be dissolved. (p. 182)

So I consider it important to approach my life, and the lives of the clients with whom I work, with curiosity for the unknown and with a sense of adventure. And so my therapeutic work is enlivened by attention to my own presence, the subjective encounter of my clients, and by consciously leaning into the moment.

Integrating the many views I have discussed within this writing, and pursuing these tenets in my lived experience, allows me to feel strengthened in my personal life and in my professional work. Freed to move out of the confinement of rote evidence-based models, I am able to actively court the present moment with my clients. I am able to accompany them with presence and curiosity into the unknowns that exist in the movement toward growth. In this, I experience the return of heart and spirit to the therapeutic human encounter.

References

Bugental, J. F. T. (1965). *The search for authenticity: An existential-analytic approach to psychotherapy.* New York, NY: Holt, Rinehart and Winston.

Bugental, J. F. T. (1999). *Psychotherapy isn't what you think.* Phoenix, AZ: Zeig, Tucker & Co., Inc.

Freedman, D. H. (2010, July/August). Why scientific studies are so often wrong: The streetlight effect. *Discover Magazine,* 55-57.

Friedman, H. L., & Hartelius, G. (2013). *The Wiley-Blackwell handbook of transpersonal psychology.* West Sussex, England: Wiley-Blackwell.

Gurdjieff, G. I. (1963). *Meetings with remarkable men.* London, England: Penguin.

Hastings, A. (1991). *With the tongues of men and angels: A study of channeling.* Holt, San Francisco, CA: Rinehart and Winston.

James, W. (1958). *The varieties of religious experience: A study in human nature.* New York, NY: New American Library.

Khan, I. H. (1982). *The art of being and becoming.* New Lebanon, NY: Omega Publications.

Laing, R. D. (1967). *The politics of experience.* New York, NY: Pantheon Books.

Ohlsson, B., Hausman, M., & Zaentz, S. (Producers), & Forman, M. (Director). (1984). *Amadeus.* [Motion Picture]. USA: Warner Home Video.

Polster, E. & Polster, M. (1973). *Gestalt therapy integrated: Contours of theory and practice.* New York, NY: Bruner/Mazel.

Rogers, C. (1961). *On becoming a person: A therapist's view of psychotherapy.* New York, NY: Houghton Mifflin.

Scotton, B. W., Chinen, A. B., & Battista, J. R. (Eds.). (1996). *Textbook of transpersonal psychiatry and psychology.* New York, NY: Basic Books.

Rosenberg, M. (1999). *Nonviolent communication: A language of compassion.* Encinitas, CA: PuddleDancer Press.

Walsh, R., & Vaughan, F. (Eds.). (1993). *Paths beyond ego.* New York, NY: Penguin Putnam.

Watts, A. (1972). *In my own way: An autobiography.* New York, NY: Pantheon Books.

24

Mutato Nomine de te Fabula Narratur:
With the Name Changed
the Story Applies to You

Cornelia Pinnell

THIS WRITING IS MEANT to be deeply personal. It is born out of my personal experiences, and it is influenced by my readings, by my encounters with patients in my clinical work, and by discussions with colleagues and students. The process of writing itself has been fragmented, as I often found myself exhausted physically or emotionally, and conflicted when choosing among my competing roles and duties. It is my hope that my personal story will have relevance to others, clinicians and patients alike, who, like me, are facing a loved one's dying process and developing courage, compassion, and self-compassion—"De te fabula narratur."

The cycle of life is multilayered and complex; it holds joys and sorrows, predictable events and unforeseeable ones, challenging and transformative twists and turns. Personal and professional aspects of my life have been closely intertwined and have influenced each other in ways that do not cease to amaze me. I grew up in Romania, during the years of the "golden epoch" of Ceausescu's reign. My parents came from families that survived World War I and World War II; they were political refugees who had lost everything they owned more then once and were separated repeatedly from their roots, and from their extended families, friends, and communities. They started their lives again and again, picking up the pieces and building anew. My early years were carefree, and life was simple. I played with the other kids in my neighborhood and had many friends at home and in school, unaware of the difficulties and the oppression experienced by the adults living and working in a totalitarian regime. In my family and in my community I felt loved and safe, and I was never alone; I felt I belonged to many overlapping and interlocking social circles. The Romanian culture is collectivistic and family-oriented; it is also fatalistic and tragic. My cultural and family heritage taught me about the (tragic) givens of existence; about choices, freedom and responsibility; and about being interconnected, belonging, and living with purpose. I also learned that profound changes can occur in the blink of an eye, that tragedy and loss are part and parcel of existence, of the human condition. I learned that we are free to choose how we respond to the specific circumstances of our lives.

I became a psychologist, despite the presidential decree that abolished the psychology programs in Romania at the end of my first year of studies. In retrospect, I can recognize the pattern of choices that have led me to where I am today, as my life path has unfolded. As a young adult, and confronted with the realities of life within a dictatorship, I chose to emigrate. I immigrated to the United States, initially with the status of legal alien, then permanent resident, eventually becoming an American citizen. I left everything behind, like many generations in my family before me. I experienced culture shock and future shock. I felt uprooted and alone, living in a foreign land, being apart from and not belonging. I had died metaphorically to one world, to be reborn in the New World, not knowing if and when I could reconnect with my family and friends. I experienced many losses, and I was painfully aware of the permanence of my choices, of their far-reaching consequences, of the reality that I could never go home again. And I was determined to create a new life for myself and for my child. I was also determined to become a psychologist.

I have been a clinical psychologist for almost two decades. Existential philosophy, which I discovered as a teenager, has been the bedrock for my philosophical musings and self-reflections, and for my efforts to make sense of life—mine and others. Existentialism, particularly humanistic existentialism, has also been central to my professional work, both as a clinician and as an educator. I continued to read, and I searched for mentorship in existential therapy, beyond my graduate training years. I felt honored to start the basic training in existential-humanistic psychotherapy, entitled Unearthing the Moment, under the guidance and mentorship of James Bugental and Myrtle Heery. I completed the basic and the advanced training, and I have continued my involvement in ongoing trainings. Moreover, I have taught graduate students about existential philosophy and existential psychotherapy.

My experience as a psychology educator and clinician has been, again and again, that the professional and the personal are closely intertwined, influencing each other in profound ways. During the early years of my existential-humanistic training, I also experienced such professional and personal synchronicities. The theme of one of these early trainings was old age, illness, and mortality. I remember distinctly listening intently to all the presenters; each one was describing the complex experiences of aging and of taking care of an ailing spouse. Among the speakers was Elizabeth Bugental. I was touched by their candid self-disclosures. I was moved to tears by their accounts of love and pain, of dedication and devotion to their life partners. For me, they were a model of humanity, and I felt inspired. I also felt awe, pain, and fear, thinking of a distant future. At the same time, I distinctly remember thinking that, despite our shared humanity, "This does not apply to me!"—at least not at that time. Little did I know how relevant that experience was for me, AT THAT TIME.

Recently, I read and re-read Elizabeth Bugental's (2005) words from her book *AgeSong, Meditations for Our Later Years*: "I notice as I grow older the increasing simultaneity of love and pain," (p. x) and "We live our lives and, if we're lucky or maybe smart, or both, we do mostly what we meant to do. Then it ends," (p. x) and "With conscious choices and an ability to stay in the moment, we might even bring joy and quiet pleasure to this final life phase" (p. x). I remembered our walks and our talks, our laughter and tears, and I understand her words differently now. It is no longer only an intellectual understanding, nor one that involves only empathy and compassion for someone who was advancing in age and who had been a primary caregiver for her beloved spouse, following his stroke. My new understandings go deeper, organically deep into my bones. I, too, experienced being a primary caregiver for my beloved husband, who was diagnosed with cancer a few months after that impactful training, and who died shortly thereafter. I have also experienced being a primary caregiver for my beloved mother, following her heart attack and strokes. My new understandings come from my lived experience, a shared experience now. It is not the same to read about such experiences in the pages of a book, or many books. It is different to live through illness and frailty and helplessness and death; to face IT squarely and have IT be a part of my life, day in and day out.

Almost four years ago, my 83-year-old mother nearly died following a heart attack and several silent strokes. She has never been the same! She had been a vibrant woman who had aged with grace. We had had a very close relationship; she had not only been my mother, but also my best friend, a teacher, and a mentor. She had represented a model of humanity, not only for me, but also for countless generations of her students at Babes-Bolyai University, where she taught philosophy for almost four decades. My mother had taught me about life, love, and friendship; she had taught me love for knowledge and philosophy; and she had inspired the desire to contribute to society and create a better world. Among the lessons I learned from my mother are: (a) we can choose an optimistic outlook on life in the midst of tragic circumstances and, related, my awareness that there is good luck embedded in bad luck; (b) the importance of "washing away the soot" and cleansing the soul from negativity at the end of each day, not allowing it to accumulate over time—we used to drink a "peace tea" every evening, to let go of unwanted sources of negativity; and (c) we can choose, and we can act every day to make our lives beautiful and meaningful. Even though my mother has lost her memory of who she had been and of everything she had known, she has continued to teach me lessons about life and death, about growing old, about taking care of someone who is slowly leaving life. She lives with me in our home, and I have been the primary caregiver for her, as she has not been able to complete even the most basic tasks of daily living. I have felt like a lifeline for my mother for almost four years now.

Myrtle looked at me with her penetrating blue eyes and said, "You have to write about it while it is happening! Afterwards, it changes, and you know it." Driving away from Sedona that April day, I was thinking of Myrtle's words and remembering her gaze, which touched my heart. I knew very deeply that she was right. And yet, I have postponed for years writing about a very painful experience I have been living. During the drive back home, I felt surrounded by beauty, like in the Navajo prayer of the beauty way. The desert was green, with golden blooms of brittlebush and palo verde and waves of pale orange blooms from desert mallow against the intense blue sky. The beauty filled my soul and gave me strength. For a long time, I have wanted to share my experience as a primary caregiver for my mother, and I kept postponing and postponing. I had started to write before and then I had to stop, tears rolling down my face. Maybe this time it will be different!

"I came to pick up my mom's meds," I told Beth, the pharmacist. We have known each other since I started my regular visits to the pharmacy, and we have often talked about our mothers. "How is your mother?" she asked me. "She is getting weaker every day, losing her life force little by little," I answered. "How is your mother?" I asked her. Beth's 96-year-old mother has been living in a skilled nursing facility for many years. I knew Beth visited her mother several times a year. This last visit was difficult. "It is so hard, you know, when you spend time and you talk with your mother, and all of a sudden your mother looks at you and says, 'And who is your mother, deary?'" Beth also found out that her sister was diagnosed with cancer. Her voice broke as she was telling her story, eyes downcast, and her face full of the grief of losing her mother. I understood her pain so well! Her story and her pain were echoing the story of so many others, including my own. I, too, missed my mother—the beautiful, vibrant, smart, wise, witty, funny, kind woman I had considered a role model, my closest friend, and a source of inspiration. I remembered my mother's words, uttered in various situations, and so fitting now—"De te fabula narratur."

If we live long enough, we will have a spouse, parent, sibling, child, or friend for whom we will become the primary or secondary caregiver. I am an adult and only child, and have been a primary caregiver in my home for my mother, who has been very frail and very ill for a long time. The role of caregiver brought about significant changes in my life, as it does for all primary or secondary caregivers. The adjustment to these changes is stressful. Although the new role can be meaningful and rewarding, the new caregiving duties likely bring about emotional turmoil and physical exhaustion. I have experienced both. Usual challenges include added responsibilities pertaining to housekeeping, supervision of medication, maintenance of hygiene, assistance with bathing, incontinence, and so on, along with increasing social isolation. If the caregiving occurs in the home, modifications may be necessary to transform the living space and adjust it to the needs of the suffering individual—for example, accommodations for the use of a walker or wheelchair, adding grab bars in the bathroom, and reorganizing the bedroom. Professional caregiver help, palliative medical care, or hospice care are also available. All these changes result in physical, financial, social, and emotional stress for the primary caregiver (Shaevitz, 2012).

All too frequently caregivers forget to take care of themselves. It is paramount for the caregiver to stay active and healthy, remain socially engaged, maintain friendships and close relationships, avoid depression, and engage in pleasurable activities (Shaevitz, 2012), to continue to live life with gusto.

I am not alone in mourning the slow loss of a loved one—parent, spouse, life partner, sibling, child, or friend—through death, or through little losses that add up day after day, week after week, creating a prolonged goodbye. The knowledge and awareness of shared humanity, of shared experiences with countless others, brings little comfort, but a sense of connection and humility when facing the great equalizer. Aging and death are part of life! Quoting La Rochefoucauld's maxim "Le soleil ni la mort ne se peuvent regarder en face" (p. 275), Yalom (2008) advised his readers to stare into death. His afterword to *Staring at the Sun* ended with this thought:

> It is my hope that by grasping, really grasping, our human condition—
> our finiteness, our brief time in the light—we will come not only to

savor the preciousness of each moment and the pleasure of sheer being but to increase our compassion for ourselves and for all other human beings. (Yalom, 2008, p. 277)

My knowledge of philosophy, psychological theory and research literature on lifespan tasks and challenges, mindfulness and compassion, loss and grief, the challenges of caregiving, and the danger of compassion collapse is blended with my life experiences. I believe that my teaching and my clinical work have been enriched by my personal life experiences, as I benefitted personally from my professional knowledge and skills. I am continuously drawing from many sources to nourish my soul, to become a better teacher and healer, a better human being. I believe I have grown in my capacity to be with and to listen respectfully and compassionately to another human being who experiences the pain of loss, or isolation, or meaninglessness, or to someone approaching the end of life. . . . I have grown in my ability to sit with the pain of another and, together, to learn from it with self-compassion and compassion for each other.

The details of our lives may be as different as our paths are unique. I discovered that my life path involves taking care of my frail and ill mother, as a primary caregiver, while she is slowly transitioning through the last stages of her life. I want to have the courage and the fortitude to be able to meet her needs with love and respect, preserving her dignity. I pray to be able to take care of her not only with sadness and pain, but also to be able to be present with her in each precious moment. I want to be able to recognize the moments of emotional connection: the little joys and the laughter, which are also part of this process of saying a long goodbye. My path also involves sharing my experiences with my students in teaching about aging, death and dying, caregiving, and end-of-life care; about compassion for the person who is experiencing physical and emotional pain in the process of dying; about compassion for those who experience the loss of a loved one and for the caregivers; and last, but not least, about self-compassion—all within an existential-humanistic framework.

As I opened my eyes, I heard my mother's voice. I could not make out her words. I went to greet her and say, "Good morning," but I found her fast asleep. Most likely she spoke again in her sleep, as she often does. I am still surprised when her speech while asleep is more coherent than when she is awake. "Thank you," she often says during the day, acknowledging the help she receives from those around her, since she cannot do anything for herself. She often says these words at night as well, during her dreams. I am deeply moved by the way her gratitude shines through, day and night, and by the way the essence of her soul shines brightly through the darkness of her psyche. This inner light of her being helps me stay strong in my daily commitment to take care of her, despite innumerable physical and emotional challenges.

At age 87, my mother spends most of the day in bed and sleeps long hours, like an infant. Sometimes she seems confused and scared, yet she seldom complains of anything. When she is awake, she is mostly joyful and playful. She enjoys listening to music, she responds to beauty, flowers, children's faces and their voices. She likes to sing, and she joins in singing tunes from my childhood and from her youth, as we connect on a bridge of beauty. She greets everyone with a kind gaze and a smile. Sometimes she says, "Hello," or "Servus," but her ability to use words has narrowed significantly. When I told her about the universe, the cosmos, and about chaos, hoping that she would resonate to concepts she used to feel passionate about, she listened, and then she asked me, "What does chaos mean?" When I tell her about current events, local and world news, she listens. I often wonder how much she actually understands about what is happening around her. I remember my shocking realization that she did not recognize parts of her body. And yet, in her interactions with a French Canadian hospice nurse, my mother thanked her repeatedly in French. At times, she surprises me and her other caregivers with funny comments, which make sense in context. One afternoon, while Maria (a caregiver) was thinking of her husband being late for an event, my mother commented, "At least he has good intentions," and Maria started laughing, surprised by the timing of the comment. Even though she cannot articulate her experience any longer, I see in her eyes whether she is emotionally present with me or not. Her comments to me are at once painful and moving; although she does not know who I am, nor who she is, she asks me at times, "Are you my mother, or am I your mother?" Occasionally she says, "I am so glad to know you! You are very kind to me." One day, recently, she said, "Sint trista. Sint pe drum (I am sad. I am on my way)." Another day she told me, "Sint moarta (I am dead)," making me think about the multiple layers of meaning of her words. And so the long goodbye continues—every day a bit more, every day a bit farther. I am witnessing her being in two worlds and her gradual disconnection and disengagement from THIS world and from life.

References

Bugental, E. (2005). *Agesong: Meditations for our later years.* San Francisco, CA: Elders Academy Press.

Shaevitz, M. H. (2012). *Caregiving is a group effort: A primer for geriatric caregivers and those receiving care.* Unpublished manuscript.

Yalom, I. D. (2008). *Staring at the sun: Overcoming the terror of death.* San Francisco, CA: Jossey-Bass.

Resources

American Society on Aging: www.asaging.org/
Home Modifications: www.homemods.org
Local agencies on aging/Eldercare Locator: www.eldercare.gov
National Hospice and Palliative Care Organization: www.nhpco.org
National Institute on Aging: www.nia.hih.gov

25

~~~

Soul and Intentionality of This Book

Myrtle Heery

LIFE IS A GREAT MYSTERY. How much will this book influence your mysterious journey in living and dying? Will your actions be changed personally and professionally because of something you have read in this book? How did I come to be here in this moment writing the last chapter of this book? What brought you to read this book? Questions of intentionality are part of being human. The questions existed long before psychology and psychotherapy. Questioning continues to prompt the study of psychology, the study and healing of the soul (psyche means soul). And the answers to questions are profoundly influenced by our diverse backgrounds and different understandings, interests, desires, and impulses prompting our journey in living here and now. Perhaps you are finishing reading this book or you just randomly opened to this page. But here you and I are together, despite our diverse backgrounds in space and time, contemplating soul and intentionality.

My Soul's Roots

I grew up in the southern part of the United States, where soul food has its roots. Vangie, our black maid, used to fix herself soul food and eat quietly by the ironing board. The house had a special smell when she cooked. When I watched Vangie cook, I saw she used mostly what she called "throw-ins." There was no recipe. There were basic ingredients, of course, but these alone did not produce soul food. It was the cook, Vangie, with her knowledge, experience, and intuition of what to throw into the pot and when. The result was unique and delicious every time. Yalom (1998) touches on this phenomenon of "throw-ins" in a healing psychotherapy as well as in expert cooking. I remain in awe of how Vangie cooked and who she really was. I often sat by the ironing board asking her the obvious and forbidden questions that only a child would ask. "Why is your skin black? Why is my skin white? Why are we different?"

"Honey, we just look different but we really aren't so different inside. Now hush up and think about it." Vangie would continue her precise ironing while singing songs to the Lord. I would watch her with great intensity and think as she had instructed me. Finally, she would look up from the ironing board and say, "Now go do your homework, child, or you will do nothing but iron the rest of your life." Vangie never gave a verbal answer to that question—or many other questions that I asked. Instead, she introduced me to my great natural capacity to search inside myself for the answers. I discovered inner searching (Bugental, 1999) as a profound process that I have supported and encouraged through psychotherapy. As a natural psychotherapist, Vangie would firmly remind me that the hour was up and I needed to attend to my external life—a continual reminder to balance the inner subjective world with the external objective world.

When I was a child, Vangie seemed the wisest person in the world. Her presence fed my soul. Her carefully chosen words and long silences became the foundation of my commitment to what the Zen tradition calls "no mind," the ability to hold emptiness in relationship, a space where differences meld and truth is lived in the moment (Levine & Levine, 1995, p. 215). This truth would later support me through many hours of psychotherapy. (Heery, 2001, pp. 90-91)

And when my carefully chosen words come out, it is in my lyrical southern accent. The long vowels and humor that follow always lighten moments that might otherwise be tense. I have deliberately chosen to keep my accent and practice it with my southern friends who live in California. Questions cloaked with the sweet sound of music lighten everyone's soul in the moment.

Soul

What is behind this pull to ask, to search for meaning of differences, of living and dying? Behind the many paradoxes in living and dying, underlying it all, is the soul's drive for meaning. I use the term soul here as an individuated aspect of spirit. Soul is a manifestation of spirit in a physical body. The soul is that aspect of being-ness that temporarily manifests and inhabits a physical body. The soul uses that body to act in the physical world, dealing with all the perceived limitations of time, space, and physical embodiment that we experience here. After death the soul soars like a bird, if you will, flying free once again after its tenure in the world of form.

A nice thought for relieving some death anxiety of what happens after we die. But is it actually true, this idea of the soul flying free after it leaves the body? Some rationalists say "dead is dead." In an interview I had with Albert Ellis, M.D. (Ellis, 2000), founder of Rational Emotive Behavior Therapy (REBT), he affirmed "dead is dead" with great intensity. We all answer the question of what happens after we die in our unique way, but the question is there for each of us.

The following is my experience of not what can happen after death, but rather how I have made meaning of what happened in my objective world in relation to death (Heery, 2011).

I struck a deal with Jim (Dr. Bugental) toward the end of his life. If there was a life after death he would send me a message I could not mistake. About a week after he died I was waiting in my office for a client, and a picture fell off my office wall, landing at my feet. It was a poster from an International Transpersonal Conference, with the words "Individual Choice and Universal Responsibility." I found tears welling up. I was not sure, but it seemed to be the promised message. Being a stubborn student, I had to get one more message. Later that day there was a letter in my mailbox from a local mortuary with the following message: "You too will die one day! Today and only today you can purchase your cremation for 50 percent off." OK, I got it. These words reminded me of one of Jim's frequent phrases, "pointing with your elbow," which Jim used to emphasize the necessity yet limitation of words in attempting to describe one's subjective experience." (pp. 126-127)

My personal experience of losing a loved one affords me mindful awareness and support to others in bereavement. Bereavement is an intense experience that can open a bereaved person to larger or transpersonal realms of reality. As a result of these experiences, an ongoing subjective relationship with those who have died becomes not only consoling but grounded in the objective world (Heery, 2001). I have had the great honor of being part of this grounding. Not only did my bereavement clients develop a relationship with the deceased, but I also began to have a relationship with the deceased, (i.e., having the same birthday as the lost loved one, another time being surrounded by dragonflies as I stepped outside my office following a session where my client had shared that her deceased child adored dragonflies). I have had many dreams of the deceased loved ones, including an eagle that kept flying higher and higher to be affirmed the next day in session when I learned that the client's deceased child loved eagles. All of these experiences opened me to the ongoing supportive relationship with the client, myself, and the deceased loved one. There are many of these experiences that over and over provide evidence of the subjective experiences being bridged to objective experiences.

Mystery is infinite, not finite. Mystery is the latent meaning always awaiting our discovery, and it is always more than our knowing in the objective world. Mystery points to the subjective world where implicit meanings are waiting to be *transformed* into explicit meanings in living experience. (Heery & Bugental, 2005, p. 253)

Creating space for this mystery is a mindful, subjective-based psychotherapy and is supported by intentionality.

Intentionality

Take a moment now and go inside. Ask yourself, "What do I seek, yearn for, or desire for myself?" Notice the impulses that arise. Soon you find through your searching process that some impulses come up more strongly than others. As you sit with the question of what you truly seek and desire for yourself, you see that some impulses arise and then fade, while others have a strength of their own that impels your inner being to be, to become. These are the seeds in your consciousness that will be watered by forces both opposing and supporting.

You have now visited the first stage of intentionality, wishing. I wish I could express my ideas clearly in this chapter. I wish . . . (you fill in the blank). Each of us is very familiar with wishing.

In 1969, existential philosopher and psychologist Rollo May expanded on the various stages of intentionality in his book *Love and Will* (May, 1969). May elaborates on wishing as the first stage of intentionality when he says, "Only by admitting and affirming the immediate wish can we get to the deeper level of what one genuinely wishes" (p. 247). I come closer to a genuine wish by first letting the thoughts arise around the wish, taking their own unique shape and form in my mind, and then drawing my attention to the internal energy around this wish, the soul's wish.

The next stage of intentionality raises and intensifies wishing to wanting. Wanting forms a bridge so that wishing moves closer to the objective world, bringing meaning closer to our experience. The soul wishes to bring the subjective into the objective world now. On the conscious level the individual reflects the soul's larger wanting by turning attention to the energy surrounding this wanting. Once the soul has taken on a physical body, this act of wanting moves toward the issue of meaning. On some very deep level, we are asking, "What am I doing here?" The pulse of life is continually moving toward meaning.

The search for this meaning moves from wishing and wanting to the next stage of intentionality, willing. At this stage, consciousness is directed from the subjective realms to the objective realms. Will can often get blocked by the inability of the individual to relinquish, to move forward with one intention of that moment. Intentionality moving into the objective world is known as responsibility.

Will must be raised into responsibility: the ability to respond and take action or actualize and interact Do I continue to write this chapter in spite of the fact that I must return calls, buy groceries, and so on, or do I give it up as unfinished because those other impulses are calling more strongly? The ability to respond and relinquish options is vital to implementing an intention in the objective world. We choose to drop an activity or complete it; our personal choice is to act or not to act. Do I forget this chapter or do I hold the wishing and wanting around the chapter as I venture out to the market? This choice expands the work as I return to it after going to the market So there is an overlap in activities on the physical level as they bleed into and nourish each individual intention through the individual's overall intentionality. Yet I must make a choice to actualize this chapter and interact with the results of the completed chapter. I will have to choose fewer social engagements, including market shopping, but not at the expense of self-care. When intentionality moves into the objective world, choice and relinquishment become pivotal to the outcome on the objective world.

We bring intentionality to bear on every level in our lives. It may be something as small as getting out of bed to start the day or a bit more complex to wake up and bring forth the dream world into this objective world. As I sit with my clients, I am mindful of their struggles with intentionality around finding authentic work, facing a life-threatening illness, ending an unworkable relationship, or grieving the loss of a loved one and the great task or relinquishment in order to achieve what they feel "called" to actualize in the world. Many intentions die daily for the chosen few to be actualized in this world. But the commitment to actualize some is essential in making meaning of living.

All of these experiences—no matter how small—in some larger sense are part of the search for meaning in our existence. Writing a paper, work, relationships, grieving, etc. are all part of the larger picture of being in this world and attempting to make meaning out of our time here. Meaning is essential to living; there is a continual flow toward meaning during one's lifetime. The spirit expresses itself through the soul and the intentionality of being here and now. Listening with mindful awareness is essential in the process of moving inner levels of consciousness (subjective) to the outer levels of consciousness (objective).

In many venues psychotherapy has become known as a hand-holding process: one person needing help and the other person listening with empathy, helping to reframe the pain and hopefully providing an opportunity for healing and transformation. This process is mostly thought of as a one-way street, the healer doing the healing. This simplistic view is just not so. The healing process involves mutual activation of intentionality for both healer and healed, therapist and client. More recently neuroscience has brought to light the expansion of the brain with new neuron pathways as we mindfully listen to ourselves and others with compassion versus judgment (Siegel, 2007). This recent interface of mindfulness and brain development research is exciting to psychotherapy and intentionality. For some, there is a science of the soul developing. There is actual objective proof of the subjective world transforming itself into the objective world.

This transformation is a waking up process that is rich for both psychotherapist and client. The journey of actualizing intentions often includes when and how an individual gets stuck. Resistance is part of subjective-based therapy. Working through resistance brings us face to face with fear, which can defeat intentionality. Fear is a clever, treacherous adversary, as I well know and am sure you, the reader, also know. It has no decency, respects no law or convention, and shows no mercy. It goes for your weakest spot, which it finds with unerring ease. It begins in your mind, always. One moment you are feeling calm, self-possessed, and happy. Then fear, disguised in the garb of mild-mannered doubt, slips into your mind like a spy. Doubt grows. You become anxious.

For fear, real fear, such as shakes you to your foundation, such as you feel when you are brought face to face with your mortal end, nestles in your memory like a gangrene: it seeks to rot everything, even the words with which to speak of it. So you must fight hard to express it. You must fight hard to shine the light of words upon it. (Martel, 2001, pp. 160-161)

This deeply rooted fear in all of us is embedded in our finitude, our inevitable death, and the fact that our life as we know it will end Paradoxically, we often live our death by attempting to fix time and all that it encompasses: people, places, and circumstances. The experience of facing continual change is a fundamental part of being human, yet many of our cherished cultural beliefs imply that we will or should achieve an unchanging stability or permanence. Our expectations for our lives thus are often at odds with our life experiences. This circumstance is part of our pattern of expectation that we will "perfect ourselves" or "complete our education" or "finish psychotherapy." Each of these postulates the human state as one of finite and fixed possibilities that will safely materialize if one but lives properly. Our fears become rooted around these unattainable permanent states of being.

A mindfulness practice, whatever practice best suits you, brings each of us back into the capacity to observe the inner and outer truth of impermanence and the unknown. Being mindful of our subjective world enhances the will to make conscious and clear choices, not based on fear, but based on compassion, courage, hope, resilience, and tolerance. We all have fears in living, in becoming who we wish and want to be—psychotherapists and you, the reader, included. Our potential in actualizing our soul's intentionality is grounded in being mindful of choices.

We have ideals, values, talents, emotions, and aspirations stacked all around our inner and outer homes. We intend to start realizing them almost any day now. This is non-being or a type of death. Living in the past or waiting for some magical future is when mindfulness of the now can be attended to in subjective-based psychotherapy.

When a computer doesn't work, when a line carries no power, when a battery is drained, the objective world for that moment is dead. How much deader is a man or woman who is not realizing his or her own being from the inside out?

I have had the great honor in the last couple of years to consult with psychotherapists working with veterans. Their caseloads include vets from Vietnam through the Iraq and Afganistan wars. Each psychotherapist has had an "inside experience." They have each served in a war. They know the experiences they are listening to from the inside out. Facing death anxiety straight on and then returning to family life in the United States with all the memories of war trauma is difficult and challenging for veterans. For a vet to then become a psychotherapist assisting other vets is a deeply rewarding experience, which includes transforming some of the most cruel acts of humanity—war and its far-reaching aftereffects.

These psychotherapists were using many objective, evidence-based psychotherapies, but these theories and applications were not enough. Suicide rates continued to rise in this client population no matter what objective theory was being implemented by different therapists. They did not want to abandon their objective models of psychotherapy, but wanted to include an emphasis on the subjective world of the client to see if the outcome of their psychotherapy—both with individuals as well as groups—would change. I was called in for consultation regarding application of the existential-humanistic model to treating trauma. Of course, the first item on the agenda was the *presence* of the psychotherapist and evidence of vicarious traumatization, the effect of listening to multiple trauma cases (Pearlman & Saakvitne, 1995).

The first outcome of these consultations was a substantial reduction in stress, as a result of being open and honest about the high level of stress caused by so many cases of potential and actual suicide. I often ask the question in all my groups whether process, consultation, or task groups: How many of you have experienced what was just shared by this participant/colleague? Immediately a show of hands or "yes" resounds in the room, pointing to the universality of the experience (Yalom, 2005). No one wants to be alone with stress. First, acknowledging the fact of the stressors to others present in the same boat, brings not only relief, but choices of self-care and support for each other actualizing ongoing self-care. Practicing some form of mindfulness individually and collectively is a big component of self-care for these psychotherapists. Experiencing emotional extremes of tears and laughter together immediately formed an inner and outer connection of healers who are now far more effective with their individual clients and groups. I often speak about awareness of and using the immediate moment in psychotherapy, what is alive is what is now.

> It is important to distinguish sharply between experiencing and information about experience. Experiencing happens now. Information may speak about life but is not itself living. Information is once removed from experiencing. What is alive is moving, is choosing, is changing, is breathing, is active. In some measure, what is alive is always unpredictable, beyond certainty. Life is incessant movement, always going forward into the next moment. Bodies change, thoughts, change, emotions flow—there is no final form of any aspect of life. Without flow, an organism is dead. Psychological reality is always the present, the ever-moving, never-repeatable present. As one client so poignantly phrased her grief over the loss of her sister, "I do not know if the next moment will be a tear of longing to see her or laugh over a joke we shared." (Heery & Bugental, 1999, p. 27)

The existential-humanistic model of psychotherapy deals openly with death, grief, and loss. The fit with the Veterans Administration (VA) psychotherapists has been perfect. A couple of reactions from VA psychotherapists are, "I feel that this model facilitates openness and reduces tension in the psychotherapeutic relationship," and "I have been able to use the existential-humanistic model in just about every session. I have found it to be extremely effective when noticing my own feelings in the moment."

I frequently talk to them about their own death anxiety and dreams of their clients and invite continued openness to include dimensions of transpersonal experiences with their clients. The shift from the client to themselves and to working with their clients with mindfulness from the inside out (not the outside in) has been an authentic experience for everyone: psychotherapists, clients, and me. I am honored to serve them and watch the ripple effect through their clients' continued changes. I have witnessed psychotherapists actualize these models with traumatized individuals and to also use evidence-based psychotherapy as needed. The baby is not thrown out with the bath water, and the tail does not wag the dog!

Your Call and Response

Take a moment to gather your self-compassion and then ask again, "What do I seek, yearn for, or desire for myself?" Notice the impulses that come up more strongly than others, the ones that do not fade. Perhaps this book has watered some latent impulses making them consistently strong. These impulses have a strength of their own that impel your inner being to be, to become. These are your seeds in your consciousness, your soul's calling. I invite you to answer this call as the authors in this book have, by using all of your being—to actualize your soul's call through your unique process of intentionality.

References

Bugental, J. F. T. (1999). *Psychotherapy Isn't What You Think*. Phoenix, AZ: Zeig, Tucker & Co., Inc.

Ellis, A. (2000). *Albert Ellis on REBT,* DVD. Mill Valley, CA: Psychotherapy. net.

Heery, M. & Bugental, J. F. T. (1999). Unearthing the Moment. *Self and Society, 27*(3), 26-27.

Heery, M. & Bugental, J. F. T. (2005). Meaning and Transformation. In E. van Deurzen & C. Arnold-Baker (Eds.*), Existential perspectives on human issues* (pp. 253-264). New York, NY: Palgrave Macmillan.

Heery, M. (2001). A Humanistic Perspective on Bereavement. In K. J. Schneider, J. F. T. Bugental, & J. Fraser Pierson (Eds.), *The handbook of humanistic psychology* (pp. 433-446). Thousand Oaks, CA: Sage.

Heery, M. (2001). Inside the Soul of Russian and American Psychotherapy Trainings, *Journal of Humanistic Psychology, 42*(2), 89-101.

Heery, M. (2011). Pointing with my elbow: Remembering James F. T. Bugental, 1916-2008. *Journal of Transpersonal Psychology, 43*(2), 124-127.

Levine, S. & Levine, O. (1995). *Embracing the Beloved*. New York, NY: Doubleday.

Martel, Yann. (2001). *Life of Pi* Orlando, FL: Harvest book, Harcourt, Inc.

May, Rollo (1969). *Love and will.* New York, NY: Norton & Co., Inc.

Pearlman, L. A. & Saakvitne, K. W. (1995). *Trauma and the therapist.* New York, NY: W. W. Norton & Company.

Siegel, D. (2007). *The mindful brain: Reflection and attunement in the cultivation of wellbeing.* New York, NY: W. W. Norton & Company.

Yalom, I. D. (1998). *The Yalom reader.* New York, NY: Basic Books.

Yalom, I. D. (2005). *The theory and practice of group psychotherapy* (5th ed.). New York, NY: Basic Books.

About the Contributors

Michael Barbee, Psy.D. (California Institute of Integral Studies, 2001), licensed psychologist in private practice and in community mental health in San Francisco, CA. Dr. Barbee leads an existential-humanistic supervision group in his role as a clinical supervisor for psychology doctoral interns. For seven years he has participated in the Unearthing Trainings, completed the basic and advanced trainings, and continues annual advanced trainings. Prior to his psychology doctorate, Dr. Barbee obtained degrees in pastoral care and counseling and in art therapy. His publications include "Transsexual Identity Formation: A Visual Narrative Approach and Men's Roles and Their Experience of Depression" in the *Art Therapy Journal*, "Conflicts in the Coming Out Process" in *The Therapist's Notebook*, and a contribution to *Working With Images: The Art of Art Therapists*. He is also a practicing artist and shows his work periodically. He can be reached at MichaelBarbee@hotmail.com.

Sarah Burdge, Ph.D. (Institute of Transpersonal Psychology, 2006), licensed psychologist in private practice in Menlo Park, CA. Dr. Burdge teaches a wide range of graduate psychology classes, including clinical practicum at Sofia University. In 2006 she was awarded the APA, Division 32 Jourard Award for her dissertation research. She has presented at numerous APA and other conferences, beginning in 2004 on topics ranging from the use of phenomenological awareness in research to peace advocacy. She has also made presentations to local Bay Area psychological associations on the use of existential and spiritual practices in clinical domains. She supervises clinicians in training using existential-humanistic principles at StarVista and Sofia University. Dr. Burdge began Unearthing the Moment Trainings over a decade ago, completed the basic and advanced trainings, and continues with annual trainings and monthly consultations. She can be reached at drburdgephd@aol.com or www.sarahburdgephd.com.

Kate Calhoon, Psy.D. (Colorado School of Professional Psychology, 2007), licensed psychologist in private practice in Denver, CO. She works with adolescents, individuals, and couples with specialized training on eating disorders, trauma, and couples skill-building and communication. She has completed basic and advanced trainings for Unearthing the Moment and continues with yearly trainings. She co-authored the chapter "The Myth of Obedience: Existential Analysis of American Beauty" (Calvert, Calhoon, Fehl, Gregory) in the book *Existential Psychology East-West* (Editors: Hoffman, Yang, Kaklauskas, 2009) and was a panel presenter for "Facilitating Transformation With Eating Disorders Through the Lens of the Existential Givens" at the 2011 Annual Conference of the Society of Humanistic Psychology, Chicago, IL. Dr. Calhoon is a sports enthusiast, runner, wife, and mother of two busy boys and two rowdy dogs. She can be reached at kkcalhoon@yahoo.com or www.drkatecalhoon.com.

Thea Comeau, M.Ed., is a Ph.D. student in counseling psychology at McGill University in Montreal, Canada. She has taught, presented, and consulted extensively on self-care and wellness for helping professionals, including the International Meaning Conference in Vancouver, Canada, 2010, and at various universities throughout Canada and the United States. Thea's clinical work has focused on work with survivors of sexual violence; she is currently practicing with students at the McGill University Counseling Services. Her current research is exploring the role of values in growth following traumatic experiences. She has completed the basic and advanced Unearthing the Moment Trainings and continues yearly advanced trainings. She can be reached at thea.comeau@mail.mcgill.ca.

Pamela Cronin, M.A. (Notre Dame De Nemur University, 1996), M.F.T., is in private practice in Burlingame, CA, where she works with children, families, couples and individuals. After writing her Master's Thesis on "Life

Satisfaction and the Aging Population" in 1996, she developed a special interest in the aging process and now assists families and individuals who are coping with aging, grief, loss, death, and dying. She continues to perform research, to write, and to develop ways for families to nurture mutually beneficial relationships, in the moment, with an awareness of the aging process. She continues to support and facilitate the development of and work related to the "Balancing of the Selves." She has published a chapter on "Living the Facts: The Largest Aging Population" in *Awakening to Aging*, 2005. Pamela has volunteered at Kara, supporting grief and loss groups for individuals and families, including uncomplicated or complicated loss; volunteered at the Friendship Line, a telephone support system for isolated elders; and volunteered and worked at the Center for Domestic Violence Prevention as a volunteer coordinator and community educator. She has worked with individuals, and facilitated groups for men and women involved in domestic violence, and developed and implemented a support group for the children of women in recovery. She has completed basic and advanced trainings for Unearthing the Moment and continues with yearly trainings, monthly consultations, and is a teaching assistant with Dr. Heery for an ongoing training in California. Pamela also serves on the IIHS Advisory Board. She can be reached at apcronin25@gmail.com.

Steve Fehl, Psy.D. (University of the Rockies, 2011), is Director of the Center for Growth, in Colorado Springs, CO, where he sees individuals and couples. Dr. Fehl is a regular contributor to the New Existentialist blog, as well as a contributing co-author of chapters in *Explaining Evil*; *Existential Psychology East–West*; *Miracles: God, Psychology, and Science in the Paranormal*; and *Whole Person Health Care*. Prior to earning his doctorate he served Lutheran parishes in Texas, Michigan, California, Minnesota, and Colorado. His research interests include Lesbian, Gay, Bisexual, and Transgender (LGBT) issues; faith and spirituality; spiritual abuse; existential theology; and the role of spirituality in existential psychology. He has completed basic and advanced Unearthing the Moment Trainings and continues yearly advanced trainings. He can be contacted at fehl@center4growth.com.

Christopher S. M. Grimes, Psy.D. (Forest Institute of Professional Psychology, 2004), Licensed psychologist, Director of the Program for Psychology & Religion at St. Louis Behavioral Medicine Institute, and Assistant Clinical Professor of Family and Community Medicine at St. Louis University School of Medicine The Program for Psychology & Religion provides multidisciplinary evaluations and treatment for clergy, both men and women. He has completed the basic and advanced Unearthing the Moment Trainings and continues yearly advanced trainings. He maintains research and writing interest in the area of psychology, religion, spirituality, and wellness. He can be contacted at the Program for Psychology & Religion by visiting http://www.slbmi.com.

Deborah Haarstad, M.A. (Professional School of Psychological Studies, 1984), M.F.T., is in private practice in Santa Rosa, CA. She has completed the basic Unearthing the Moment Trainings and continues with the advanced trainings. She has been a volunteer for Hospice of Petaluma, CA, since 2008. As a group facilitator at hospice she has co-written an eight-week workshop titled "Beginning Again," created to assist bereaved partners making the transition into the next chapter of their lives. She is the publisher of *Group Therapy Update*, a directory of psychotherapy groups in Sonoma County, CA. She can be contacted at deborahhaarstadmft.gmail.com or deborahhaarstadmft.com.

Christopher T. Harrison, Ph.D. (Institute of Transpersonal Psychology, 2009), is a licensed psychologist in private practice in Redwood City, CA, where he specializes in treating substance use disorders. He is an adjunct faculty member at the California Institute of Integral Studies and Sofia University. He is the former Clinical Director of The Sequoia Center, an alcohol and drug addiction treatment facility in Redwood City, CA. Dr. Harrison has also worked at the Stanford University School of Medicine, where he helped to develop and deliver a smoking cessation protocol for a National Cancer Institute funded study on nicotine dependence in adolescents. In addition to his interest in addiction research and treatment, Dr. Harrison is passionate about helping others to explore and implement practical methods to cultivate peace and wellness in daily life. He has completed the basic and advanced Unearthing the Moment Trainings and continues yearly advanced trainings. Chris can be contacted by e-mail at bewell@drchristopherharrison.com or through his website at www.drchristopherharrison.com.

Sandra Harner, Ph.D. (Fordham University, 1995), is a licensed psychologist and vice president of the Foundation for Shamanic Studies. She studied in The Art of the Psychotherapist Trainings with James F. T. Bugental, was a teaching assistant in the basic and advanced trainings, and continues in the annual trainings of Unearthing the Moment with Dr. Heery. Her private psychotherapy practice focuses on clients with serious health concerns from an existential-humanistic perspective. She has researched the psychological and immunological effects of shamanic journeying. Her recent book, *Ema's Odyssey: Shamanism for Health and Spiritual Knowledge,* is a presentation of one woman's spiritual search through Harner Shamanic Counseling.

Myrtle Heery, Ph.D. (California Institute of Integral Studies, 1987), M.F.T., has been in private practice in Petaluma, CA, for over 30 years. She focuses on helping individuals and couples bring to consciousness clear communication first with themselves, then with others. Her psychotherapy applies existential-humanistic and transpersonal principles. Dr. Heery founded the International Institute for Humanistic Studies in 2000 and now serves the organization as director and primary instructor for the Unearthing the Moment program, a series of trainings focusing on mindful applications of existential-humanistic and transpersonal psychotherapy. She co-edited *Awakening to Aging,* 2005, a collection of essays on conscious aging. In addition, she has published articles and chapters on a variety of psychotherapeutic topics, including an article published in the United States and Russia on "The Soul of Russian and American Psychotherapeutic Trainings." She has lectured at universities in Beijing and Shanghai, China, and Edmonton, Canada; and conducted trainings in the United States, Canada, Europe, Mexico, and Russia. She is a lecturer in the Psychology Department at Sonoma State University, Rohnert Park, CA, and an associate core faculty member, Sofia University/Institute of Transpersonal

Psychology, Palo Alto, CA, where she teaches group theory and process. Her passion is teaching and facilitating national/international trainings for psychotherapists and a variety of helping professionals. She leads monthly consultation groups, consults with VA Center therapists, and conducts individual consultations by phone. Dr. Heery can be contacted at www.human-studies.com or mheery@sonic.net.

Louis Hoffman, Ph D. (School of Psychology, Fuller Seminary, 2001), licensed psychologist, is an executive faculty member and director of the Existential, Humanistic, and Transpersonal Psychology Specialization at Saybrook University, San Francisco, CA. Additionally, he is co-director of the International Psychology and Socially Engaged Spirituality Certificates at Saybrook. Dr. Hoffman completed the basic and advanced Unearthing the Moment Trainings and continues attending the yearly trainings. He has served as a president of the Society for Humanistic Psychology, co-founded the Zhi Mian International Institute of Existential-Humanistic Psychology, serves on the Honorary Scientific Committee of the 2015 World Congress for Existential Therapy, and co-founded the International Conference on Existential Psychology held biannually in China. An avid writer and speaker, he has written numerous journal articles and book chapters as well as having five books to his credit including *Existential Psychology East-West* and *Brilliant Sanity: Buddhist Approaches to Psychotherapy*. Dr. Hoffman serves on the editorial boards for the Journal of Humanistic Psychology, The Humanistic Psychologist, Janus Head, and PsycCRITIQUES: APA Review of Books. He has been active in providing therapy, supervision, and training, including starting a training clinic with his wife in Colorado that offered practicums, internships, and postdoctoral residencies rooted in an existential approach. Most importantly, he is a husband to a wonderful wife and father to three wonderful children. He can be contacted at lhoffman@saybrook.edu.

Mary Jane Hooper, M.A. (Texas Woman's University, 1995), M.F.T., C.G.P., has been in private practice for 16 years in Fort Worth, TX, where she continues to see adults, couples, and families, and leads psychotherapy process groups. In addition to her private practice, in 2003 she completed the labyrinth facilitator training with Dr. Lauren Artress of Grace Cathedral in San Francisco, CA. She led the labyrinth ministry at St. Joseph Catholic Church, Dallas, TX, from 2003 to 2010, where hundreds of people walked the labyrinth under her leadership. She and her husband Win Hooper, J. D., lead retreats focused on soul journeys in Pagosa Springs, CO. She has completed the basic and advanced training in Unearthing the Moment and continues organizing and participating in advanced trainings in Fort Worth, TX. In addition, she presented at the Extended Unearthing the Moment Training CA 2013 on the use of poetry in psychotherapy. Integration of the spiritual with the psychological is foremost in her personal and professional life. She can be contacted at maryjanehooper.com or maryjanehooper@aol.com.

Gina Touch Mercer, Ph.D. (University of Houston, 1996), licensed psychologist, wife, and mother, has been practicing and teaching family and clinical psychology for 17 years. Dr. Mercer has a fellowship in geriatric psychology and specializes in aging and family issues. She has completed the basic and advanced Unearthing the Moment Trainings and continues advanced yearly trainings. She has co-written an *Instructor's Guide to the WAIS-IV*, presented at the International Alzheimer's Association annual conference, and conducted training in family therapy in Romania. Dr. Mercer is currently conducting workshops and retreats to help families manage life transitions, chronic illness, and dementia. She is in practice in Phoenix, AZ, and online at www.familyroutes.org.

Deborah Partington, Psy.D. (Arizona School of Professional Psychology, 2003), is a licensed psychologist in Phoenix, AZ. She divides her time between working in community mental health supervising doctoral and master's interns in psychology and private practice, where she sees adults and couples. She has completed the basic training in Unearthing the Moment. Professional associations include current Chair of the Ethics Committee of the Arizona Psychological Association and Member at Large of the Arizona Psychoanalytic Society. She enjoys world travel and is publishing *Telling Stories*, a novel constructed of interconnected short stories a young woman creates in her journey in psychotherapy. She can be contacted at deborahpsyd@q.com or www.deborahpsyd.com.

Cornelia Pinnell, Ph.D. (Ohio University, 1996), licensed psychologist, was born in Romania. She studied psychology, philosophy, and history at "Babes-Bolyai" University in Cluj-Napoca, Romania. She completed her M.A. in Clinical Psychology at Towson State University and her pre-doctoral internship at Indiana University Medical Center. She is currently professor (core faculty) at the Arizona School of Professional Psychology at Argosy University, where she has taught a variety of graduate courses, including Advanced Experiential and Existential-Humanistic Therapy. She has been a licensed psychologist in private practice in Glendale and Carefree, AZ, since 1998. She is on the Advisory Board of the International Institute for Humanistic Studies and assists Dr. Heery in teaching basic and advanced Unearthing the Moment courses in Arizona. She has completed basic and advanced trainings in Unearthing the Moment and continues participating in the annual trainings. She has made a presentation at the Extended Unearthing the Moment Training CA 2013 on the topic of "Compassion and the Dying Process." She has published extensively in hypnosis and other areas of psychology in various psychology journals. Dr. Pinnell can be contacted at cpinnell@argosy.edu.

Makenna Berry Newton, Ph.D. Candidate at Saybrook University, is completing her dissertation on "A Qualitative Evaluation of Proposed Recommendations for an Existential-Humanistic Multiculturally Informed Practice With Those Experiencing Homelessness and/or Poverty." She has completed a Master's in Nonprofit Management and has completed the basic and advanced Unearthing the Moment Trainings. She was an invited co-presenter of "In-Difference, Inequality and Injustice: Humanistic Perspectives on Multicultural Issues in Mental Health Treatment" at the 6th Annual Society of Humanistic Psychology Conference in 2012. Her research and practice interests are in cultural competency, relational and existential-humanistic psychotherapy, integrated health care, qualitative research, and social change and transformation. Her chapter in this book is a reflection of her early professional and personal history with the experience of homelessness and poverty. Makenna can be contacted at makennaberrynewton@gmail.com.

Cynthia S. Sauln, Ph.D. (Institute of Transpersonal Psychology/Sofia University, 2013), has a certificate in Spiritual Guidance and received a certification in dream work from the Marin Institute of Projective Dream Work (MIPD) in 2011. She has led dream groups at Sofia University and privately in Palo Alto, CA. Cindy has completed the basic and advanced trainings and continues annual trainings for Unearthing the Moment. Her clinical experience has been applying the existential-humanistic and transpersonal model in psychotherapy with adults, children, and their families in community mental health and school settings. Cindy's special interests and research include incorporating spirituality and expressive arts in psychotherapy, as well as exploring the varying ways people of all ages find meaning from their dreams. She lives with her family in Palo Alto, CA, and can be reached at csauln@gmail.com.

Amy Sharp, Ph.D. (Institute of Transpersonal Psychology, 2013), explored the role of pain and suffering in the transformative work of long-term psychotherapy for her dissertation research. Dr. Sharp's clinical experience includes working with children, working with underprivileged adults in a residential rehabilitative center, and long-term therapy with adults in a community mental health clinic. Her clinical training also includes the basic and advanced courses, Unearthing the Moment. Dr. Sharp is currently completing her postdoctoral hours conducting assessments in the emergency room of a local hospital in Mountain View, CA, and is writing an article to be published on her research on transformative work of long-term psychotherapy. She is an editor of professional works and can be reached at amyksharp@gmail.com.

David Schulkin, M.A. (Institute of Transpersonal Psychology, 2008), M.F.T., has been in private practice in Santa Cruz, CA, since 2010 seeing teenagers, adults, couples, and families and leading psychotherapy process groups. He has completed the basic and advanced courses in Unearthing the Moment and continues the advanced trainings twice a year. He lives with his wife and son in Santa Cruz. In addition to his work as a psychotherapist, he is an avid surfer who has been teaching surfing since 1998. Teaching surfing has influenced his therapeutic approach and helped him develop the ability to adapt to various dynamic environments, such as working with the complexities of people's lives and interpersonal interactions To learn more about David, visit his website at www.davidschulkin.com or contact him at 831-515-8489.

Barbara F. Strouzas, M.A. (Holy Names University, 1996), M.F.T., has been in private practice in Livermore, CA, since 2001. Her areas of specialty include adolescent and family issues, addiction, and anger management. Her experience includes working with Alameda County Juvenile Probation counseling adolescents involved in the justice system, leading Domestic Violence groups with court-ordered adult perpetrators, and she volunteers in her community as the Mental Health Advisor for a juvenile diversion program for the local police department. She is an Adjunct Professor at Holy Names University (Oakland, CA), where she teaches graduate master's students Domestic Violence, Group Psychotherapy, Marriage and Family Counseling, Introduction to Practicum, and Practicum. In addition she lectures for local schools and philanthropic groups. She has completed basic and advanced trainings for Unearthing the Moment and continues advanced yearly trainings. Barbara can be reached at bobbistrouzas@yahoo.com or 925-960-0910.

Ilyssa Swartout, Psy.D. (Arizona School of Professional Psychology, 2002), licensed psychologist in private practice in Glendale, AZ, with specialty in infertility. She completed her supervised doctoral internship at Treatment Assessment Screen Center (TASC). From 2001–2002, Dr. Swartout provided clinical services for clients in the criminal justice system and in an Arizona State Prison. She is currently a certified Gestalt therapist (2002), a certified EMDR therapist (2013), and facilitator, National Bereavement Association (2003). She has completed the basic and advanced Unearthing the Moment Trainings (2006) and attends yearly trainings. She also serves on the Board of Directors for IIHS and is a teaching assistant for the Arizona trainings with Dr. Heery. She has taught graduate courses in humanistic, existential-humanistic, and experiential theory and therapy at American School of Professional Psychology/Argosy University, Phoenix Campus and Midwestern University. Dr. Swartout has presented for several organizations in Arizona on a variety of topics including: Preventing Clinician Impairment, The Existential-Humanistic Model for Incarcerated Individuals, Understanding the Personality Disorders, Understanding Anxiety, Understanding Depression, How To Cope With the Stress of Infertility, and collaborated in presenting a three-day workshop on Couples and Family Therapy in Romania. Dr. Swartout also helped develop a Motivational Enhancement section for a substance abuse program manual, composed of 12 lessons to motivate participants to be receptive to the core lessons of the program for TASC, Spring 1999. She can be contacted at Growing Edges, LLC by visiting www.yourgrowingedges.com.

Rex R. Vogan II, Psy.D. (Argosy University-Phoenix, 2007), licensed psychologist, received his doctoral degree in clinical psychology with a specialization in sport psychology. He founded in 2009 and is executive director of Pinnacle Behavioral Health, a multidisciplinary private practice located in Northern Virginia. He has a dual focus in clinical and sport psychology issues, with a particular interest in the emotional and psychological recovery from sport injury. He began his existential-humanistic training with the International Institute for Humanistic Studies in 2004 with its Unearthing the Moment two-year training program. Since the completion of this course, he has attended yearly advanced trainings in existential-humanistic psychotherapy held in California. He works with adolescents and adults from an emotion-focused, depth-oriented, and present tense perspective. He can be contacted at www.pinnbh.com or drvogan@pinnbh.com.

Daniel B. Wasserman, Ph.D. (University of Maryland, College Park, 1984), licensed psychologist in private practice in Prescott, AZ, with over 35 years of full-time clinical experience. He completed an internship at the Michigan State University Counseling Center in 1979-80 with an intensive focus on psychotherapy. For the next four years, Dr. Wasserman worked in community mental health at the West Yavapai Guidance Clinic in Prescott, AZ. He served on the adjunct faculty of Prescott College from 1982-88 and has been in private practice since 1984. Psychotherapy with individuals, couples, and groups has been the main focus of his professional practice, which also includes a divorce mediation component. Dr. Wasserman is the co-author of two previously published articles/book chapters, one on program evaluation research in community mental health centers and the other on time-limited psychotherapy, respectively. He has engaged in Sufi studies for over 35 years and in Fourth Way Consciousness studies for the past 3½ years. Both of these systems inform his therapy work deeply. Married with two adult children, Dr. Wasserman travels far and wide to visit his adventurous daughter, so far in Europe, Asia, and Africa. Dr. Wasserman can be contacted at docdocdaniel@ yahoo.com.

Mark C. Yang, Psy.D. (Fuller Theological Seminary, 1994), licensed psychologist and co-founder and director of the Zhi-Mian International Institute of Existential-Humanistic Psychology (http://zhimianinstitute.com/home), whose mission is to promote existential-humanistic psychology and provide counseling skills training to mental health professionals in Asia. Dr. Yang is also an adjunct professor, the director of the Existential-Humanistic Programs in Asia, and the co-director of the International Psychology Certificate Program at Saybrook University (www.saybrook.edu). Saybrook University was started by the founders of the American humanistic psychology movement. Dr. Yang is actively involved in the training and supervision of psychology students from the existential-humanistic perspective throughout Asia. Dr. Yang's professional interests include: existential psychology, individual and group psychotherapy, grief and bereavement counseling, legal and ethical issues in clinical practice, and cross-cultural psychology. Dr. Yang was born in Taiwan and immigrated with his family to the United States when he was 9 years old. He can be contacted at markcyyang@gmail.com.

www.ingramcontent.com/pod-product-compliance
Lightning Source LLC
Chambersburg PA
CBHW020340270326
41926CB00007B/257